BEETHOVEN
THE CREATOR

BY ROMAIN ROLLAND

The Great Creative Epochs:
I
FROM THE EROICA TO
THE APPASSIONATA

De Luxe Edition

TRANSLATED BY
ERNEST NEWMAN

GARDEN CITY PUBLISHING CO., INC.
Garden City   New York

CONTENTS

The Author and the Publisher *page*	11
Introduction	17
CHAPTER I.—1800.—Portrait of Beethoven in his thirtieth year	23
II.—The *Eroica*	59
III.—The *Appassionata*	103
IV.—*Leonora*	205
Breuning wrote on 2nd June, 1806	261
To the Reader	263
Appendices :	
NOTE I.—Beethoven's Deafness	265
II.—A Beethoven Sketch-Book of 1800	291
III.—The Brunsvik Sisters and their Cousin of the *Moonlight*	297
REFERENCES	333

LIST OF ILLUSTRATIONS

Portrait of Beethoven (1814). Engraving by Blasius Höfel after a drawing by Louis Letronne; with a dedication by Beethoven to his friend Franz Wegeler. (Reproduced from the original engraving by permission of Artaria & Co., Vienna)
Frontispiece

	Page
Reproduction of the bill of Beethoven's first public concert in Vienna	24
Original covers of works by Beethoven	24
Portrait of Joseph Haydn	40
Portrait of Giulietta Guicciardi (probably in the *Moonlight* period, about 1801/2). (Miniature found among Beethoven's papers)	40
Facsimile Letter	54
Portrait of Princess Maria Christina Lichnowsky	56
Portrait of Prince Karl Lichnowsky	56
Manuscript title-page of the *Eroica*, with the dedication to General Bonaparte afterwards erased	62
Miniature portrait of Beethoven by Christian Horneman (1802/3)	72
Silhouette of Beethoven at 16	72
Portrait of Beethoven (1800/1). Engraving by Johan Josef Neidl after a drawing by Gandolf Stainhauser	72
A page of the *Eroica* manuscript	82
General view of Heiligenstadt	88
The church at Heiligenstadt	88
The Graben, Vienna	94
A page of the *Appassionata*	162
A page of the *Fidelio* manuscript	216
Portrait of Giulietta Guicciardi, Countess Gallenberg (probably in 1815)	216
The Kohlmarkt, Vienna, in Beethoven's time	232
The Michaelerplatz, Vienna, in Beethoven's time	232
St. Peterplatz and Church, Vienna	248
General view of Vienna	248
Portrait of Wilhelmine Schroeder-Devrient (1822), at the time of her début in *Fidelio*	264
The Vienna Theatre in which *Fidelio* was first performed	264

ILLUSTRATIONS

St. Stephen's Church, Vienna … 264
Portrait of Josephine Brunsvik, Countess Deym (Miniature) … 312
Portrait of Giulietta Guicciardi, Countess Gallenberg … 312
The Empress's Garden, Vienna … 322
Portrait of Countess Therese von Brunsvik. (Original portrait by Kallhofer, hitherto known only in the mediocre reproduction by J. B. Lampi, engraved by W. Unger, and in the copy, made by Therese herself, that is now in the Beethoven House in Bonn) … 328

The smaller illustrations evoke aspects of Vienna in Beethoven's day. That on p. 61 shows the Heiligenstadt house in which he wrote the Testament.

NOTE BY AUTHOR AND PUBLISHER

THE AUTHOR and the publisher have the agreeable duty of thanking all those who have helped them in the production of this book. On every side they have met with the kindest willingness to be of service. The great "Beethovenian" families (let us give them that glorious title!) in whose archives are preserved the souvenirs of their ancestors' friendship with Beethoven, the collectors of musicology, the great musical libraries, have all placed their documents at our disposal: many of these have not been published hitherto.

Among them is the fine original portrait of Countess Therese Brunsvik by Kallhofer, which is now in the castle of Korompa, and for the excellent reproduction of which we have to thank the Countesses Chotek.

Thanks to the friendly courtesy of Countess Carla Lanckoronska, we were able to obtain from Prince Lichnowsky the portraits of two of the protectors of the youthful Beethoven—Prince and Princess Karl Lichnowsky.

Dr. Stephan von Breuning, of Vienna, gave us permission to reproduce Horneman's charming miniatures of Giulietta Guicciardi and Beethoven, that came to him from his grandfather, the devoted friend of the composer.

Giulietta's granddaughter, Baroness Gisela Hess-Diller, has been kind enough to supply us with two other portraits that are not so well known, and a picture of the pretty *Contessa* of the *Moonlight* sonata.

Herr Julius Wegeler, of Koblenz, most cordially offered us the facsimiles of some valuable letters from the magnificent Beethoven collection of the Wegeler family.

We have to thank also the following :—

Prof. Dr. Johannes Wolf, Director of the Staatsbibliothek, Berlin, for a page of the *Fidelio* manuscript, as well as the title-pages of some of Beethoven's works ;

Hofrat Dr. Eusebius Mandiczewsky, Director of the Vienna Gesellschaft der Musikfreunde, for the title-page and another page of the *Eroica* ;

Artaria & Co., of Vienna, for a perfect proof of the original engraving of the portrait of Beethoven by Letronne and Blasius Höfel ;

The Universal Edition, Vienna, for the facsimile of the *Moonlight* sonata ;

Gustav Bosse, of Regensburg, for the galvano-portrait of Wilhelmine Schroeder-Devrient ;

Kistner & Siegel, of Leipzig, for the galvano-portrait of Countess Deym ;

The Verlag der Oesterreichischen Staatsdruckerei, of Vienna, for the reproductions of the picturesque engravings of Vienna in Beethoven's time;

The Directors of the Nationalbibliothek, Vienna, for the portrait of Haydn and for the bill of Beethoven's first concert in Vienna;

M. Henry Expert, Director of the Bibliothèque du Conservatoire, Paris, for a page of the *Appassionata*.

To all our friendly collaborators we offer our sincerest thanks, to which we are sure we can add those of the public.

The author wishes to express his particular gratitude to Mlle. Dr. Marianna de Czeke, who has been occupied for some years in preparing for publication the still unpublished Journal of Therese von Brunsvik, and who has generously given him the benefit of this treasure, as well as of her fine erudition. He would add also his most grateful homage to Therese's grand-niece, Baroness Irène de Gerando, *née* Teleki, who did him the exceptional favour to allow him to make the acquaintance of those moving and truly sacred Confessions, which he has been careful to use with the most pious discretion.

FROM THE *EROICA*
TO
THE *APPASSIONATA*

INTRODUCTION

We may smile at the simplicity of those newcomers who, bound like ourselves to the rolling wheel of time, imagine that only the past passes, and that the clock of the spirit comes to a standstill at their midday! These young generations, that cherish the illusion that the new form obliterates for ever the ancient forms but will itself never be blotted out, fail to see that even while they speak the wheel is turning and the shadow of the past already twining itself about their legs.

Let us raise ourselves above this kingdom of shadows! We know that everything must pass—we and you, all that we believe in, all that we deny. The suns themselves are mortal. Yet the beams they gave out thousands of years ago still bear their message through the night; and thousands of years later we see by the light of these extinct suns.

I will refresh my eyes, a last time, at the sun of Beethoven. I will say what he was for us—for the peoples of a century. What that is I know better to-day than I did when, as a young man, I poured out my song to him. For at that time his light, unique as it was, penetrated us. To-day the shock of the meeting of two epochs of humanity—of which the war has been not so much the separation as the landmark at the cross roads, where so many runners have come to grief —has had this advantage, that it has forced us to come to full conscience of ourselves, of what we are, of what we love. . . . I love, therefore I am. And I am that which I love.

We had become so accustomed to living in our Beethoven, to sharing with him from our infancy the bed of his dreams, that we had failed to perceive to what degree the tissue of his dreams was exceptional. To-day, when we see a new generation detaching itself from this music that was the voice of our inner world, we perceive that that world was only one of the continents of the spirit. It is none the less beautiful for that, none the less dear to us; nay, it is dearer still. For only now do our eyes clearly perceive its delimiting lines, the definite contours of the imperial figure that was our *Ecce homo*. Each great epoch of humanity has its own, its Son of God, its human archetype, whose glance, whose gestures, and whose Word are the common possession of millions of the living. The whole being of a Beethoven —his sensibility, his conception of the world, the form of his intelligence and of his will, the laws of his construction, his ideology, as well as the substance of his body and his temperament—everything is representative of a certain European epoch. Not that that epoch modelled itself on him! If we resemble him, it is because he and we are made of the same flesh. He is not the shepherd driving his flock before him; he is the bull marching at the head of his herd.

In painting his portrait, I paint that of his stock—our century, our dream, ourselves and our companion with the bleeding feet : Joy. Not the gross joy of the soul that gorges itself in its stable, but the joy of ordeal, of pain, of battle, of suffering overcome, of victory over one's self, the joy of destiny subdued, espoused, fecundated. . . .

And the great bull with its fierce eye,[1] its head raised, its four hooves planted on the summit, at the edge of the abyss, whose roar is heard above the time. . . .

ROMAIN ROLLAND.
October 1927.

---

[1] Drawn by Letronne, engraved by Höfel.

CHAPTER I

1800 : PORTRAIT OF BEETHOVEN IN
HIS THIRTIETH YEAR

Reproduction of the bill of Beethoven's first public concert in Vienna

Original cover of works by Beethoven

Original cover of works by Beethoven

CHAPTER I

1800: PORTRAIT OF BEETHOVEN IN HIS THIRTIETH YEAR

THE MUSIC of Beethoven is the daughter of the same forces of imperious Nature that had just sought an outlet in the man of Rousseau's *Confessions*. Each of them is the flowering of a new season.

I admire these youngsters who shake their fist at Rousseau, at Beethoven! It is as if they were falling foul of the spring or the autumn, the inevitable fall of the leaves, the inevitable shooting of the buds! Rousseau and the *Sturm und Drang*, these April showers, these equinoctial storms, are the signs of the break-up of an old society and the coming of a new. And before the new can take shape there must be an emancipation of man as individual. The claim of individualism in revolt is at once the token and the harbinger of the Order that is on the way. Everything at its own time ! First the Ego, then the Community.

Beethoven belongs to the first generation of those young German Goethes (less different than one thinks from the old Lynceus !) (1), those Columbuses who, launched in the night on the stormy sea of the Revolution, discovered their own Ego and eagerly subdued it. Conquerors abuse their power : they are hungry for possession : each of these free Egos wishes to command. If he cannot do this in the world of facts, he wills it in the world of art ; everything becomes for him a field on which to deploy the battalions of his thoughts, his desires, his regrets, his furies, his melancholies. He imposes them on the world. After the Revolution comes the Empire. Beethoven bears them both within himself, and the course they run in his veins is the circulation of the blood of history itself ; for just as the imperial Gesture that had to wait for Hugo to find a poet worthy of it inspired its own Iliad—the Beethoven symphonies of the years before 1815—so, when the Man of Waterloo has fallen, Beethoven *imperator* also abdicates ; he, too, like the eagle on his rock, goes into exile on an island lost in the expanse of the seas—more truly lost than that island in the Atlantic, for he does not hear even the waves breaking on the rocks. He is immured. And when out of the silence there rises the song of the Ego of the last ten years of his life, it is no longer the same Ego; he has renounced the empire of men; he is with his God.

But the man whom I am studying in this first volume is the Ego of the period of combat.(2) And I must sketch his portrait in the rough. For if it is easy enough to see at a glance, after the lapse of a century, in what respect this mountain is part of the range of a distant epoch, it is necessary also to distinguish the respects in which it dominates the range, and the declivities, the precipices, the escarpments that separate it from its attendant peaks. True, the Ego of Beethoven is not that of the Romantics; it would be absurd to confuse these neo-Gothics or impressionists with the Roman builder. Everything that was characteristic of them would have been repugnant to him—their sentimentality, their lack of logic, their disordered imagination. He is the most virile of musicians; there is nothing—if you prefer it, not enough—of the feminine about him.(3) Nothing, again, of the open-eyed innocence of the child for whom art and life are just a play of soap-bubbles. I wish to speak no ill of those eyes, which I love, for I too find that it is beautiful to see the world reflected in iridescent bubbles. But it is still more beautiful to take it to you with open arms and make it yours, as Beethoven did. He is the masculine sculptor who dominates his matter and bends it to his hand; the master-builder, with Nature for his yard. For anyone who can survey these campaigns of the soul from which stand out the victories of the *Eroica* and the *Appassionata*, the most striking thing is not the vastness of the armies, the floods of tone, the masses flung into the assault, but the spirit in command, the imperial reason.

BUT BEFORE we speak of the work, let us consider the workman. And first of all let us reconstitute the carpenter's frame-work—the body.

He is built of solid stuff well cemented; the mind of Beethoven has strength for its base. The musculature is powerful, the body athletic; we see the short stocky body with its great shoulders, the swarthy red face, tanned by sun and wind, the stiff black mane, the bushy eyebrows, the beard running up to the eyes, the broad and lofty forehead and cranium, " like the vault of a temple," powerful jaws "that can grind nuts," the muzzle and the voice of a lion.[4] Everyone of his acquaintance was astonished at his physical vigour.[5] " He was strength personified," said the poet Castelli.

"A picture of energy," wrote Seyfried. And so he remained to the last years,—until that pistol shot of the nephew that struck him to the heart.(6) Reichardt and Benedict describe him as "cyclopean"; others invoke Hercules. He is one of the hard, knotty, pitted fruits of the age that produced a Mirabeau, a Danton, a Napoleon.(7) He sustains this strength of his by means of vigorous ablutions with cold water, a scrupulous regard for personal cleanliness, and daily walks immediately after the midday meal, walks that lasted the entire afternoon and often extended into the night; then a sleep so sound and long that he thanklessly complained against it!(8) His way of living is substantial but simple. Nothing to excess; he is no glutton, no drinker (in the evil sense of the word) as some have wrongfully described him.(9) Like a good Rhinelander he loved wine, but he never abused it—except for a short period (1825-1826) with Holz, when he was badly shaken.(10) He was fonder of fish than of meat; fish was his great treat. But his fare was rough and countrified: delicate stomachs could not endure it.(11)

As he grows older, the demon that possesses him brings more and more disorder into his way of living. He needs a woman to look after him, or he will forget to eat; he has no hearth of his own. But there is to be found no woman who will devote herself absolutely to him; and perhaps his independence would revolt in advance against the rights that devotion of this kind would establish over him.

Yet he likes women, and has need of them; they occupied a greater place in his life than in that, I will not say of a Bach or a Handel, but of any other musician. I will come back to this point. But though his avid nature cries out for love, and though love fled from him less than has been supposed (as we shall see later, he fascinated women, and more than one offered herself to him), he is on his guard against them, on his guard against himself. His sexual continence has been exaggerated. Certain entries of the year 1816 in his journal(12) testifying to his disgust, testify also that he has had experience of the light-o'-love. But his conception of love is too lofty for him to be able, without a sense of shame, to degrade it in these—to use his own word— bestial (*viehisch*) unions. He ended by banishing the sensual from his own passional life; and when Giulietta Giucciardi, the beloved of the old time, still beautiful, comes to him in tears and offers herself to him, he repulses her with disdain. He guards the sanctity of his memories against her, and he guards his art, his deity, against contamination : " If I had been willing thus to sacrifice my vital force," he said to Schindler, " what would have remained for the nobler, the better thing ? "

This governance of the flesh by the spirit, this strength of constitution, both moral and physical, this life without excess, ought to have assured him an unassailable health: Röckel, who in 1806 saw him nude, splashing about in the water like a triton, said that "you would have predicted he would live to the age of Methuselah."

But his heredity was flawed. It is more than likely that he derived from his mother a predisposition towards tuberculosis; while the alcoholism of his father and his grandmother, against which he fought morally, must have left its mark on his system. From early days he suffered from a violent enteritis; also, perhaps, from syphilis (13); his eyes were weak, and there was the deafness. He died of none of these, however, but of cirrhosis of the liver. Moreover, in his last illness there were fortuitous circumstances that brought about the fatal result,—first of all pleurisy, the result of the furious return from the country to Vienna in an ice-cold December in a milkman's cart, without any winter clothing; then, when this first trouble seemed to have been stemmed, a fresh outburst of anger that brought on a relapse. Of all these cracks in the building, the only one that affected the soul—and that terribly—was, as we know, the deafness.

[BUT AT

BUT AT the point of departure of about the year 1800 —for other men it would have been a point of arrival— when, in his thirtieth year, he has already won the foremost place for himself by the side of the venerable Haydn, his strength appears intact, and he is proudly conscious of it. He who has freed himself from the bonds and the gags of an old rotting world, freed himself from its masters, its gods, must show himself to be worthy of his new liberty, capable of bearing it; otherwise, let him remain in chains! The prime condition for the free man is strength. Beethoven exalts it; he is even inclined to over-esteem it. *Kraft über alles!* There is something in him of Nietzsche's superman, long before Nietzsche. If he can be fierily generous, it is because such is his nature and because it pleases him to distribute royally, to "friends in need," largesse from the booty he has won.(14) But he can also be pitiless, lacking in all consideration, as, indeed, he sometimes is. I refer not to those furious outbursts of rage in which he respects no one, not even his inferiors(15); he professes at times a morality of the stronger,—*Faustrecht*: "Strength is the morality of the men who stand out from the others, and it is mine."(16)

He is rich in scorn—scorn for the feeble, the ignorant, the common people, equally so for the aristocracy, and even for the good souls who love and admire him; a scorn of all men, terrible in itself, of which he never quite succeeded in purging himself. As late as 1825, for instance, he says: " Our epoch has need of powerful spirits to lash these wretched, small-minded, perfidious scoundrels of humanity."(17) In a letter of 1801 to his friend Amenda he speaks thus insultingly of a man (Zmeskall) who will remain faithful to him to his last breath, and who, to share with him the terrors of his last days, has his own sick body carried to a house near that in which Beethoven is undergoing the final agony: " I rate him and those of his species only according to what they bring me; I regard them purely and simply as instruments on which I play when I please."

This bragging cynicism, that he displays ostentatiously before the eyes of the most religious of his friends, bursts out more than once in his life, and his enemies fasten upon it. When Holz, about 1825, is about to become intimate with him, the publisher Steiner lets him know that it is very good of him to do anything for Beethoven, who will cast him aside, when he has made use of him, as he does all his *famuli*; and Holz repeats the remark to Beethoven.

Imputations of this kind are belied, at every period of his life, by the torrent of his warm humanity.(18) But we must recognise that the two currents, vast love, vast scorn, often came to a clash in him, and that in the full flush of his youth, when victory broke down all the flood-gates, the scorn poured out in torrents.

May gentle souls forgive me! I do not idealise the man: I describe him as I see him.

But it is here we become conscious of the antique sublimity of the destiny that smites him, like Œdipus, in his pride, his strength, just where he is most sensitive — in his hearing, the very instrument of his superiority. We remember the words of Hamlet:

> . . . and that should teach us
> There's a divinity that shapes our ends,
> Rough-hew them how we will.

We who, at a century's distance, can see that tragedy for what it was, let us prostrate ourselves and say, "Holy! holy! Blessed is the misfortune that has come upon thee! Blessed the sealing-up of thine ears!"

The hammer is not all: the anvil also is necessary. Had destiny descended only upon some weakling, or on an imitation great man, and bent his back under this burden, there would have been no tragedy in it, only an everyday affair. But here destiny meets one of its own stature, who "seizes it by the throat"(19), who is at savage grips with it all the night till the dawn — the last dawn of all — and who, dead at last, lies with his two shoulders touching the earth, but in his death is carried victorious on his shield; one who out of his wretchedness has created a richness, out of his infirmity the magic wand that opens the rock.

LET US return to the portrait of him in this decisive hour when destiny is about to enter; let us savour deliberately the cruel joy of the combat in the arena between the Force without a name and the man with the muzzle of a lion!

This superman over whose head the storm is gathering (for the peaks attract the thunderbolt) is marked, as with smallpox, with the moral characteristics of his time—the spirit of revolt, the torch of the Revolution. They declare themselves already in the Bonn period. The youthful Beethoven has attended at the University the lectures of Eulogius Schneider, the future public prosecutor for the department of the Lower Rhine. When the news of the taking of the Bastille comes to Bonn, Schneider reads from his pulpit an ardent poem that arouses the enthusiasm of his pupils. In the following year the *Hofmusicus* Beethoven subscribes to the collection of revolutionary poems in which Schneider hurls in the face of the old world the heroic defiance of the democracy that is on the way:

"To despise fanaticism, to break the sceptre of stupidity, to fight for the rights of humanity, ah! no valet of princes can do that! It needs free souls that prefer death to flattery, poverty to servitude. . . . And know that of such souls mine will not be the last!"[20]

Who is it that is speaking? Is it Beethoven already? The words are Schneider's, but it is Beethoven who clothes them with flesh. This proud profession of republican faith is arrogantly carried by the young Jacobin — whose political convictions will indeed change in time, but never his moral convictions — into the upper-class salons of Vienna, in which, from the days of his first successes, he behaves without ceremony towards the aristocrats who entertain him.

The elegance of a world that is nearing its end has never been finer, more delicate, more worthy of love (in default of esteem) than on this the eve of the last day, when the cannon of Wagram were to arrive. It recalls Trianon. But these grand seigneurs of Vienna on the threshold of the nineteenth century, how superior they are, in taste and culture, to their princess in exile, the daughter of their Maria Theresa! Never has an aristocracy loved the beauty of music with a passion more complete, or shown more respect for those who bring down the blessings of it to mortals. It is as if they would win pardon for their neglect of Mozart, who had been thrown into a common grave. In the years between the death of poor Wolfgang and that of Haydn the Viennese aristocracy bends the knee before art, pays court to artists : its pride is to treat them as equals.

The 27th March, 1808, marks the apogee of this consecration, the royal coronation of music. On that date Vienna celebrates the seventy-sixth birthday of Haydn. At the door of the University the highest aristocracy, accompanied by the musicians, awaits the son of the Rohrau wheelwright, who is coming in Prince Esterhazy's carriage. He is conducted into the hall with acclamations, to the sound of trumpets and of drums. Prince Lobkowitz, Salieri, and Beethoven come to kiss his hand. Princess Esterhazy and two great ladies take off their cloaks and wrap them round the feet of the old man, who is shaken with emotion. The frenzy, the cries, the tears of enthusiasm, are more than the composer of the *Creation* can bear. He leaves in tears in the middle of his oratorio, and as he goes out he blesses Vienna from the threshold of the hall.

A year later, the eagles of Napoleon swoop down on Vienna ; and Haydn, dying in the occupied city, carries the old world to the tomb with him. But the young Beethoven has known the affectionate smile of this old world that so nobly throws the mantle of its aristocracy under the feet of the artist, and he despises it; he tramples the mantle underfoot. He is not the first of these peasants of the Danube and the Rhone (the first two of them were Gluck and Rousseau) to see the proud nobility anxious to please them, and who revenge themselves on it for the affronts that generations of their own class have had to endure. But whereas the "Chevalier Gluck" (a forester's son), who is artful by nature, knows how to blend the permitted violences with what he owes to the great, and even how to make these violences an advertisement for himself, and whereas the timid Jean-Jacques bows and stammers and does not remember until he is descending the stairs all the bold things he should have said, Beethoven blurts out straight to their faces, in the crowded salon, the contempt or the insult that he has on his tongue for this world. And when the mother of Princess Lichnowsky, the Countess von Thun, the noble woman who had been the friend of Gluck and the protectress of Mozart, falls on her knees before him and begs him to play, he refuses without even rising from his sofa.(21)

How kind this princely house of Lichnowsky is to him! They have adopted this little savage from Bonn as a son, patiently set themselves to hewing him into shape, all the while taking infinite pains to avoid rousing his susceptibilities. The princess shows him the affection of a grandmother (the word is Beethoven's own); "she would put him under a glass so that no unworthy breath should touch him"; and later we have the story of that soirée at the Lichnowsky palace in December 1805, at which some of his intimates are trying to save *Fidelio*, which Beethoven, after the first failure, has refused to revise, and the princess, who is already mortally ill, appeals to the memory of his mother and conjures him " not to let his great work perish."(22) Yet only a few months after that it will need only a word that seems to him to be directed against his independence for Beethoven to smash the prince's bust, run out of the house, and bang the door behind him, vowing that he will never see the Lichnowskys again.(23) " Prince," he writes to him on separating from him, " what you are you are by the accident of birth ; what I am, I am of myself. There are and there will be thousands of princes. There is only one Beethoven."(24)

This spirit of proud revolt breaks out not only against the people of another class but against those of his own, against other musicians, against the masters of his own art, against the rules : " The rules forbid this succession of chords : very well, I allow it."(25)

He refuses to take for granted the edicts of the classroom ; he will believe only what he has himself experienced and tested. He will yield only to the direct lesson of life. His two teachers, Albrechtsberger and Salieri, confess that he owes nothing to them, for he has never been willing to admit that they taught him anything ;

his real master was his own hard personal experience. He is the rebellious archangel: according to Czerny, the astounded and dismayed Gelinek said, " There is Satan in this young man ! "

But patience ! The spear of St. Michael will bring forth the God concealed in him. It is not from a vain pride that he refuses to bow before the judgments of authority. In his day, people thought it monstrous that this young man should regard himself as the equal of a Goethe and a Handel.(26) But he was.

If he is proud before others, he has no pride before himself. Speaking to Czerny of his faults and his imperfect education, he says, " And yet I had some talent for music ! " No one has ever worked harder, more patiently, more tenaciously, from his first days to his last. The theoreticians whom he rejected at twenty he returns to and re-reads at forty ; he makes extracts from Kirnberger, Fux, Albrechtsberger, Türk, Philipp Emanuel Bach,—and this in 1809, after he has written the *Pastoral* and the C minor !(27) His intellectual curiosity is enormous.(28) Near the end of his life he says, " Now I am beginning to learn." Patience ! already the iron is emerging from the fusing ores. The jealous passion for glory, that is nourished by the rivalries of the virtuosi and the exciting contact with the public, is only, as it were, an infantine skin eruption. When his friends, says Czerny, speak to him of his youthful renown, he replies :

Portrait of Joseph Haydn

Portrait of Giulietta Guicciardi (probably in the *Moonlight* period, about 1801/2). (Miniature found among Beethoven's papers)

"Ah! nonsense! I have never thought of writing for renown and glory. What I have in my heart must out: that is why I write." Everything is subordinated to the imperious voice of his interior life.

EVERY TRUE artist has within himself, diffuse and intermittent, this dream-life that flows in great streams in the subterranean world of him. But in Beethoven it attains to a unique intensity; and that long before the closing of the doors of his hearing blockade him from the rest of the universe. Think, for example, of the magnificent Largo e mesto in D minor in the sonata Op. 10, No. 3,—that sovereign meditation that dominates the vast plain of life and its shadows! It is the work of a young man of twenty-six (1796). And the whole of Beethoven is already there. What maturity of soul! If not so precocious as Mozart in the art of smooth harmonious speech, how much more precocious he was in his interior life, in knowledge and mastery of himself, of his passions and his dreams! His hard childhood, his premature experiences developed these aptitudes early. I see Beethoven as a child as his neighbour the baker used to see him, at the window of that garret of his that looked out over the Rhine, his head in his hands, lost in his " beautiful, profound thoughts."(29) Perhaps there is singing within him that melodious lament, the poetic adagio of his first pianoforte sonata.(30) Even as a child he is a prey to melancholy ; in the poignant letter with which his correspondence begins we read, " Melancholy, that for me is an evil almost as great as illness itself. . . ."(31) But even in the early days he has the magic power to win free of it by fixing it in tones.(32)

But conqueror or conquered, he is always alone. From his infancy, wherever he may be, in the street or in the salons, he isolates himself with a peculiar strength. Frau von Breuning used to say, when he was thus lost in the distance, oblivious of everything, that he had his *raptus*.(33) Later this becomes a gulf in which his soul disappears from the sight of men for hours and days. Do not try to recall him ! That would be dangerous : the somnambulist would never forgive you.(34)

Music develops in its own elect that power of concentration on an idea, that form of *yoga*, that is purely European, having the traits of action and domination that are characteristic of the West : for music is an edifice in motion, all the parts of which have to be sensed simultaneously. It demands of the soul a vertiginous movement in the immobile, the eye clear, the will taut, the spirit flying high and free over the whole field of dreams. In no other musician has the embrace of thought been more violent, more continuous, more superhuman.(35)

Once Beethoven takes hold upon an idea, he never lets it go until he possesses it wholly. Nothing can distract him from the pursuit.(36) It is not for nothing that his piano playing is characterised by its legato, contrasting in this respect with the Mozart touch,(37) that was delicate, pointed, clean-cut, as well as from that of all the pianists of his own time. In Beethoven's thought, everything is connected, and yet it appears to gush out in torrents. He controls the thought, and he controls himself. He appears to be delivered up to the world by his passions; but in fact no one can read the thought that is moving in the depths of him. In these early years of the nineteenth century, Seyfried, who studies him at close quarters both in drawing-rooms and at home (they live in the same building), is struck not so much by the traces of emotion in his face as by its impassiveness: "It was difficult, even impossible," he says, "to read either approbation or dissatisfaction on his face [when he was listening to music]; he remained always the same, to outward appearance cold and reserved in his judgments. Within him the mind was working without respite; the fleshly envelope was like a marble without a soul."

This is a different Beethoven from the ordinary

conception of him as looking like King Lear in the storm! But who really knows him? One is always inclined to accept the impression of the moment.

In his thirtieth year his mind is a formidable equilibrium of opposing elements. If in the outer world he gives free rein to his passions, in his art he holds their mouth in with a bit controlled by a wrist of steel.

He rejoices in improvisation; it is then that he comes to grips with the element of the unforeseen in genius; the subconscious forces are unchained, and he must subdue them. Many of the great musicians have been masterly improvisers, especially in the eighteenth century, when music, its joints still supple, cultivated the faculty of free invention. But this public of connoisseurs, that only yesterday had been spoiled by Mozart, unanimously vows that in this field no one can compare with Beethoven. They agree also that in the whole art of Beethoven itself there is nothing to compare with the unheard-of power of his improvisation.[38] It is difficult for us to form an idea of it,[39] in spite of the fact that expert pianists like Ries and Czerny have described for us its inexhaustible wealth of ideas, its bewildering posing and solving of difficulties, its unexpected sallies, its swirl of passion. These professionals, on their guard as they are, fall as easy victims to the conqueror as the others. Wherever he happens to be playing, says Czerny, there is no resisting him; the public is staggered. " Apart from the beauty and originality of the ideas, there was something extraordinary in the expression." Aloys Schlösser speaks of his " poetic fury." Beethoven is like Prospero : he calls up spirits from the very depths to the very heights.(40) The listeners break into sobs : Reichardt weeps bitterly : there is not a dry eye anywhere. And then, when he has finished, when he sees these fountains of tears, he shrugs his shoulders and laughs noisily in their faces : " The fools ! . . . They are not artists. Artists are made of fire : they do not weep."(41)

This aspect of Beethoven—his contempt for sentimentality—is hardly known.(42) They have turned this oak into a weeping willow. It was his listeners who wept ; he himself has his emotion under control. " No emotion ! " he says to his friend Schlösser at parting : " man must be strong and brave in all things."(43) We shall see him give Goethe a lesson in insensitivity.(44)

If he ignores in his art the torments that ravage his inner life, it is because he wills it so. The artist remains master of them ; never do they sweep him away. Has he been their plaything ? Well, it is his turn now ! He takes them in hand, and looks at them, and laughs.

I HAVE been describing so far the man of 1800, the genius as he was at thirty—with the big, repellent traits that indicate an abuse of strength, but strength indubitably, an immense interior sea that does not know its own boundaries. But there are grave risks that it may lose itself in the sands of pride and success. This God whom he bears within himself, will he prove to be a Lucifer?

I do not use the word "God" as a mere figure of speech. When we speak of Beethoven we have to speak of God: God to him is the first reality, the most real of realities; we shall meet with him throughout all his thinking. He can treat him as an equal, or behave as his master. He can regard him as a companion to be treated roughly, as a tyrant to be cursed,[45] as a fragment of his own Ego, or as a rough friend, a severe father *qui bene castigat*. (The son of Johann van Beethoven had learned as a child the value of this treatment.) But whatever this Being may be that is at issue with Beethoven, he is at issue with him at every hour of the day: he is of his household, and dwells with him; never does he leave him. Other friends come and go: he alone is always there. And Beethoven importunes him with his complaints, his reproaches, his questions. The inward monologue is constantly *à deux*. In all Beethoven's work, from the very earliest, we find these dialogues of the soul,[46] of the two souls in one, wedded and opposed, discussing, warring, body locked with body, whether for war or in an embrace who can say? But one of them is the voice of the Master: no one can mistake it.

Towards 1800 Beethoven, while still recognising it, contends with it. The struggle goes on again without intermission. Each time the Master imprints his burning seal on the soul. And he waits and watches for the fire. As yet comes only the first flame, kindled by the feeble breath of Beethoven's religious friend Amenda.(47) But the flame and the pyre are ready. Only the wind is wanting!

It comes!

THE MISFORTUNE that descends on him between 1800 and 1802,(48) like the storm in the *Pastoral*—though in his case the sky never clears again—smites him in all his being at once; in his social life, in love, in art. Everything is attacked: nothing escapes.

First of all, his social life: and that is no small matter for the Beethoven of 1800! Imagine the brilliant position of an artist who has given to the world in five years the first ten pianoforte sonatas (among them the *Pathétique*), the first five sonatas for piano and violin, the first eight trios, the first six quartets (thrown at Prince Lobkowitz's feet in a single sheaf), the first two piano concertos, the septet, the serenade ! And these are merely the most famous of the works, those whose fires are still unpaled after a century. Conceive to yourself the treasures of poetry and of passion that this young genius has poured into them—the melodic grace of them, the humour and the fantasy, the unleashed furies, the sombre dreams ! A whole new world, as, indeed, his contemporaries, especially the younger of them, immediately perceived (49) ; as Louis Schlösser put it, " the musical hero whose genius has unchained the interior infinite and created a new era in art."(50)

This piano music and chamber music (for the impetuous genius has had the rare patience not to attempt the conquest (51) of the symphony until after he has made himself master of the whole domain of *Kammermusik*), enjoys an unprecedented popularity. Before he is thirty years of age he is recognised as the greatest of all clavier composers ; and as regards other music, only Mozart and Haydn are regarded as his equals. From the first years of the century he is performed all over Germany, in Switzerland, in Scotland, in Paris (1803). At thirty he is already the conqueror of the future.

Take now a look at this conqueror, this Beethoven of thirty, the great virtuoso, the brilliant artist, the lion of the salons, who fascinates youth, kindles transports, and thinks little of this elegant, vibrant, refined world, though he has need of it—(he has always lived in it, from the time when, as a child, he became a little *Hofmusicus*; when he emerges from his father's poor hearth, or now, at Vienna, from his untidy bachelor's rooms, it is always to breathe the most aristocratic atmosphere in Europe and taste the intoxication of it)—this Beethoven whose bad manners the good Princess Lichnowsky has patiently polished, and who affects to despise fashion but for all that carries his chin well up over his fine white three-deep cravat, and out of the corner of his eye looks proudly and with satisfaction (though at heart a little uneasy) at the effect he is creating on the company,[52] this Beethoven who dances (but how?), this Beethoven who rides a horse (unhappy animal!),[53] this Beethoven, whose charming humour, whose hearty laugh,[54] whose delight in life, whose concealed grace and elegance (very much concealed, and yet there!) find expression in ravishing works like the Bonn *Ritterballet* (1791), the *Serenade* of 1796, the exquisite Variations on *Vieni amore* (1791), on a Russian dance tune (1795–1797), on an air from *La Molinara* (1795), the frisky German dances (1795–1797), the youthfully happy waltzes and *Ländler*.[55] Do not fall into the error of regarding this man as unsociable. He may clash with this society, but he cannot do without it. And that fact gives us the measure of what it must have cost him later to be deprived of it.

Dв

But for the moment he is enjoying it. He is its favourite. Yet the poor plebeian young man knows how precarious is this favour, this attachment, how much of irony, benevolent or malevolent, there is blended with it—the suspicious young bumpkin believes in his heart that it is so, and he is right ; he knows that these noble admirers are on the look-out for his gaucheries, his absurdities, his weaknesses, and that (we know this sort of friend!), however much they may like him, to-morrow they would not mind throwing him over. Observe that he has not troubled to conciliate them : he conciliates no one ; that is a natural impossibility with him ; he would rather die than mince the truth. If he has many a devoted Mæcenas, he has also, it goes without saying, enemies, jealous rivals whom he has mortally offended, virtuosi whom he has discomfited, embittered colleagues,(56) fools whom he has deflated, and even young artists whom he has not gone out of his way to flatter. He is rough with people who show him their insipid works ; and he lacks the address to build round himself a clientèle of obsequious disciples (all he has, at the most, is one or two professional pupils).(57) Never was anyone less the " dear Master " than he.

He is alone on his tight-rope ; below is the gaping crowd awaiting the false step. He gave them no thought so long as he was sure his body was whole. To be one against them all rejoiced him ; he sported with vertigo.

... But to-day, now that destiny has dealt him a grievous wound? Imagine the man on the tight-rope suddenly becoming dizzy. What must he do? Confess that he can no longer see clearly? He clenches his teeth: so long as there is a glimmer of light for his eyes he will go forward.

The imminence of the night that is about to descend on him increases the fury of creation in him.

AND IT increases love.

Beethoven is a man possessed with love. The fire burns unceasingly, from his adolescence to the shadows of his last days. "He was never without a love affair," one of his intimates tells us. Sensitive to beauty, he can never see a pretty face without being smitten, as we learn from Ries. It is true that none of these flames lasts very long: one expels the other. (He is coxcomb enough to boast that the most serious of them lasted only seven months.) But this is only the outer zone of love. Within it there are sacred passions, of the kind that leave for ever in the soul the *Wonne der Wehmut*, the wound that never ceases to bleed. There are the " little friends "(58); there are the women he has been in love with; and there is the " Immortal Beloved." Between the one kind and the other it is often difficult, where a Beethoven is concerned, to draw a dividing line : more than one of these little affairs commences in jest and ends by being serious.

Every variety of passion and of love is contained in these first years of the century, just when his malady is about to immure him. There is not a day when he is not surrounded in some Vienna salon or other by a swarm of young girls, several of whom are his pupils — that kind of pupil he never refused !—while all pay him court. Let us insist on this fact, which at first sight is astonishing ! He is the fashion ; it is he who writes for Vigano and la Casentini the new ballet, *Die Geschöpfe des Prometheus* (The Creations of Prometheus) given at the Court Theatre on the 28th March, 1801.

In every epoch the virtuoso, the artist who is in the public eye, has attracted women. Beethoven has always exercised a fascination over them.[59] Ugly and common as he appears at first sight, unpleasant as the first approach to him may be, hardly has he begun to speak or smile when all of them, the frivolous and the serious, the romantic and the quizzical, are at his feet. They notice then that he has a fine mouth,[60] dazzling teeth,[61] and " beautiful speaking eyes that mirror the changing expression of the moment, by turns gracious, agreeable, wild, angry, menacing."[62] No doubt they laugh at him,[63] and are delighted to find ridiculous things in him that they can quiz him about : these indeed are their defence, for without them he would be dangerous ; in this little duel of hearts they assure their advantage over him. And of course there can be no question of these young girls, beautiful, rich, titled, letting the adventure go any further than a drawing-room flirtation. No one will blame them for that ! What surprises us rather is that the heart of more than one of them is touched. The women's letters published by La Mara and M. A. de Hevesy(64) often mention Beethoven, "who is an angel!" And even while they are making fun of him their imagination is sometimes a trifle too occupied with him. They take him about with them in their castles in Hungary ; and behind the thickets, at night, sweet words pass, kisses are exchanged —perhaps promises too, that are only thistledown on the wind. (But we hear the wind blowing hot and furious through the presto agitato of the finale of the *Moonlight* sonata.)

These years 1799-1801 see the beginning of the intimacy with the two related families of the Brunsviks and the Guicciardi.(65) He loves the three cousins, Tesi (Therese), Pepi (Josephine), and Giulietta by turn and all together. (They are aged respectively twenty-five, twenty-one and sixteen.) And his feelings are reciprocated, as well as they can be by these volatile creatures, intoxicated with their spring,—the beautiful and coquettish Giulietta, the fascinating Josephine, who is tender and proud (the one of the three who most truly loved him at this time), and the serious (though not so serious then as later!) Therese Brunsvik, who remained so long uncertain of herself and unhappy. Giulietta carries the day over her rivals; she unchains a tempest of passion in Beethoven. It is not to her, however, that the letter of eleven years later to " the Immortal Beloved " is addressed.(66) But in November 1801 she is " this dear girl, this enchantress " (*ein liebes, zauberisches Mädchen*), who has captured Beethoven's heart, and by whom he believes himself to be loved.(67) She alone dissipates the clouds of melancholy and misanthropy that have gathered about him since he became haunted by the " spectre of deafness,"(68) only to let them descend again, alas, more crushingly than before!

Precisely because he feels the trouble approaching—that mortal infirmity that soon he will no longer be able to conceal!—he feels the need to fly to a woman for refuge. And now it is not a question merely of love, but of marriage.(69) From now until 1816 this will be his constant hope—and his constant deception. The poor man sees the light going out, and he searches for the faithful hand that will guide him. But who will reach him that hand? It will not be any of the women who then attract him. Apart from their pride of caste—and if they themselves have none, their families see to that for them—what means of existence has he to offer

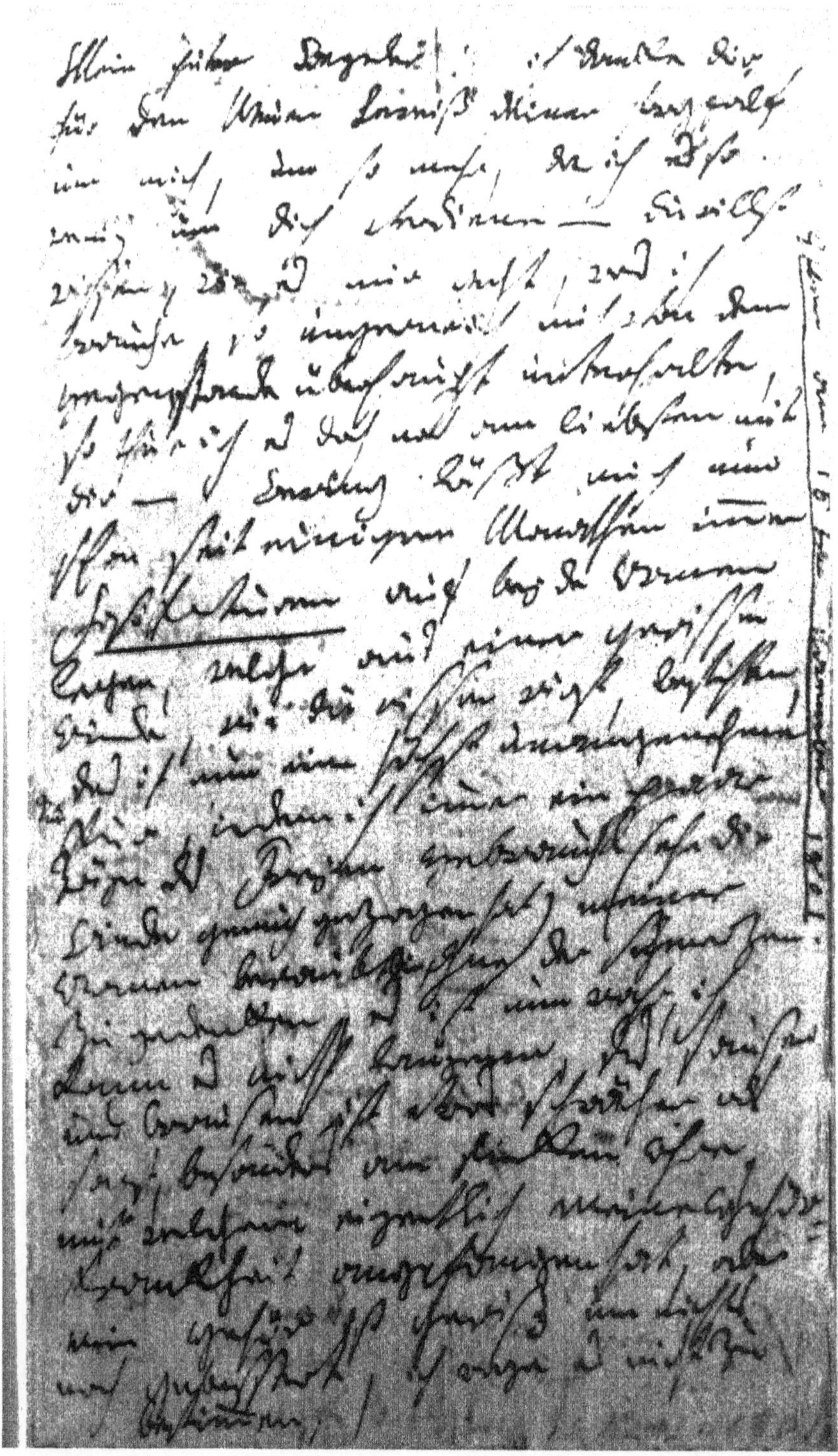

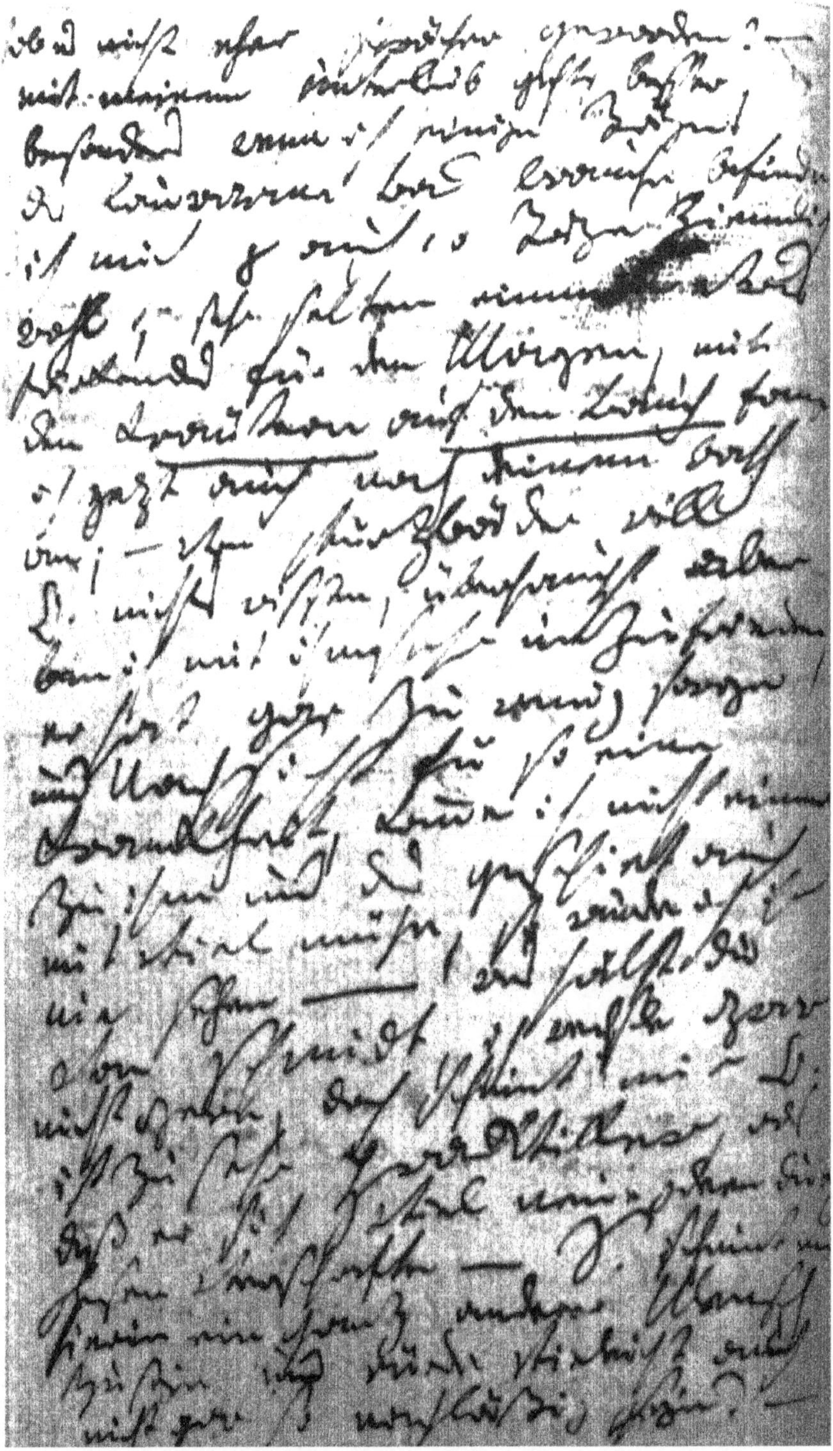

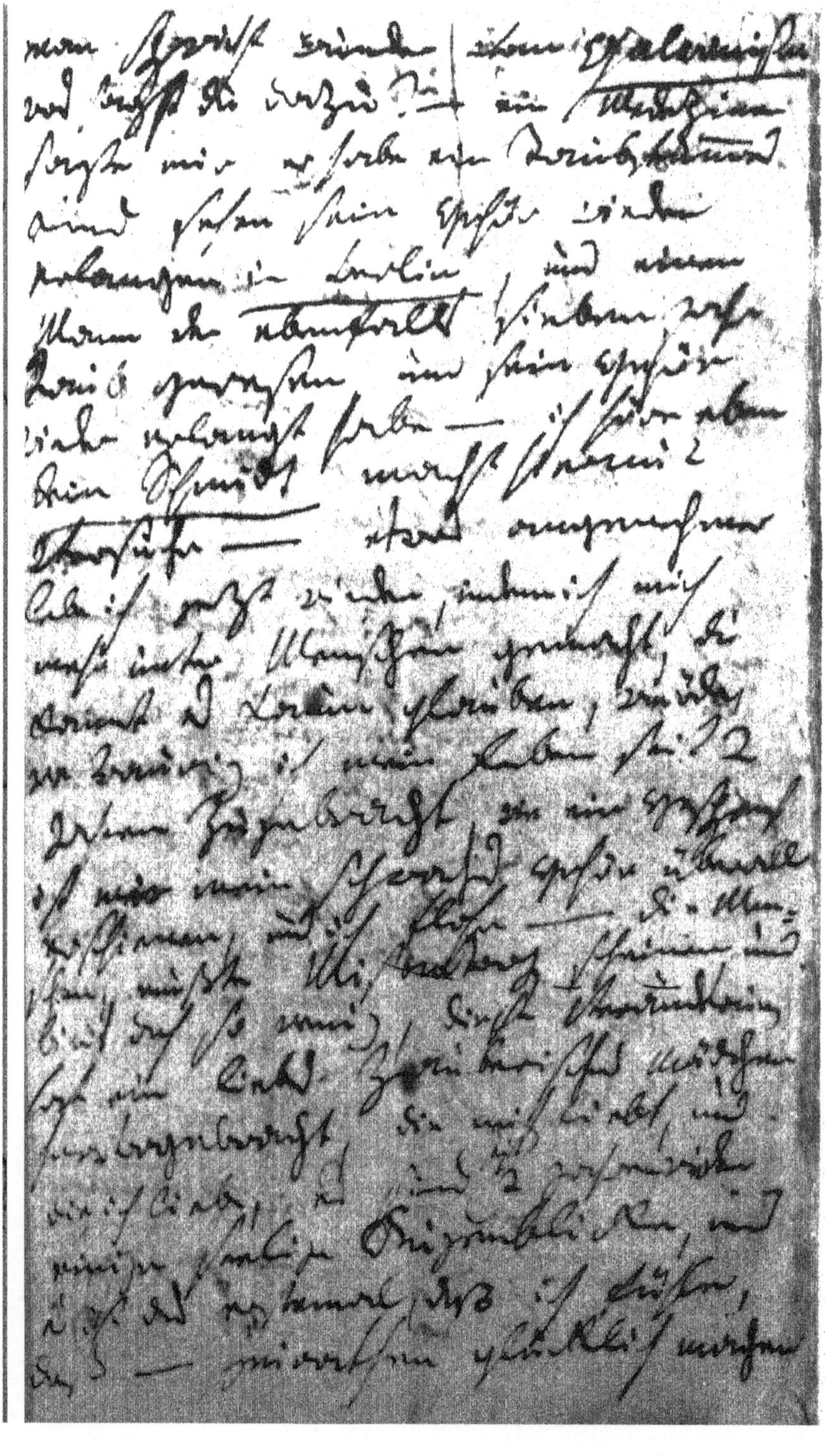

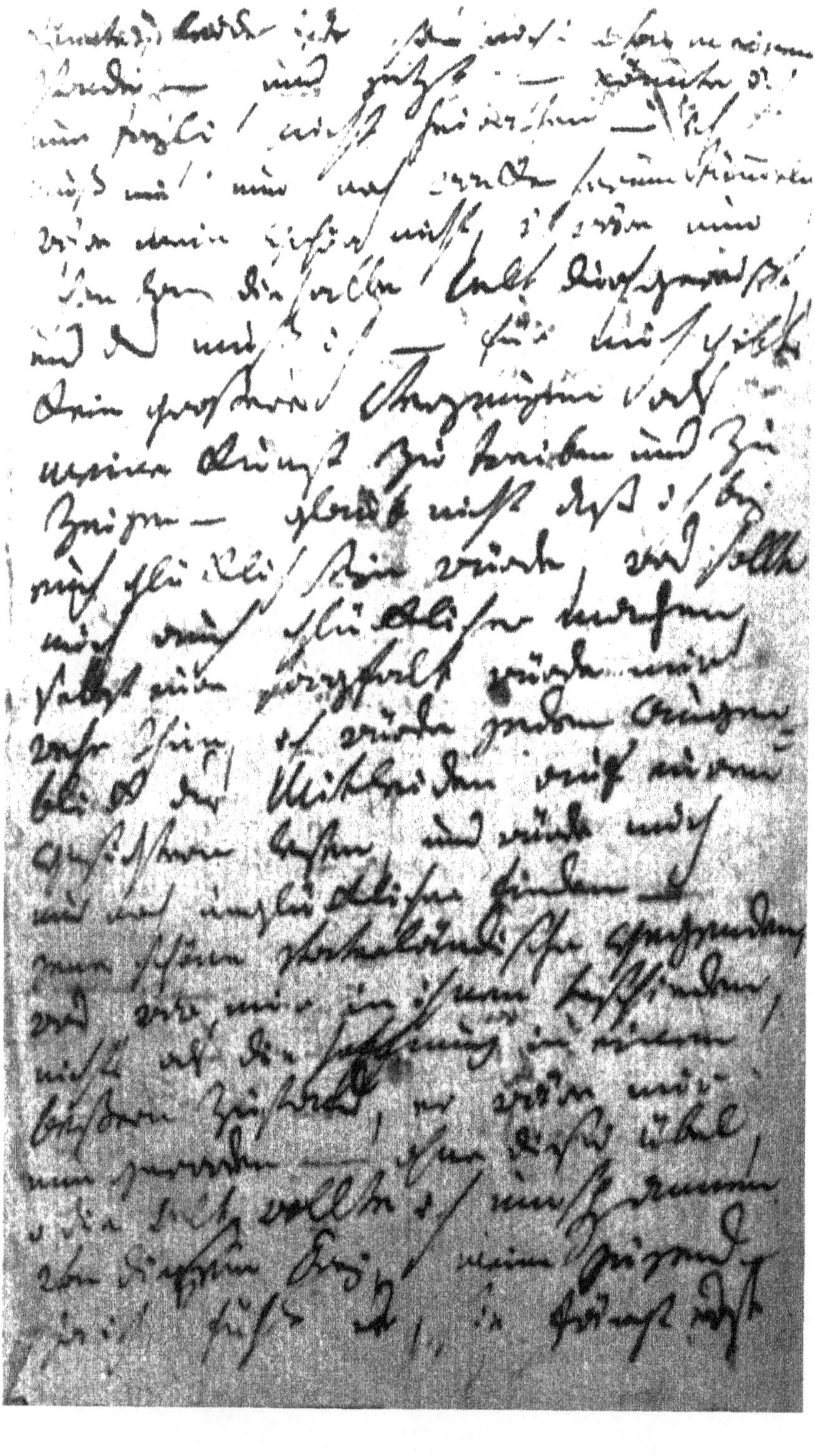

them?(70) Until the first onset of his malady he has lived without thought for the morrow. At present his compositions bring him in little, he does not see to getting paid for the lessons he gives, he exists on provisional pensions that are always wounding to his susceptibilities. To lay anything by he would have had to tour Germany and Europe as a virtuoso. The idea occurs to him.(71) But the deafness comes on so swiftly that already the project makes him uneasy. In any case it would be years before he could amass sufficient to marry on.

Giulietta does not wait for him. She marries— a double affront, this!—a musician (and what a musician!), a man of the world, an amateur, a handsome fellow, one of those dandies who play at being the great artist, without having the faintest idea of the gulf there is between insipidities like theirs and a work of genius. This little Count Gallenberg, a cub of twenty, will have the impertinence, at the orchestral concerts of the winter of 1803, to put side by side with the symphonies of Beethoven his own overtures, pieced together out of Mozart and Cherubini; and Giulietta is no more conscious of the difference than he is.(72) She marries him on the 3rd November, 1803, a year and a half after Beethoven had dedicated *alla Damigella Contessa* the sorrowful *Sonata quasi una fantasia*, Op. 27, No. 2 (the *Moonlight*).(73) The illusion had been short-lived; and already the sonata showed more suffering and wrath than love. Six months after this immortal ode, Beethoven, in despair, writes the Heiligenstadt Testament (6th October, 1802).

THERE ARE biographers who love to read their hero a lesson. Beethoven's have not spared him in this respect. All through the monumental works that Thayer and his German successors have devoted to him (74) they set themselves to prove that Beethoven well deserved his troubles—almost, even, his deafness!

It is true: his crime was not to know how to adapt himself to ordinary standards. They show no less zeal in demonstrating that, all in all, he was not so unhappy! Again it is true; the unfortunate man had within him the immense joy of the symphonies. But when they use his laughter as an argument against his sorrow they show themselves lacking not only in a sense of grandeur but in the most elementary humanity. History, in the hands of conscientious savants who go to the archives for the life of a man but forget to look for it in the man himself, is a form of treason. I do not wish to be unjust. These men, with the patience of

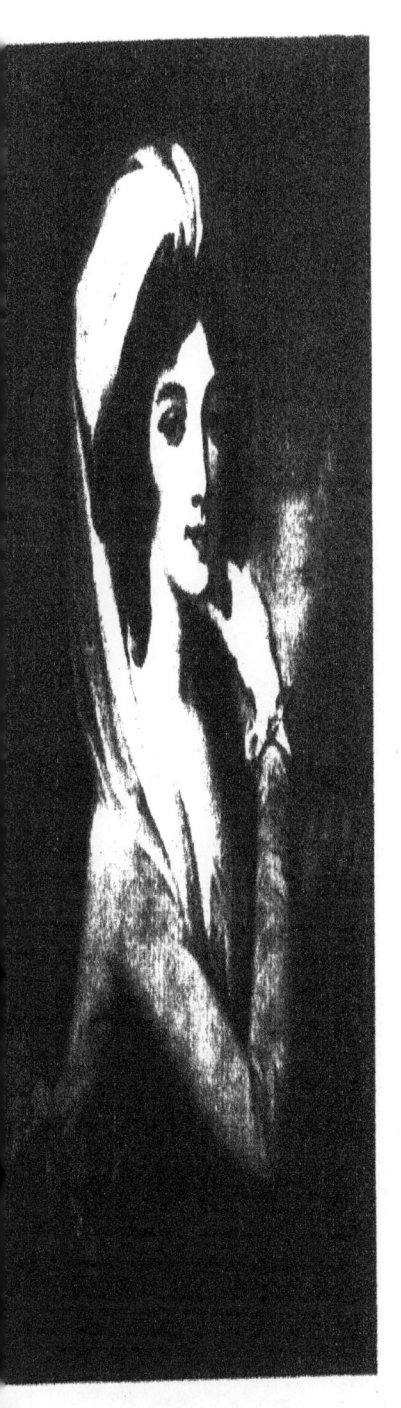

Portrait of Princess Maria Christina Lichnowsky

Portrait of Prince Karl Lichnowsky

ants, have meticulously amassed a treasure of documents for which we cannot be too grateful to them; and every now and then there comes a glow into the blood of the good musicians that they are, that makes them render fine homage to the perfection of the art. But how destitute of life they are, and what a sealed enigma life remains to them! They have no psychology. And nowhere do they suspect the true proportions of the hero. They measure him with the measuring rod of ordinary men. They are right, and they are wrong. Their measuring rod authorises them to declare the mountain lacking in proportion; that is because they see it from below. The mountain, in its turn, would have the right to tax them with that " spirit of smallness " (*Geist der Kleinlichkeit*) which Beethoven abominated, and which, in a moment of irritation, he attributed to one of his good friends.

Beethoven would not be Beethoven if he were not *too much* of whatever he was. I do not praise him; I do not blame him; I am trying to paint him *whole*. Whoever would understand him must be able to embrace the excess of his contrasts, that brings about his mighty equilibrium. Yes, Beethoven is capable—at any rate in his youth—of feeling joy and sorrow almost simultaneously. The one does not exclude the other; they are the two poles of his " electrical genius "; (75) it is by means of these that he discharges and re-charges his formidable vitality. The most extraordinary thing about him is not his enormous capacity for suffering and loving but the elasticity of his nature. Of this the crisis of 1802 is the most magnificent example.

Beethoven is felled to the ground ; never has a more heartrending cry of despair than this testamentary letter (which was never despatched) been torn from a human breast. He measures his length on the ground,—but, like the Titan of the fable, only to raise himself again at a bound, his strength multiplied by ten. " No, I will not endure it ! " . . . He seizes destiny by the throat. . . . " You will not succeed in bowing me utterly down."

In natures such as this, the excess of suffering determines the salutary reaction ; the strength increases with that of the enemy. And when the prostrated one finds himself on his feet again he is no longer merely one man : he is the army of the *Eroica* on the march.(76)

CHAPTER II
THE EROICA

CHAPTER II

THE EROICA

TO GREAT lives there comes in their June prime an hour of plenitude, ardent and spring-like, when the spirit of the sap splits the bark, and, from dawn to evening, the whole tree is at once flower and fruit, wing and song. The imprisoned forces, the genii of joy and those of sorrow, the demon of the species, the frenzied thrust of the creative need, break through the narrow let of the flood-gates of the days, and, out of the furnace of Being, project the flood of the God, the unknown Self. In moments such as these, trials, sickness, and the most grievous wounds all serve to liberate the stream; the pick of suffering pierces the soul and makes an issue for the fire. And the soul's laceration is the spirit's intoxication. Who can say that the one negates or is inconsistent with the other? They are one; they are the rhythm-beat of genius. As long as his strength keeps growing, the harnessed joy and sorrow bear him on; he makes of them his team, which he drives where he will. He it is who wills the route. His energies rise up in legions. But he holds them bound; he assembles them and launches them to the conquest of the interior world.

I am not playing with words! These images are only reflections, shadows of fire that dance across the roadway. Let us enter into the forge! Let us see if ever a Napoleonic will has more victoriously manipulated an incandescent mountain of molten matter! Even in the life of a Beethoven, itself exceptional, this period of three years is unique. It rightly bears the title of *Eroica*. It is an Etna; and within, the Cyclopes are forging the shield of Achilles.

WE CAN follow every blow of the hammer. By a singular good fortune there have been preserved for us almost

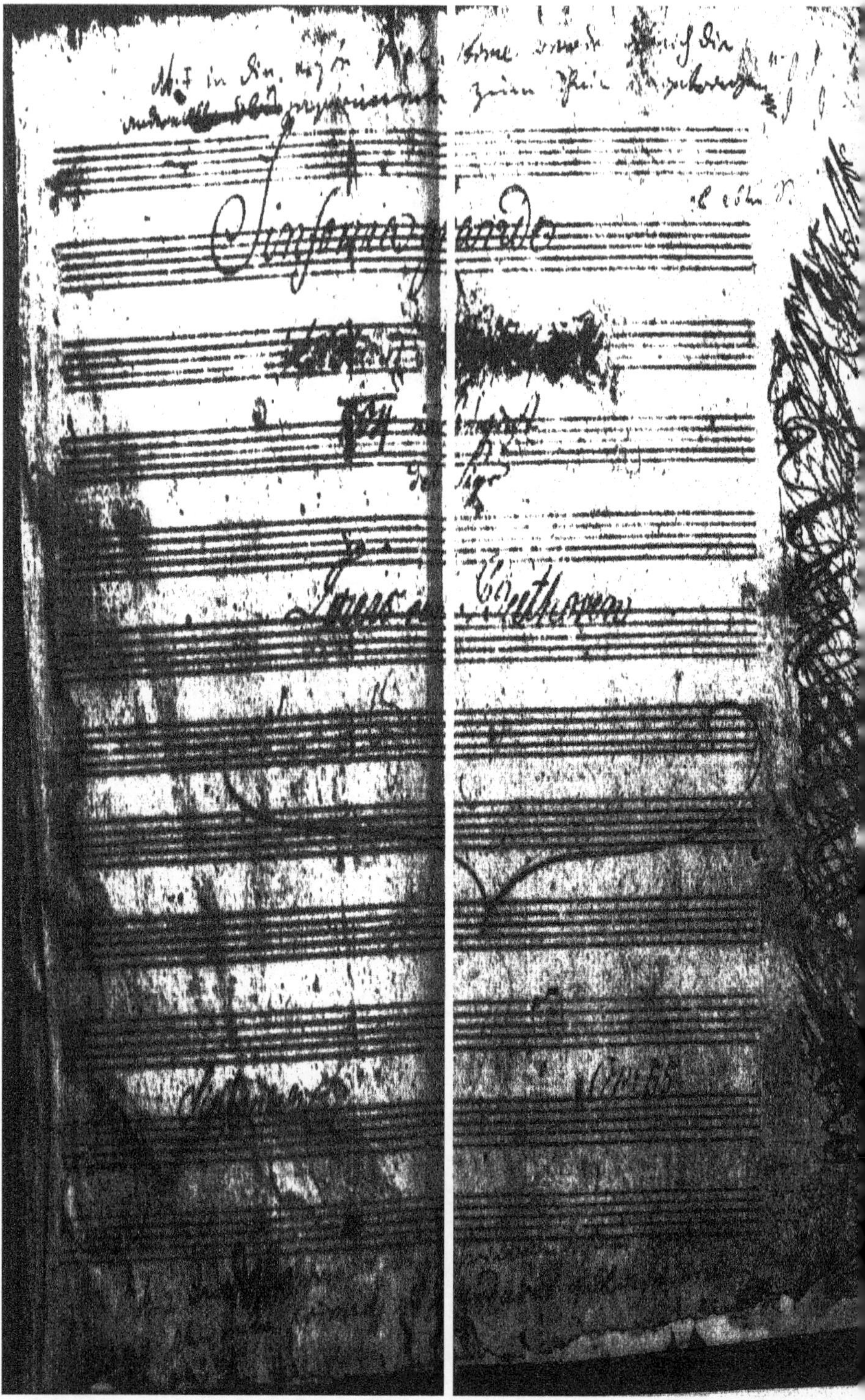
Sinfonia grande

the whole of the Sketch-Books (77) from the autumn of 1801 to the spring of 1804. And the details into which I am about to enter will prove, I hope, to the musician who mistrusts a poet's judgments on music, that this poet, before he begins his song, has used his eyes. He has even seen, as he went along, that more than one musician who has spoken on the subject of Beethoven, whether to extol or to depreciate him, has listened to him very absent-mindedly, otherwise how are we to account for those incredible errors of judgment that attribute to this master-builder of Roman vaults, this *imperator* of the will to order, of the inexorable and sovereign reason, a romantic anarchy and a sentimental disorder?

It is at Heiligenstadt, then, that he has been since the commencement of the summer of 1802, in a big house outside the town, belonging to a peasant, standing on an eminence from which the Danube and the plain can be seen away in the distance, with the blue line of the Carpathians on the horizon. . . .

"*Laudeturque domus, longos quæ prospicit agros!*"

He is wrapped in the silence of the fields; for Dr. Schmidt has advised him to spare his hearing, and he would conceal his infirmity from men. He is alone with his demons,—slighted love, hope, grief, the whole concert of the inner voices. And as long as summer and hope endure, the tree has blossomed with youth and joy. He has just finished the second symphony.(78)

But October has come,—October, that chills the sun, that of the fields and that of the blood. . . .

Der hohe Muth der mich oft in den schönen Sommertägen beseelte—er ist verschwunden . . . (" The lofty courage that often possessed me during the lovely days of summer has fled ").(79)

And now the cold of the grave and the odour of annihilation. In the lone house at Heiligenstadt, in these sunless days, a death-roar is wrung from Beethoven. A mournful Testament; the groans of the chained Prometheus have come to us over that century of battles and revolutions, have filled our sky, and still move the heart of humanity !(80)

But the man in his death agony—what did *he* hear in answer to his cries ? From the depth of the woods around him, where the future *Pastoral* sleeps under the October rains,(81) the appealing cry of the Testament is answered by the mysterious horn-call of the *Eroica* . . . " Lazarus, arise ! "

Ries tells us that Beethoven wrote (he really means conceived and commenced) the *Eroica* at Heiligenstadt. Now Beethoven returned to Vienna in November: it is clear, then, that the first idea of the monument sprang up in him on the very morrow of the Testament. Perhaps he had hardly penned the last lines of this—the farewell to joy,(82)—when the spirit of life convulsively upheaved the tombstone and the lightning that had just struck the man rebounded from him.

Nottebohm attributes the opening pages of the Sketch-Book to October.(83) And in the earliest pages appear tentative sketches for the first, second, and fourth movements of the *Eroica*; then come four long sketches, each of them with variants, for the first section of the first movement; then a number of short sketches; —and all the rest follows. The brain is taken possession of by the interior vision; Beethoven never pauses now till the work is finished. But what hammering on the anvil, and what a shower of sparks!

We observe that the first long sketch, which at one stroke projects the whole design of the first part of the first movement, hollows out the river bed, draws with a sure and heavy line the contour of the summit, the melodic peaks, the succession of lights and shades, the sequence of the modulations—this first casting presents already, along with the projection of the

EB

big heroic theme, its plaintive downward bend at the fifth bar :—

[musical notation]

Hesitation of the still troubled soul to follow the injunction given it by the invisible Master, the call to action, to the great destiny ! . . . And this throws the light of day on that " October night " in which the bleeding heart of Beethoven received, in a clap of thunder, the heroic mission, and, for a moment, grew faint and wavered. . . . But the imperious flood takes possession of him again and carries him along :—

[musical notation]

Beethoven has thus received, from the very first instant, the revelation as a whole, the impulse and the general atmosphere of the first part of the movement. But if the weighty machine is now posed on the rails, and, endued with its essential organs, the themes and principal motives of its first half, begins to move, all the rest is still to find ; the second half of the first part is still in the haze ; and even in the first half how heavy this haze hangs on the workman's heart! Before he arrives at the thirtieth bar he loses, not his direction, but the sustaining breath; he repeats himself, becomes involved in the mire, pulls up short; and, returning on his steps, he indicates, by means of one of his customary signs :—

"*Vi—de*"

his hero's progress by means of a variant of the first text, that introduces the gigantic, long-striding motive:—

A following sketch, completing this design, adds to it some syncopations that complete its characteristic of contracted muscles and gripping fingers, in a mighty effort to scale the peaks :—

Later on, his lucid economy of the elements he is employing will make him reserve this athletic motive for the combat of the second part. But in this first part he introduces, at bars 25 and 26, those syncopated sforzati against which, as against a triple obstacle, the course of the hero is brought up with a shock, but which, caught up and broken by his youthful vigour, only heighten the effect of invincibility :—

Passing motives of the first part are indicated : the first, tender and plaintive, is at first barely suggested, and even then suddenly broken off :—

It is like a cry of a bird in the forest. . . . Then it awkwardly pulls itself together and gets going again, feeling its way : it first of all achieves its right rhythm :—

then its line :—

which it will later lose again in its hesitations, at last recovering it and settling down in it firmly and finally.

The other motive, with a rhythm like a cavalcade, comes into full being from the first :—

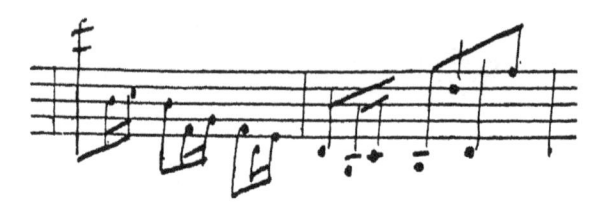

and remains fixed in all the sketches. But how many times must it have been carded and unravelled before arriving at its definitive form ! What superfluous agitations, what stampings and tramplings, Beethoven must have erased from his idea ! Sometimes the second sketches increase the chaos by the very act of trying to win free of it ; and it is only in the last ones, after the ultimate rigours of criticism and after a furious tension, that the artist achieves the broad, continent, flawless line. The combat is all the more exhausting because Beethoven, quitting the inspired opening, pierces to the tangled heart of the movement, stripping from it, shred by shred, the most exquisite details of expression, such as this :—

wearing himself out in unheard-of efforts to achieve the conclusion of the first part, recommencing and again recommencing without advancing, stuck in some banal clogging harmony or other, until suddenly he finds himself free of the bad dream.

As for the second section,—the famous *Durchführung* (84) —who will ever be able to say what it contains of days and nights and weeks of battle? Here is an Austerlitz of music, the conquest of an empire. And Beethoven's has endured longer than Napoleon's. It took him longer to realise it; for he, himself and alone, was *imperator* and army.

Let me remind the reader who has not much technical knowledge of music what the *Durchführung* of a sonata or a symphony is. It signifies the "Middle Empire,"— the section between the first exposition (and repeat) of the themes and their final conclusive return. It is here that the creative imagination gives itself up to the constructive manipulation of the stated motives, which it transposes and combines in twenty different ways. Ever since the *Eroica* this section has been the peculiar field of genius (often it remains unoccupied!). There the composer lives and moves at the very centre of the cosmos of his thought, like the God who takes in his hand the substance of the worlds and projects it into moving architectures, suspended above the void.

Beethoven's predecessors saw in this section little more than a means of dialectical transition between the exposition of the thesis and its conclusion ; and they used it for a display (though always discreet, for that was a polished age) of their skill in the art of elegant thematic debate. With Mozart the *Durchführung* never exceeds in length two-thirds of the first section ; often he keeps it down to one-third.(85) Beethoven until now had followed this example. With the *Eroica* he suddenly ruptures the tradition ; his *Durchführung* is longer than the first section by as much as two-thirds—250 bars as against 147.(86)

Theoretically this should result in disproportion, the first exposition of the themes (the substance of the discourse) being lost in the oratorical " development " (if the term " development " be applicable here). But nothing of the kind happens. As a matter of fact, for more than a century the effect of the symphony, its empire over the millions of human beings who have trod in turn the banks of this river of sound, come precisely from this prodigious *Durchführung*. The marvelling admiration of criticism has never ceased to grapple with this phenomenon. We find ourselves faced with one of the most stupendous problems of construction that has ever been posed and triumphantly resolved in music,—an *ars nova* as involved, as condensed, at once vertiginous and sure, as a Gothic vault ; the same involutions unfolding themselves under the firm controlling hand of geometric reason, the science (is it instinctive or conscious?) of numbers ruling the intoxicated play of the imagination.

Now what was the first form taken in Beethoven's mind by the conception of this monument, the harmony of whose masses and the equilibrium of whose buttresses we are about to study?

According to the sketches, before having even traced the plan of this section he had already settled on the course of the modulations—the colour before the line,—and on the key in which the lovely lyrical episode :—

was to enter. And as soon as he has begun to outline his plan, which is still rather formless, he decides upon the famous dissonances—the first two bars of the principal theme, brusquely evoked out of a mist, held in suspense for a moment, then tearing their way through the cloud :—

This magical return (in the third section), the shock of which invariably surprises the ear, and seems even to many instructed listeners a mistake or a caprice, is willed from the very first design of the movement, even before anything of the remainder has been decided upon.(87) And the will maintains the conception through all the following " states " of the engraving, right to the end.

We thus have two essential elements of the first casting :

(1) The modulation, which indicates the declivities of the stream and its direction.

(2) The rapids, the whirlpool, the breakwaters.

That is everything.

It is now for the will to explore the lay-out of the country. The will, in artists of the second rank, is a sort of tepid and consciously applied reason : with Beethoven it is always alight with genius, as much as, or even more so than, the first inspiration. For, as I shall have the occasion to show some day,(88) the essence of this genius residing in his subconsciousness he does not know himself until he is revealed to himself; and this revelation happens with each blow of the pick on the rock that sends the rough splinters flying from the enveloping stone, with each thrust of the spade into the clay that encloses the idea ; it is himself he unearths by the sweat of his brow. The obscure but powerful instinct knows where it should go; the spirit has sensed the direction of the tunnel that is to be dug. But it does not know the surprises reserved for it in the bowels of the mountain, the resources, the obstacles it will encounter there. And out of these very obstacles the energy of genius will fashion an element of strength and solidity.

The innumerable sketches for this second section show with what tenacity and what sovereign self-criticism he laboriously establishes, one by one, the layers of his vast structure. He brings to the task a marvellous sense of rhythms and numbers, of the opposition of masses and of colours, of the preparation of effects, of how to throw the principal accent into high relief, how to disengage the great outlines in all their nobility and intensity. Hence the drama of this march with titan strides, a drama that seems to mount *crescendo*, and is about to cover the world, but crashes down to ruin, making way for the sudden twilight in which, as if beneath the dust, the shattered giant pants. And out of this dust, in a murmuring silence, on the very verge of death, there emerges in largest outline the unexpected summons of the heroic theme, renewing the action and soon bringing victory.(89)

Two men have sought to discover the hidden laws of this colossal architecture,—Hugo Leichtentritt, in his *Musikalische Formenlehre* (1911), and Alfred Lorenz, in a penetrating analysis entitled *Worauf beruht die bekannte*

Wirkung der Durchführung im 1. Eroicasatze. Eine Untersuchung. (90) Each has been surprised at the discovery of the relations of the numbers that between them determine the various members of the structure, the mighty framework of the *Durchführung*. Lorenz obtains these four main divisions :

    I. 54 bars.
    II. 64 ,,
    III. 54 ,,
    IV. 60 ,,

The first and second divisions form a symmetrical opposition—thesis and antithesis ; the third and fourth effect the synthesis. And the *Durchführung* as a whole constitutes a perfect sonata, a complete symphony, at the core of the symphony.

Moreover, if, in accordance with the directions, we repeat the first section of the allegro, the numbers of the three sections (the first with repeat, the *Durchführung*, and the final section with the coda as apotheosis) give this astonishing equilibrium :

    298—250—294.

Not, of course, that Beethoven has measured his proportions with a line ! It is his instinct that has established them, in the night of thought. And it is precisely this that kindles our admiration.

Let us not forget that Beethoven had here no model

to guide him. He discovered a New World: he discovered himself! The *Eroica* is Columbus's caravel, the first to reach an unknown continent,—a new style, to which the future has rightly given the name of its first explorer. But what other explorer has ever shown such a surety in his discovery, such a mastery over the work of whose mass and range he himself had no suspicion until he had embarked upon it? We of to-day see only the result; we no longer reflect upon the exhausting groping revealed in the sketches, the furious labour of the fevered and tortured solitary who has attached himself, like Michael Angelo, to the ceiling of his Sixtine, and bolted and barred himself in until he has solved the problem of the numbers and forms he has let loose, and subdued it to his will. But it is because we are obscurely conscious, in the victorious result, in the equilibrium and symmetry of the suspended masses, of the heroic passions of the battle, it is for this reason that he intoxicates us. And the curious thing is that this *Eroica*, the most novel of Beethoven's works, and therefore, one would have thought, the one that it should have taken the longest to understand, was the one that very soon became the most popular.(91)

I know that an exhausted élite holds cheap this popularity, to which itself can never attain; it would like to see in it a stigma of commonness. And it goes without saying that we share its disdain when the popularity of a work is bought at the price of its lowering itself to the level of a mean facility, of common bad taste. But when, underneath these first strata of commonness, the artist is vigorous enough to delve down to the great laws of the general life and the essential rhythms of the soul, the masterpiece of the individual genius becomes, without effort or intention on his part, the natural expression of all humanity. And I affirm that this oneness is the highest harmony that can be realised on earth. Beethoven has accomplished it in the *Eroica*. Like Gluck, whose work he admired,(92) but with the torrential flood of an inexhaustible inspiration that was denied to Gluck, he was able to build for his own delight and offer to the new century—in that epoch that, by dint of revolutions and battles of empires, inaugurated the reign of the masses,—the first incomparable models of a monumental style, proportioned to the number, the spirit, and the vision of assembled thousands. He did not abolish the lines of his great predecessors,—that sonata form that Haydn and Mozart had recently so lovingly perfected ; but he adjusts the fabric to his great shoulders, to the amplitude of that chest of his in which there beats the heart of a whole world. He is in the line of those master-builders of imperial Rome, who took the cupola and the vault that had hitherto served for tiny structures and gave them a more spacious organisation. As early as 1808, the Beethoven quartets reminded Reichardt of

Michael Angelo raising the cupola of Brunelleschi on the Pantheon of Agrippa. But while in the grandiose intellectualism of Michael Angelo, the master-workman, the line is dry, cold and abstract, Beethoven's line is always full and moist with sap, like the spring-filled tree-trunks of the fine Gothic portals. All is flesh and blood. Right from the bursting of the dam by the two imperious opening chords :—

which, in accordance with a frequent habit of Beethoven, seem to have been placed at the head of the work only after this was finished, as a sort of affirmation of its total will, of the sovereign *Credo*,—from this *hoc volo, sic jubeo*, the river begins to flow; and nothing can stop it until it reaches the estuary.

AND NOW that I have tried to indicate some of the hidden ways of the creative spirit in the construction of this first movement, let me dream my interpretation of it before you! It pleases you professional musicians to turn up your noses at all interpretations. But your works would not be listened to unless the tissue of their rhythmic and sonorous combinations suggested a web of successive and connected emotions to those who listen to them. And you yourselves (or those of you who can rise above the low-water mark of the mere journeyman) can write nothing that will endure if the forces of your whole being, your ideas as well as your emotions, are not engaged—even if you are unconscious of it. Let us claim the right, then, to dream the work of art after (or, perhaps, before?) having looked at and run our hands over its naked body. In dreams is often divination; one sees better with the eyelids closed.

Let us brush from our path, first of all, the too simple anthropomorphic explanation that builds on the title—"Bonaparte"—that Beethoven first of all wrote on the title page and then tore out.(93) In a mind like that of Beethoven, wholly absorbed in itself, its passions, its combats, and its God, the external world counts merely as a reflection, an echo, a symbol of the interior drama. Moreover, Beethoven is incapable of seeing the life of other beings as it is: his own is too vast; for him it is the measure of everything; he projects it into everything.

Other artists, such as Mozart and Haydn, who are less preoccupied with themselves, find room within themselves for the observation of the external world. Mozart takes other souls to himself; Haydn has a shrewd eye for them, and a roguish touch. Beethoven scarcely ever emerges from himself; but this Self is a universe. Even the exterior nature that he sees becomes immediately incorporated with it, loses its own character, takes the form and the odour of the Beethoven cosmos. Imitation —which, say what you will, has always been one of the fundamental instincts of the artist, a spring from which he draws nourishment—is in Beethoven an extremely attenuated faculty, or it is strangely transformed by the nature of the glance, always partial, always passionate, always charged with his own weighty interior life, that he directs upon things. If then Napoleon has come into Beethoven's mind it is after the act, when he searches, in the circle of the living men about him, as in a mirror, for a face that shall give back to his solitude the image of his own omnipresent self. But the first gesture of the supposed model suffices to destroy the illusion violently: and the outraged Beethoven tears out the name of Bonaparte. Hans von Bülow's error really was not much greater—though, in the circumstances, more absurd—when he foisted on to the *Eroica* the name of Bismarck! Any of us could equally well indulge in this trifling game of resemblances, in the manner of young

THE EROICA

Hamlet impudently laughing in the face of Polonius over the clouds of the Baltic. As a matter of fact, each symphony, each work of Beethoven bears one name alone—Beethoven.(94)

The great motive that dominates the symphony :—

is a personality. What matters it to us whether it is a man or an idea, the obscure voice of instinct or the lucid will? It lives and it acts. Who can doubt its existence? Simple and upright it goes forward; from its first step it is marked with the seal of its destiny, that marches to its appointed end and knows no other. The soul into which this order has entered bends, at the fifth bar,(95) under the burden. But this burden itself is its destiny, is a part of its essence; it accepts it with a sigh, and abandons itself to the stream. The overcoming of the first obstacles (bars 25 to 27) reveals to it its own energy; it takes to spouse the action imposed on it. This resounding "Aye!" (bars 35 to 45) is answered, by reaction, by the regrets of the tender and weary heart :—

(oboes, clarinets, flutes, and violins in alternation). For the moment the heart is subdued by the will (bars 55 ff.). The battle is joined between the two souls, a combat with lashing whips, with sabre blows (bars 65 ff.). The mighty motive gradually raises its head; it transforms itself into fragments, as if by that means to find a way through. But always it is met by the plaint that stays it and troubles its heart (bars 83 ff.):—

Checked in its impulse, it returns, it redoubles. The great off-beat harmonies cut sharply down (bars 123, etc.) :—

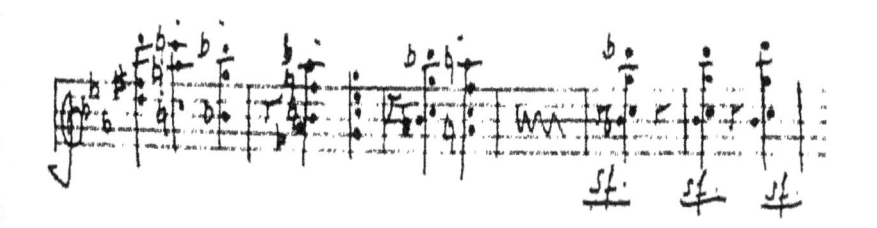

It is the confession of defeat, the renunciation of tenderness, of *Sehnsucht* (bars 132 ff.). The first section

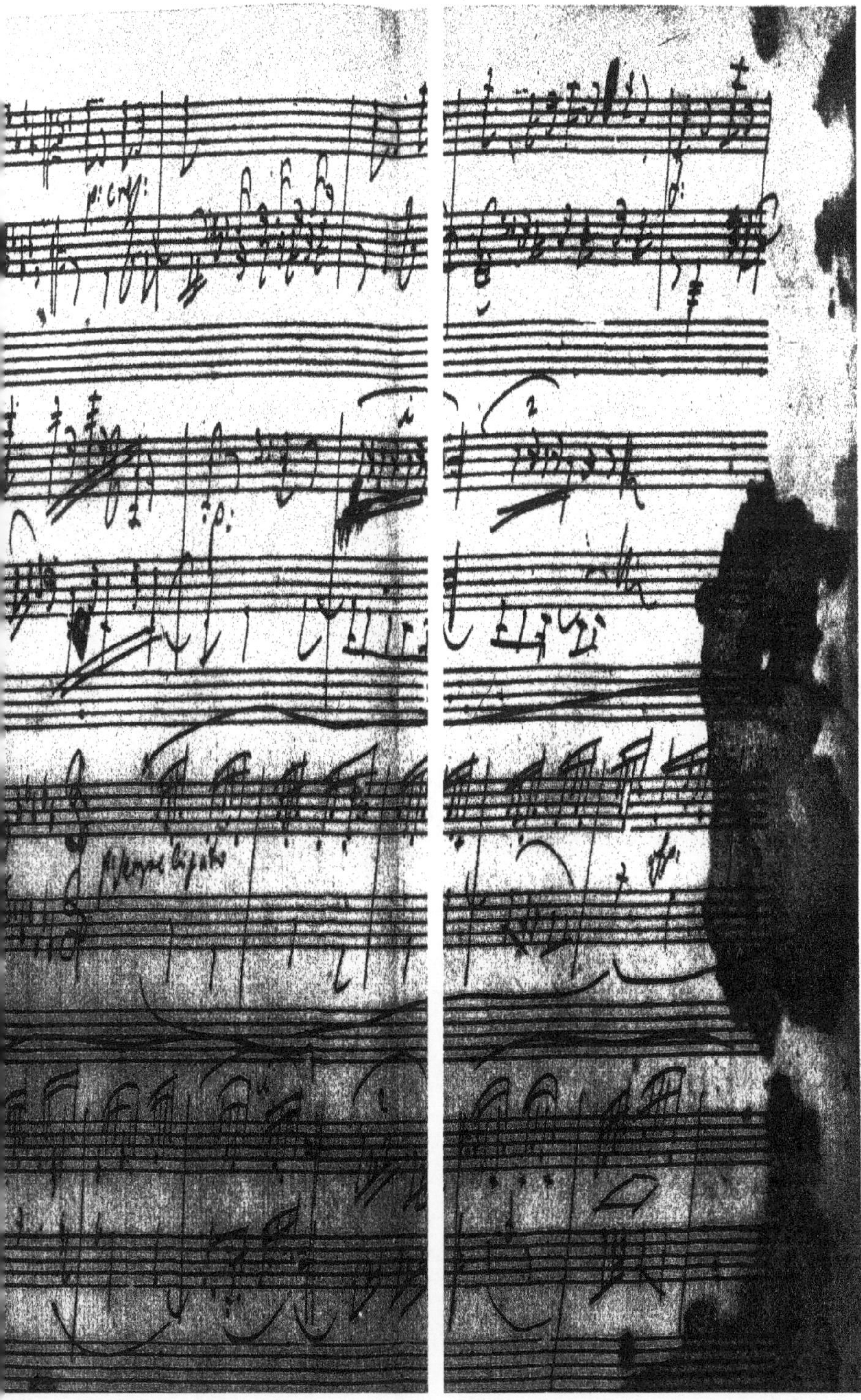

of the allegro closes with a bleeding wound, cruel harmonies that hurt :—

The spirit once more plunges into the broil, and now it is as if it has lost its way. The first battle—an inconclusive one—has been joined between the ego of love and the ego of will, in the house at Heiligenstadt, enveloped in the night of the fields.

In the second section (the *Durchführung*) the soul's field of battle becomes co-extensive with the universe, and the fresco assumes colossal proportions. As in those fabulous combats in which the giant, hacked in pieces, grows new arms, like an antediluvian lizard, the theme of the will, plunged again into the fire, hammered on the anvil, breaks up into fragments, stretches out, enlarges. It is Beethoven's hallucinatory speech to Bettina : "*I see it fly and become lost in the chaos of impressions ; I pursue it, I clasp it passionately again, I can no longer separate myself from it, I must multiply it, in a spasm, in modulation after modulation.* . . ."

On the boundless plain the innumerable theme swells to an army corps; it deploys its ample developments. The flood mounts wave on wave; but here and there islets of elegy appear like clumps of trees in the middle of the torrent. In spite of the labour of the giant blacksmith, who furiously tries to weld the opposing motives, the word of the will does not yet achieve a complete victory. In vain (bars 302–303) it realises, for a moment, the powerful homophony of major octaves :—

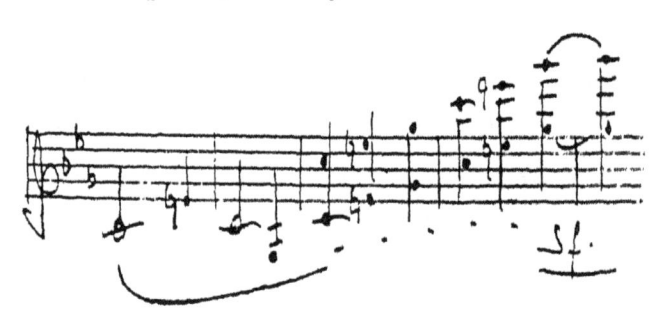

It topples over into the minor again, remounts, and once more falls; vainly it piles Pelion on Ossa (bars 341–370). Precipitated into the depths, buried under the mass, the breathless warrior tries to rise, but has no longer the strength for it; the rhythm of life is broken, seems on the point of extinction. . . . Already we hear no more—(a muffled tremolo of the strings in the silence) —than the humming of the fevered blood in the arteries. . . . Suddenly the summons of destiny is heard pianissimo against this curtain of shifting purple haze :—

The motive of heroic action, given out by the horns, rises from the abyss of death.

The whole orchestra leaps to its feet to welcome it.

It is the resurrection. All the forces of the soul resume their march towards the appointed goal. The third section of the movement begins. To it is reserved the victory. By a stroke of genius,—the idea was seemingly re-discovered, as Alfred Lorenz notes, by Wagner in *Parsifal*—it is announced first by the prophecy of the horn, then that of the flute, which, for the first time, instead of letting the motive fall, magically maintains it for five bars (transposed from E flat into F major, then into D flat) on the dominant :—

The third section, the synthesis of the other two, reproduces in a condensed form the musical drama that has just been played before us. But it does not confine itself to the customary mere repetition of this. It keeps postponing the conclusion. Mallarmé said of Wagner's *American Centennial March* that it was an Egyptian dynasty on the march. The coda of the first movement of the *Eroica* is the Grand Army of the soul, that will not stop until it has trampled on the whole earth. After the spirit has for the last time evoked, in an imperious summing-up of isolated moments of the first two parts, the abrupt fall from the full tumult of the combat into the humming silence (bars 568-570) :—

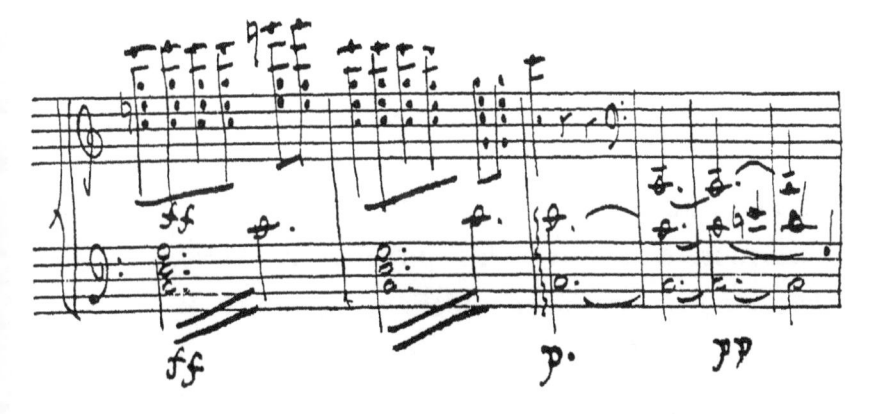

this last time it is no longer the impassible order to advance that is heard. The first theme to reappear—the motive of action—is encircled with dances :—

No more grief, no more regrets ! Even the plaint and the elegy are drawn into the epic round ; and the imperial cavalcade ends in a carousal, the dance of a jubilant people, set in motion by a hero's fist.

IN THE adagio assai, the hero is dead. Never has he been more truly alive : his spirit hovers above the coffin that is borne on the shoulders of humanity.(96)

A *Funeral March*. . . . The idea was a trite one in that epoch of heroic apotheoses ! But how Beethoven has revivified it by what he has put into it, the intimate accent, the soul laid bare—his own genius ! (In 1803, too, he was not quite divested of " eloquence," as he was to become later, in the years after 1817.) But in this eloquence there is nothing that does not come from the heart. The major *dolce cantando* is, in my opinion, the modern poem that comes nearest to the elegiac choruses of Greek tragedy ; it has the harmonious grace of Sophocles, his natural nobility, his perfection, his serene melancholy. The return to the minor is the occasion for prodigious developments of quite another character, sombre, complex, Shakespearean, with unexpected strokes of genius, the evocations of hallucination. The elegy becomes an epopee : already, in the forests

General view of Heiligenstadt

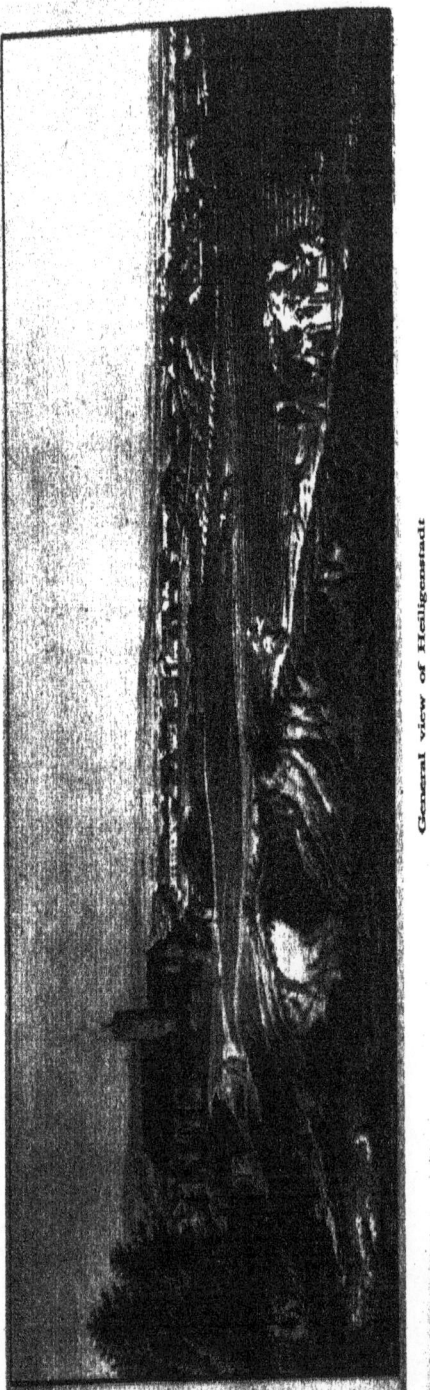

above the Rhine, we see the corpse of Siegfried being raised on the buckler. (Without Beethoven the funeral scene of the *Götterdämmerung* would never have been possible.) And the coda becomes, at the pianissimo, an exhausted murmur welling up from an abyss of sorrow.

But let us return to the Sketch-Book, and be prepared for a surprise. If ever a melody has seemed inspired, if ever a phrase has seemed to find its appointed line at the first attempt, if any work of art conveys the impression that it could never have been written otherwise, that not a single one of its accents or inflections could be changed, for they are part of it from all eternity, it is the principal motive of this Funeral March. Yet the Sketch-Book shows that Beethoven reached it only by slow stages, painfully, sweating blood and tears. The first sketch for it is commonplace :—

Beethoven, as Nottebohm shows, has had to conquer the melody bar by bar,—nay, note by note, accent by accent. Now he hits upon the characteristic droop of the March :—

And now again he finds the moving accent of a phrase, of a fragment. Each bar becomes a medley of corrections and variants :—

The fugato of the development is clearly foreseen and decided upon in advance, as well as the major tonality of the middle section. But several themes occur to him. He has within him only the prescience of the unformed mass of the nebula and of its spiral line, without, as yet, any precise conception of the design; he will have to spend night after night in his observatory in order to fix the outline that is at the heart of this cloudy density. The obscurity grows in proportion as he makes his way towards the conclusion of the movement. For the very end of it he has had to make eight completely different sketches. And from the crude padding of the first version:—

who would have expected the moving end, that comes to Beethoven only at the last moment? Is it then the fruit not of genius but of industry, as the worthy industrious talents who, most of all, are ignorant of the nature of genius, love to persuade themselves? The truth is that it is genius itself that is at work through all this industry,—genius unsatisfied, criticising the insufficiency of each attempt in turn, going to the root of the matter, and each time tearing from the matrix a portion of the pure metal it wants and that it knows to be in it. For these eight versions, these eight forms, are all in it, those on the surface as well as those in the depths. But genius does not pause until it has reached the bed-rock of the matter, and the distinguishing mark of the genius is that he is never deceived as to the relative values of one idea and another. What he discovers after numberless attempts is not the last idea but the *first*, his very own, the immediate expression of the feeling that possesses him, of the essential force from which he had been separated by an accumulation of acquired commonplaces, of cold traditions, of heavy alluvions. The genius of Beethoven resides in this intuition of the hidden " Melieur,"[97] of those depths of the spirit where lies the magic metal of inspiration.

He does not proceed at haphazard : in this sub-soil of the subconscious his will always retains the light of its control. As he himself said to Schlösser, after having described his digging operations, " And then begins in my head the working-out in the broad and the narrow, the height and the depth. . . . And as I am conscious of what I want, the core-idea never leaves me."[98]

Sometimes, however, it happens that the right idea

leaps up within him sooner than he had expected, and in a quite unanticipated shape. These irruptions are particularly frequent during this period 1802–1803, when his being and his style are rapidly changing as the result of the inward shocks that are releasing the new man in him. We have an astounding example of this in the third movement of the *Eroica*, which he commences as a minuet (*M. am Ende Coda fremde St.* [*Stretta?*]) which he carries on in this way as far as the trio (a trio in the old style), and beyond. Then, suddenly returning to the minuet, he has this :—

His pen gives a leap. He writes *Presto !* . . . Overboard with the minuet and its formal graces ! The inspired rush of the Scherzo has been found !

The final movement of the symphony cost him less time than the others, for he already had the theme he was to work upon ; and the greater part of the sketches are concerned only with the contrapuntal treatment of it. But we must not forget that the work on the theme had been done before the symphony was commenced. This motive :—

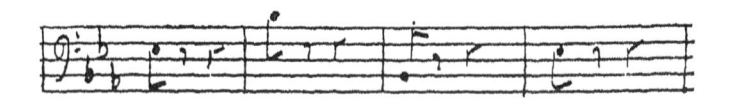

actually comes from three earlier works, in the course of which Beethoven had had time to discover its real character. And the very gradation of the three works shows us that at first this character was not recognised by Beethoven.

Begun as a simple dance and brilliant contredanse in the ballet *Prometheus* (March 1801),(99)—taken up again as a contredanse at the end of 1801(100)—then in the *Variations*, Op. 35 (spring of 1802),(101) it was still, at the time when the *Eroica* was being written, regarded by Beethoven as a motive for regular variations of the usual classical kind ; no doubt when he began this salon work he had in view, as in *Prometheus*, a sort of final gallop. But as he proceeds to manipulate his theme, throwing all sorts of lights and shadows on it, he comes upon several of its hidden souls,—the elegiac, the funereal, the heroic. When he comes to the largo of the 15th variation he sketches, without being aware of it, a big epic-dramatic scene. In the coda the death of the hero is already announced : an ending on the ordinary lines is impossible! The finale is a fugue with a suggestion of combat about it; the germ of the symphony is there. Having arrived at his goal, Beethoven returns on his steps; and now he recognises the true nature of the theme with which he had been playing,—those four mighty pillars! And the great builder sees the vast spaces he can cover with it. Then he takes it up again as the base for the last movement of the symphony, in which the variations expand to epic proportions; the contrapuntal treatment weaves it into a cluster of colossal ogival mouldings.

In this tardy discovery of the profound significance of a melodic theme we are face to face with a phenomenon of the creative subconscious to which I have elsewhere drawn attention several times in the case of Handel. It is, indeed, peculiarly characteristic of musical genius. Handel, almost always, and Beethoven frequently (as I shall show later), produce the melodic flower without being aware of the full meaning of it. (I see the æsthetes exclaiming, " Has a flower, then, a meaning ? " I reply, " Yes, for science, that is to say, for truth, and that is to say, in the last resort, for art itself; for the beautiful and the true in combination constitute the consciousness of the beautiful,—whence the beautiful in its entirety.) I pass the æsthetes by and return to the creators. Beethoven and Handel are unconscious to what tree the flower belongs, and what fruit is sleeping in it. And as they are in a hurry to gather it they often make a mistake in the application of it. Their instinct, however, remains unsatisfied; for in the course of years we see them taking up the theme again, twice, thrice, or oftener, searching it once more for a significance, a method of handling, more correspondent to its hidden being. And in some cases it is only at the very end of their lives that Handel and Beethoven(102) light upon the magic word and at last give the phrase the final turn, the accent that illuminates the definitive form.

If we want to estimate the value to the world of Beethoven's misfortune, and the increase of energy that came to him with the athletic reaction of his will against it, let us survey the route that ascends from the *Prometheus* of 1801 to the *Eroica* of 1804. In the *Prometheus* we find integrally two of the most famous pages of the future third and fourth symphonies,—the Storm in the *Pastoral*(103) and the finale of the *Eroica*(104). Exquisite sketches! But they are only toys, that the hand of genius amuses itself by taking up and dropping again. In the environment of 1800 what would have become of the toys and of the player? Listen to the slack, sleek, redundant melodies of the *Prometheus* dances. Without the scourgings of misfortune, the man who wrote them might have been (who can say?) what he himself abominated twenty years later,—a Rossini, but still fleshier, still more robust, still more Rubens-like! (And the world of to-day—who knows?—might decide that it had lost nothing by that!)

AND NOW let us—we who have been the gainers by the sport of Destiny, that used the misfortune of Beethoven to forge his greatness—let us enjoy the work that has been forged, this prodigious Scherzo, whirling and armed, this finale, dedicated to Joy and Liberty, this festival, these exultant dances and marches, these rivulets of laughter, the rich volutes of these variations! In the middle of them the Hero reappears,—the opening motive, the Destiny of life, at first unconscious of itself but now attaining its goal, that *Vollendung* (perfect accomplishment) that is Beethoven's target, and of which he often speaks in his letters. But Death also reappears,—Death, that is on the other side of Victory. This time Victory denies it. And the voice of Death is drowned in the roars of Joy, in the rush of the Revolution mob, demolishing the Bastilles and leaping over the tombs.

"*Et tout cela, c'est toi, mon enfant!*" . . .
This Grand Army, these heroic charges, these disasters,

these victories, these tombs and these games . . . all are in you,—*are* you. . . .

And even all this does not suffice to fill this Self-Universe!

In these superhuman days there fly, from the anvil on which Beethoven is forging the *Eroica*, the sparks of ten other planets—the *Pastoral* symphony (the impetuous motive of the double basses (105) in the village festival):—

Leonora (the rapturous duet):—

(followed by the first five numbers of the opera); the *Waldstein* sonata, Op. 53 (with as many sketches and retouchings as for the *Eroica* : and, as with the symphony, the freshness and the animation that seem so spontaneous are,—as we shall see later when we come to study the sonatas—the fruit of long labour, achieved only after all sorts of stumblings and fumblings); the opening of the fourth piano concerto, in G major, Op. 58:—

the Scherzo of the C minor symphony, suddenly coiling and uncoiling its massive cobra folds (106) :—

and already Fate knocking at the door! (107) :—

as well as a flood of sketches for smaller works in all genres,—*Military Marches and Retreats, Variations, Bagatelles, Lieder* (including the famous Gellert hymns), *Canons, Klavier-Uebungen* (piano exercises), *Andantes, Allegrettos.* And in addition to all this, big works that he projected but never found time to write,(108)—two unknown symphonies, one of them a *lustige Sinfonia* (merry symphony), and a Mass ; while on the final page, on the interior of the cover, we find the actual title (therefore the idea) of the Kreutzer sonata, Op. 47 (*Sonata scritta in un stilo brillante* [this is crossed out] *molto concertante, quasi come d'un concerto*).

All this between October 1802 and April 1804 ! A jet of fire, a rain of stars in the night, an eruption of God, projecting the worlds that have been torn from his substance ! What a midsummer eve !

It is to be observed that in proportion as the rhythm of creation accelerates, the works expressive of joy increase—*Pastorals, Dawns*,[1] sunny concertos, *Lustige Sinfonia*. So true is it that, if the primary principle of creation be a wound, the blood that spurts from it is sovereign joy. Even at the price of the direst suffering, creation is Joy. And all the rest is nothing.

Years later (in 1817), after Beethoven had already written eight of his nine symphonies, the poet Christopher Kuffner having asked him which of them was his favourite, Beethoven unhesitatingly replied, " The *Eroica*." " I should have thought the C minor," said Kuffner. " No, no ! the *Eroica* ! " And after more than

---

[1] *Translator's Note :—L'Aurore* is the title given by the French to the *Waldstein* sonata.

a century we think as he did. The *Eroica* is a miracle even among Beethoven's works. If later he went further, never did he take so big a single stride. It is one of the Great Days of music. It inaugurates an era.

CHAPTER III

THE APPASSIONATA

CHAPTER III

THE APPASSIONATA(109)

IN THIS same year 1804,(110) in the summer following the completion of the *Eroica*, Beethoven, walking one day with Ries in Döbling, kept humming all the time the finale of the *Appassionata*. And in his piano music he was achieving a victory analogous to that he had just won in his orchestral music.

[TO ESTIMATE

TO ESTIMATE this victory we must cast a glance over the whole field, and replace the work at the end of the long avenue of sonatas leading up to this summit. I do not, however, advise anyone who wants to understand Beethoven's evolution to look for this guiding thread in the judgments of the critics and of the public during the last hundred years. A more astounding confusion could not be imagined. Each contradicts the other. It is not merely that the public differs from the critics; these differ among themselves And the clashing reasons are not only of different orders (technique and sentiment, construction or expression), but also of the same order, strictly technical and æsthetic. The same sonatas have been allotted turn by turn by competent judges to the first or the second rank, have been pronounced original or conventional. And when it so happens that two judges agree as to the exceptional quality of a work, it is for opposite reasons.

During a whole epoch, the sonata in B flat major, Op. 22, was regarded by the æstheticians as non-Beethovenian.(111) In our own day it is picked out from its companions as being one of those rare works in his first manner that are really Beethovenian.(112) Famous musicians, such as Rubinstein, have regarded the G major sonata, Op. 31, No. 1, as a particularly uninteresting work for Beethoven. Other excellent artists, such as August Halm,(113) salute it as one of the *glorreichen*

Augenblicke (114) of his career and of musical history. And while the great piano poems of the first period (the *Pathétique* and the *Moonlight*, Op. 31, No. 2) are regarded by the left wing of criticism as " historical monuments of Beethoven's interior life," as Frimmel expresses it, the right wing sees in all the work of this period an artistic objectivity that excludes the interior life.(115)

Let us ignore the commentators and go direct to Beethoven; it is of him and of his nearest friends that, whenever possible, I seek counsel. Let us listen to the hints he himself has given, and then try to elucidate them from the music. This is never equivocal, never obscure; that is the smallest of his faults. In these days we should be more inclined to reproach him for his constant rectitude, his certainty, his unity.... *Ein Mensch, ein Wort!* (116) So let him speak for himself.

IN 1802, in a conversation with his faithful old friend and confidant Krumpholz, his familiar, his " fool," as he used to call him, he said : " I am not very satisfied with the works I have so far written ; from to-day I mean to open out a new path."(117) Czerny, who reports these words, adds: " Shortly afterwards the three sonatas of Op. 31 appeared,(118) and in these we can see the partial realisation (*Erfüllung*) of his intention."

On the 2nd June, 1804, when making his sketches for the second finale of *Leonora*, Beethoven interrupts these to jot down the following monologue: "June 2nd.—The finale simpler and simpler.—All piano music likewise.—God knows why my piano music still always makes the worst impression on me, especially when it is badly played."(119)

Now in the middle of the sketches for the second act of *Leonora*, Beethoven begins work on the *Appassionata*. He puts on paper the dramatic design of the first movement, then that of the finale, and some indications of the andante.

Note two cardinal points:

In 1802 he "opens a new path" with the sonatas of Op. 31. (Especially the magnificent recitative sonata in D minor, Op. 31, No. 2.) He is still unsatisfied. In 1804 he realises his "simpler and simpler!" and the idea of the work that has been gestating in him for years, in the F minor sonata (the *Appassionata*), Op. 57. Let us try to disengage the significance of these two facts.

What is the reproach he brings against his earliest sonatas? What is it that distinguishes Op. 31 from them?

In virtue of what is it that Op. 57 carries the ascending line to its highest point?

Our epoch is inclined to underestimate Beethoven's first manner. That is a mistake, but it is easily accounted for. During the last ten years of his life his art and his personality underwent so profound a metamorphosis, under a complex of conditions that we shall study later, and that constitute one of the most shattering dramas of destiny and the soul (he has bequeathed to the future a musical testament the characteristics of which have become indelibly engraved on the century's memory), that he has himself made us forgetful of his first achievements; the cathedrals the old master erected in Op. 106, Op. 110, Op. 111, have thrown their vast shadow over the earlier buildings. But it would be a profound error to ignore the originality of these. To say, as is the habit nowadays, that they are only a prolongation or an "imitation"[120] of the art that preceded them, the forms and spirit of which they paraphrase, to say that in them Beethoven "is still under the influence of the *style galant* of Philipp Emanuel Bach, Haydn, and Mozart,"[121] and that these first twenty-two sonatas "are, as a whole, below the best works of the composers of the preceding period,"[122] is to forget the upheaval they wrought in the mind of the generation that heard them for the first time,—the furies and transports that greeted them, the ostracism meted out to them by the musicians who were in bondage to the older style, and the ardent enthusiasm they evoked in the young.

We have a light on the situation in the story of Moscheles discovering the *Pathétique* sonata,(123) and in the coarse invective that classical criticism showered on the sonata in C minor, Op. 10.(124) On the one hand the self-appointed musical pontiffs of the preceding epoch expressed themselves with regard to the young Beethoven exactly as the academic Press did some thirty years later with regard to the author of *Cromwell* and *Hernani* : the romanticism of his style made the perukes bristle. On the other hand, from the commencement of the century Beethoven was for the younger German public—to whom his name had been unknown the day before—what he still is for us, his enthusiasts of to-day, —the friend, the companion, the " consoler." The first word that occurs to Moscheles when he is trying to express his debt to this new music is " solace." It is thus a moral debt. And the newest thing in this art is the man. . . . *Et homo factus est !* . . . Music is made man, the man of the new century. That is the secret of this revolution.

The first observation suggested to us by this unexceptionable testimony of so good a musician as Moscheles is the inability of formalist criticism to penetrate to the essence of great artistic phenomena, and, in the present instance, of a musical revolution. When someone has conscientiously gleaned a few ears that have fallen from the sheaf of Haydn, of Mozart, of Sebastian or Emanuel Bach, and has noted the analogy of a few of their motives or portions of their motives with those of Beethoven, as often as not he has only demonstrated his own incapacity to perceive the vital and distinctive character and the individuality of these motives. I have made a collection of a number of truly appalling examples of the mental deafness of men of science and taste, for whose applied research I have infinite respect. When Thayer discovers a passacaglia movement in the heroic Thirty-two Variations in C minor; when he finds a similarity between the first notes of the C minor symphony and a passage in the *Gradus ad Parnassum*; when he sees a " hunting piece " in the last movement (allegro agitato) of the F minor quartet, Op. 95; when a swarm of critics docilely repeat that the opening theme of the *Eroica* was suggested by the overture to *Bastien et Bastienne* (125); we ask ourselves whether these excellent musicians have ever had an inkling of the real nature of music. They read with their eyes; they see the letters; they do not hear the spirit that speaks through them; and it does not occur to them that in two words composed of the same letters it needs merely a shifting of one of the letters or a variant of one of the accents to change the word itself. We cannot be sufficiently cautious when we are searching works of art for evidence of the influences of styles. If this kind of study can lead to relatively satisfying results in the case of artists of the second rank, in whom the letter is more than the spirit, it is almost invariably deceptive in the case of genius. For the moment a genius takes an existing form in hand he fashions an absolutely new means of expression out of it ; and particularly so in music, where a single accent, a silence, a punctuation, an inflexion of the rhythm or of the line can alter everything. The greatest artists, Handel, Gluck, Beethoven, are perhaps never so authentically original as in these inimitable accents, which the generality of artists often never notice.(126) Herein is the most immaterial (or the least material) part of their art—the vibration of the Self. If we want to pierce to the essence of an artist of genius, we must go beyond the abstract or general form, beyond what is common to him with all the others, or with many of them ; we must find what is his and his alone. And the true friends of a great man love him for what is his alone. Even Clementi, whose original quality is undeniable, might have furnished Beethoven with the whole of the material for his piano sonatas without Beethoven owing to him a single one of his impulses, a single vibration of that passionate, torrential, imperious, religious soul that was his individual possession and has become one of humanity's treasures. " Solace and delight," says Moscheles in speaking of these early Beethoven sonatas, thus indicating (and remember that he was a musician by profession) the psychical character of the upheaval and the benefit wrought by this music. And precisely therein lay the principle of its novelty.(127) To-day we too often forget that the most important thing in art, even in the newest art, is the newness *of the thing said*, not the newness of the *manner of saying it*.

But the manner also counts, especially as, in the greatest artist, it is the perfect counterpart of what he is saying. If then the thing said is new, it follows that it remains hidden from him who has not perceived the originality of the form employed. And the greatest reproach I have to bring against formalist criticism, in general, is not that it fastens *solely* on the form, but that it clings to it too *closely*, like the maggot to the rind, without seeing anything beyond the strip of detail it is nibbling at. The higher criticism of æsthetic forms embraces the totality of the work and of the creative spirit. And I grant it, though with regret, the right to pass over the emotive element and the intuitive analysis of the sentiments that have inspired the work; for it soars to regions of the mind where the form is no longer merely an external mechanism but a supra-individual organism, that is one with the Law of the *Natura Naturans* and with its profound harmonies. I know of two examples of this among the modern Beethoven commentators,—

Heinrich Schenker and August Halm. Each of them deliberately confines himself, in his Beethoven studies, to the form pure and simple; but for them this is the key to the spirit. Halm, who does not, like Schenker, admire Beethoven without any reservations,—curiously enough, indeed, he does not conceal a certain antipathy of sentiment, blended with a loyal homage of the intelligence, that is constrained to recognise sovereign greatness—has never been in the least doubt as to Beethoven's superiority, which is manifest in his earliest works. And this man, who is much less impressed by the force of the passions than by that of reason, who, I repeat, confesses that he has never really loved Beethoven and has all his life felt an instinctive desire to be unjust towards him, demonstrates to the full " the astonishing self-discipline, the circumspection, the renunciation, the discretion "(128) that are characteristic of the creative spirit of the young Beethoven : " no *Sturm und Drang*, no bluff, no swagger, never an attempt at merely external effect." If an effect is produced (and how tremendous it can be!) it proceeds from the very interior of the work, " in virtue of the mighty musical organism he creates. Even in his first sonatas he has planned the work with a precision, he has mastered it with an energy, that is hardly ever exhibited by Mozart, and by Haydn only in his best work."(129)

Here, then, we have two judgments, that are different

and complementary, on Beethoven's youthful works. The musicians of his own time were chiefly overwhelmed by the soul that was revealed in them, by the violence and the charm of the emotions. The higher criticism of to-day, that concerns itself solely with the forms, sees in Beethoven, before all things, the constructive genius. Both points of view are correct, and neither of them is complete of itself; for actually there are in Beethoven two parallel streams, two forces of his nature harnessed neighing to the chariot of his creation, that he has to learn, by years of imperious discipline, to keep in line with a firm hand, so that they will go in step together. There is a double exigence—that of an unbridled Ego, and that of an inflexible will erecting a monumental work.

In the earliest sonatas we find the two side by side, turn by turn, rarely harmonised. The young Rhinelander, now settled in the city of the Danube, was the confluent of two streams flowing respectively from the East and the West. Filled with the individualist spirit of the time and its proud claims, he overflowed with an Ego that was rich in passionate joys and sorrows, lights and shadows and violent contrasts, an Ego that was as yet less profound than intense,—which was why the new era recognised itself in him, for he differed less from it, at that time, by the quality of his sentiments than by the temperature to which his brazier raised them. This Ego he knew how to deploy and display to the best advantage, to make it bread and wine for other souls, their transports, their despondencies, their meditations and their battles. . . . Jean Jacques the Confessor has become the halcyon of the tempests of the Revolution. . . .

But at the same time he had been nourished on the great moral and æsthetic tradition of the *Ancien Régime* that was dying, on that hard discipline that subordinates the workman to the work, that constructive genius that had been kept going by two centuries of disinterested labour till it had become an instinct like that of the bee; it bequeathed to him forms for his finishing, monuments like those of the Middle Ages, that were passed from hand to hand along the generations until at last the spire came to crown the edifice. He was the master-builder who had received from Bach, from the Mannheim composers, from Haydn and from Mozart the *sonata-form* to realise in all its logic, all its beauty; he felt himself called to enlarge its plan and eternise it, to be its Bramante.

These two imperative missions will govern his musical work his whole life through :—To be Beethoven, the living man of flesh and blood, the man of suffering and courage, who will never be but once, and who, obedient to the piteous vow of all humanity, will seek to prolong the duration of himself by impressing on the heart of mankind the vibrations of his fleeting existence and his idealised image:—To bring to final accomplishment the work and the style, the spirit of an epoch, that greater Being of thought—more real than the beings of a day—in which is concentrated the mysterious and tenacious essence of the soul of a century. For just as in the form of a Greek temple or a Gothic cathedral there is summed up the still-burning flame of millions of lives that have passed away, so a whole epoch of the European mind, almost the whole nineteenth century, condenses musically into this sonata-form that Beethoven was to immortalise.(130)

I cannot stop here to describe this musical form: I must be allowed to suppose that I am addressing musicians who are acquainted with the rudiments of the art. I will only remind the reader that sonata-form, that was born of the new needs of the European musical mind in the second half of the eighteenth century, is in essence a structure of this kind:—

1. The exposition of two contrasting tonalities, or themes, or groups of themes;

2. The constructive development of motives, or fragments of motives, derived from the two themes,—an intense and vigorous analysis and synthesis—constituting, step by step, the very heart of the work (this becomes peculiarly the function of Beethoven);

3. The return of the two themes, with the principal tonality finally establishing itself;

4. In the larger sonata-form, consecrated by Beethoven, a conclusion or Coda, recalling and magistrally summing up the movement as a whole.

It is thus a sort of musical dialectic, that has been the framework of an art-form that is lucid, logical, forthright, like classical tragedy. And as the classical tragedy, that corresponded to the French seventeenth-century spirit, continued, even after that spirit had completely changed, to dominate the century of Voltaire, so sonata-form has lasted on into our own day, in a Europe whose elements have been three-fourths modified and renewed.

But Beethoven represents the golden age of the form. In him it realised its plenitude ; in it he accomplished his own. Between it and him there existed a pre-established harmony.(131)

I WILL now run rapidly over the first fifteen sonatas of his youth and try to bring out their essential characteristics, correlating them with the two great currents of Beethoven's genius,—the direct expression of the personal soul, and the constructive intelligence.

The pre-Beethoven sonata(132) generally consists of

three or four movements arranged in the same order—
a fast first movement(133) that is the special domain of
sonata-form properly so-called; a melodious slow movement in what is called song-form; a short dance
(minuetto); and an extended display of sportiveness,
in rondo form. The whole structure obeys not merely
the fundamental laws of each particular genre but the
still more imperative laws of the society to which the
work is addressed,—laws of discretion, of good taste, of
both technical and moral equilibrium between the
various parts. Whatever the emotion or the humour
that possesses the artist, he must not wholly abandon
himself to it; he stands before a select public, and his
first duty is to speak for this before speaking for himself; he must conform to the rules of good company.
The first of these is, " *Ne quid nimis !* " Do not insist too
much! Any excess of expression, any too naked expression of intimate or heated sentiment, has the explosive
effect of an impropriety or a rusticity. And the only
device for making these sentiments acceptable is to
" represent " them, in the scenic sense of that term—
to make a theatrical " imitation " of them. (In my
opinion, as will appear later, Beethoven resorts to this
method in the *Pathétique* sonata). It is for this reason
that in the order of succession of the several movements
care is taken that the mind shall taste of everything
without being overborne by anything. After the first

allegro, the æsthetic character of which is particularly defined by the regular opposition of the motives employed, their entries at fixed places, and the elegant formalism of their development, the andante offers the refined sensibility a discreet aliment, delicately salted with fine wit; besides, any excess of emotion would find its way barred by the sparkling minuetto; while finally the studied ingenuousness of the rondo, the mechanical grace of its expected repetitions, recalls the listener who might be tempted to believe in the seriousness of art to the fact that it is all a play. Learned yet not pedantic, sensitive yet not doting, gathering at its choice the flowers of feeling but lingering over none of them, this exquisite art is for the lovely butterflies of the salon and is made in their image. Beethoven's Op. 27, No. 1 (the first of the two sonatas *quasi una fantasia*), presents us with the perfect type in a new and freer form.

This noble musical plaything, already vivified by the genius of Mozart and Haydn, this mundane sonata, was taken up by the young provincial from Bonn and utilised for his début in the drawing-rooms of Vienna. These he means to conquer; so he employs their language to impose on them his own thoughts. But it is not long before the contents transform the containing vessel. Even in the earliest published works(134) his personality reveals itself, under the transmitted form, in touches that should have put the custodians of the past on their guard; for they announce a new epoch of sensibility and of human energy.

Hardly has he opened his mouth (in Op. 2, No. 1), and while he is still employing the accepted words and phrases, his rough, brusque, biting accent imposes his own signature on the borrowed modes of speech. Quite unconsciously a heroic turn of mind declares itself—for example, in the first movement of Op. 2, No. 1, and in the first main subject of the first movement of Op. 10, No. 1. It has its roots not less in the audacity of the temperament than in the clearness of the intelligence that uncompromisingly selects, decides, cuts its way through. The design is sometimes heavy; the line no longer has the feline inflexions that were characteristic of Mozart and his imitators; both are direct and drawn with a sure hand; they are the shortest possible route from one idea to another, and a route laid out broadly—the great roads of the spirit. A whole people can journey along them,—soon, indeed, whole armies, with not only the heavy waggons but the cavalry. Already, in the first movement of the C major sonata, Op. 2, No. 3, we have an Empire style, square of trunk and shoulders, of a pompous strength, now and then a little tedious, but noble, sound, virile, scorning the insipid and the trifling. The first movement of the B flat major sonata, Op. 22, shows it in the purity of its strength and the austerity of its brilliance. It is the rising breath of the Napoleonic generation, that, from Paris to Vienna and from Madrid to Borodino, will score the back of the old Europe with its heavy boots.

The counterpart of this heroic tension is the pastoral reverie, in which, suddenly leaping from the saddle, the high collar of the uniform thrown wide open, the conqueror relaxes his fever and bathes in freedom. Who ever showed us fresher streams than the composer of the first allegro of the F major sonata, Op. 10, No. 2, the first allegro of the G major, Op. 14, No. 2, or the *Pastoral* sonata in D major, Op. 28? I will return to these later.

But if he shares these two tendencies, the heroic and the pastoral, with the epoch that is coming and of which he is the scald singing at the head of the marching army, what are wholly personal to him are the abysses of the soul with their clouds and lightnings, the abrupt and frequent atmospheric changes, the interior sea on which light and shadow succeed each other without transition, and where the humour of an Ariel or a Puck disports itself on the crest of the night waves. This liberation of a nature surcharged with heavy sadnesses and passions, finding an outlet in the rough leaps and bounds of caprice, will later create the expression proper to it in the wild Beethovenian scherzos. But in the earlier sonatas,—for example, in the second movement (allegretto) of Op. 10, No. 2, and the scherzo of Op. 26 (the sonata with the variations and the funeral march, in which we can detect a subconscious preparation for the *Eroica*)—these are only trying their wings.(135)

The section of these first sonatas in which the personal soul of the young Beethoven expresses itself most freely is the adagio.

Our own musical epoch,(136) that is more interested in construction than sensitive to emotion, attaches less importance to the adagios and andantes of the classical sonatas and symphonies than to their allegros. It was otherwise in Beethoven's day ; and the German public of the end of the eighteenth and beginning of the nineteenth century drank greedily of the flood of nostalgia, of *Sehnsucht*, of tenderness, hope, melancholy, that welled from the adagios of Beethoven, as from the contemporary *Lieder* of *Wilhelm Meister* (1795-1796).(137) It found in this mirror an answer to, or the echo of, the enigma of existence. To the polemic minds that are perpetually occupied with the question of pre-eminence I leave it to decide which of the two points of view is superior to the other—that of 1800 or that of 1930. For myself, I am ready to adopt either of them in turn ; I find that there are never too many points of view from which to take in a work of art, and Beethoven's works present aspects numerous enough and varied enough to call for examination from all sides. For the moment I confine myself to those mirrors of the soul, the adagios.

Although at first still impregnated with the odour of Mozart (whom Beethoven cherished for many years and venerated always), yet they are very different. Heaven preserve me from saying—superior! Two enchanted worlds lie before us. In the adagio of the first of Beethoven's sonatas (Op. 2, No. 1), the grace of expression is in part borrowed; but the sensibility is simpler, less ornate, nearer to nature; the spirit of the young composer lacks some of the nuances of that of the ripe and subtilised Mozart; if, like Mozart, he is multiple, he is nothing like so complex; the diverse elements are set out in clear contrast with each other; they do not melt one into the other by imperceptible degrees of tint; the line, which is less inflected, and traced without any rubbing out, is concerned less with ingratiating itself than with the exact transcription of the emotion. And this emotion is never a mere play. This man is of the type, so rare among artists (those of to-day would perhaps call them "unæsthetic"), that believes in everything it says, and if it did not believe in it, would have to cease to write. Sovereign artist that he was in the kingdom of his own personality, of all that he loves and hates, of his joys and sorrows, out of which he constructs a universe of his own, he would never have admitted the æsthetic dilettantism, by some called objectivism, by others syncretism, that would fain taste of everything while attaching itself to nothing, and whose Self—uncertain, unquiet, slipping away between the fingers—goes round and round like the eels in the Sargasso Sea. He is Beethoven. He is *a* man. In that resides his strength in his own epoch,—the epoch that is sealed with the name of Napoleon. In that also is his weakness, in an epoch in which " *Kaa* " changes his skin. . . . About 1800 the empire of art, like that of action, belongs not to the subtle but to the strong,—to him who dares to be himself and proclaim it imperially. The world follows him. The voice of Beethoven speaks for him : he is the emperor of the world of feeling.

The distinguishing mark of these great instrumental adagios is this : they are a direct manner of speech, with a degree of " immediacy " such as the andantes of Mozart and Haydn never had. They are vast Songs Without Words ; the words were heard beneath the notes,—so clearly, indeed, that several of them were actually sung.(138)

Let us look at a few of the types. After the two pure reveries of Op. 2, Nos. 1 and 3 (the adagios in F major and E major), in which we have the first flowering of the young man's tenderness, his first poetic plaint, we get the fine largo of the sonata dedicated to Countess Babette de Keglevics (Op. 7),(139) with its great, serious, firmly drawn melody,—frank and healthy, without a touch of society insipidity or of equivocal sentiment about it ; of all the Beethoven meditations this is the one that, while not concealing anything of itself, is accessible to everyone.(140) We have another example in the broad and thick design, just a trifle too rounded, of the adagio molto of Op. 10, No. 1 (the sonata in C minor, dedicated to Countess von Browne), in which a melodic stream makes its way along unhurriedly, opening out at the end into a placid estuary.

But it is in the monumental Largo e mesto of the sonata in D major (Op. 10, No. 3), that the full grandeur of Beethoven's soul is for the first time revealed. (The work is contemporaneous with the first attacks of the malady that ruined his life : 1798). From the opening chords, in that majestic 6/8 whose august swing so often, in Beethoven, gives the temples of his melancholy their rhythm (141) :—

the soul of the listener yields to the hand of the master. The sadness that speaks through the music is so full of his strength and of the laws of his destiny that it no longer seems, as in the preceding sonatas, the confidence of a **single being : it is the Chorus of an antique tragedy.**

THE APPASSIONATA

The personal pain here becomes the good of all; and by its very plenitude the elegy of a man expands to the epic of a race or of an epoch.

The movement falls into three great divisions. The motive of Grief once posed on the slow epic rhythm, the arms raised to heaven, a melodious *lamento* blends with the tender accents that have come from Mozart the violent contrasts that are Beethoven's own, his pathetic declamation, his Ajax sighs, the exasperation of his intolerable suffering, that finds its outlet at last in noble tears that might accompany a funeral cortège:—

In conformity with the plan of the future Funeral Marches, the second part opens with a calmly elegiac motive:—

But grief breaks in upon it once more : destiny strikes ; the tears flow forth ; broken sobs are rhythmed by the inexorable tread of the march :—

They die away—*smorzando*—*pianissimo* ; a final resurgence, *f*, *sf*, is followed by a *decrescendo* of the sobs, bringing with it a return of the majestic first theme :—

In the second ascent of the third part the mighty march of the bass, with its *sforzando* accents on the second and fifth beats :—

expresses the implacable force of the Destiny that subdues the shudders of the revolting soul, suddenly smitten to its knees and subsiding from cries to silent tears. Finally the vast sad resignation of exhaustion, the knell-like sighs, the expiring breath :—

An immense tragedy, having for its substance the soul of a people incarnating itself in its Corypheus. The royal picture of Melancholy.(142) We are reminded of the Æschylean choruses—Envy (in *Saul*), Jealousy (in *Hercules*)—dedicated by Handel to the Great Goddesses, the Eumenides. Never until this work had Beethoven realised the classic plenitude of a lyric form in which the exigencies of his Ego and the majesty of impersonal law are fused into one. And it was long before he realised it again.

The adagio of the *Pathétique* sonata (Op. 13) is, like the whole sonata (to which I shall return), a too perfect success in a theatrical form in which the actors are too visible. Notwithstanding the strict mastery, the dialogue, especially in the episode in the minor, has too external a character. At that period Beethoven was seduced by the effect of the facile dialogue between two persons or two " principles," as is evident from a curious conversation recorded by Schindler.(143)

But, by a vigorous alternation that is often to be met with in his work, and that is the very rhythm of his life, the fictive is succeeded by the real. After the objective imitation of the passions there almost invariably comes the tragic face of genuine passion.(144)

In the Op. 27, No. 2, this occupies the whole field of vision. Here the usual second movement of the sonata does not suffice. The adagio takes the first place. By an innovation that appears to be unique, the *Moonlight* begins with a monologue without words, a confession, veracious and poignant, such as one rarely hears in music. And the whole sonata, which I shall analyse later, preserves this character of spoken music, of the homophonous, direct, scarcely veiled expression of pure passion.

In no other of the Beethoven works of this period is sentiment so absolutely the ruler of the work as it is here. But in many sonatas, in almost all, indeed, the personal element intrudes into the construction and often mars the logic of it. In *Die Verliebte* (the charming sonata dedicated to Babette, Op. 7), and especially in the gracious rondo, the sentiment is like a child that runs to you and stands between your knees. In the allegro of the C minor (Op. 10, No. 1) it gives a sudden start that made the pedants howl; it becomes a whirlwind in the finale,—with its trouble of the spirit, its irregular contrasts, its abrupt stops, its organ points,—in which this *Mane Thecel Phares* takes us by the throat: a hand writes in letters of fire, on the background of the *Durchführung*, the word that Destiny will speak in the future C minor symphony(145) :—

The lack of organic development that, whatever one may say, is evident in the admirable sonata in D major (Op. 10, No. 3) comes from the variety of impressions in the composer, who does not yet dream of unifying them in a work. This phenomenon is still more visible in the famous sonata with variations, Op. 26, in which the commentators have striven hard to find the key to the order of the four movements, and more particularly the meaning of the joyous allegro that follows the Funeral March.(146) As a matter of fact, Beethoven at that time (though not later) was completely indifferent to these clashes of various impressions ; we might even say that he deliberately sought this kind of variety. His notes show that he had commenced by sketching out the last movement—the gay allegro—and then got the idea of a minuet and a sombre march in A flat minor.(147) So at that time he had in mind a work made up of variegated impressions, harmonised only by the style and by the colour of the tonalities.

The same freedom is seen in the sonata *quasi una fantasia*, Op. 27, No. 1, the sketches for which are interspersed with those for Op. 26. Here, however, the freedom finds its psychological justification in what I would call its objective character ; for rightly or wrongly I see in it less the direct impression of Beethoven than (consciously or not) of the amiable lady to whom the sonata is dedicated—Princess Liechtenstein, *née* Furstemberg, a lady of high society, elegant and charming, impressionable and changeable, whose feelings were never profound, never all-absorbing,—reverie, agitation, caprice, elegy or laughing roguishness,—everything on the surface. All this is the absolute antithesis of the sonata that follows,—the second *quasi una fantasia*, the *Moonlight*.(148)

In this, as I have said, the personal emotion governs the construction. It will be worth our while to pause a moment to analyse this unique work.

Here the sentiment breaks the usual tonal links of the melody : the composer abandons the ordinary methods of development and repetition of the motives when the psychical state is prolonged under the sway of a single obsession (as in the first movement). He does not have recourse to the device of dialoguing opposites when he is occupied simply with himself and his passionate soliloquy (as in the third movement). He deliberately rejects the symmetry of fixed periods ; he cuts into them brusquely ; he explodes, he is subject to all the surprises of passion.

And yet, by a miracle of art and of the heart, the sentiment here shows itself to be a mighty constructor. The unity that the artist does not seek in the architectonic laws of the movement or of the musical genre (149) he finds in the laws of his own passion. For all its rhapsodic form, its free recitation, the famous adagio of the *Moonlight*, the dual song (150) of which exhales its lassitude above the monotony of the mournful accompaniment, is woven all in one piece, and exactly modelled to the beautiful, simple, veracious lines of the idea. And the idea, the plaint of which moves in a restricted circle, rises slowly from its prostration to its melodic peak—the E of the 27th bar :—

thence to descend again immediately into its agitated night : it ascends a second time (at the 49th bar) without being able to stabilise itself :—

bruises itself thrice on the degree below (the D natural) :—

falls again definitively, and sinks into an exhausted silence, while, like a passing-bell, the bass alone repeats the rhythm of its sob :—

The allegretto that follows without a break ("*Attacca subito il seguente*") has been the subject of many psychological explanations; and those of Marx and Nagel, among others, show us the dangers, not to say the absurdities, of that kind of thing. I shall not venture on anything of the sort myself. But whatever vision may have hovered before Beethoven's eyes when he wrote this movement, what each of us can value with certainty for himself is the effect willed and produced by this small picture, placed where it is in the work. This happy, smiling grace must inevitably provoke—and does provoke—an exasperation of grief; its appearance goads the weeping and disheartened soul we saw at the commencement into a fury of passion.

Hence the immortal outburst of the presto agitato finale. Above a *staccatissimo* accompaniment that lashes like hail,(151) the tempest launches itself in five mad gusts.(152) There follows a frenzy that becomes a furious stamping (bars 9-14). A melodic motive, syncopated, roughly rhythmed :—

shows us Beethoven panting, a prey to his fixed idea. It is sonata-form ; but at every moment the convulsive starts of passion split the frame. A vertiginous whirlwind —from A major to E—with hammered octaves, and, the second time, more and more hurried syncopations in the bass :—

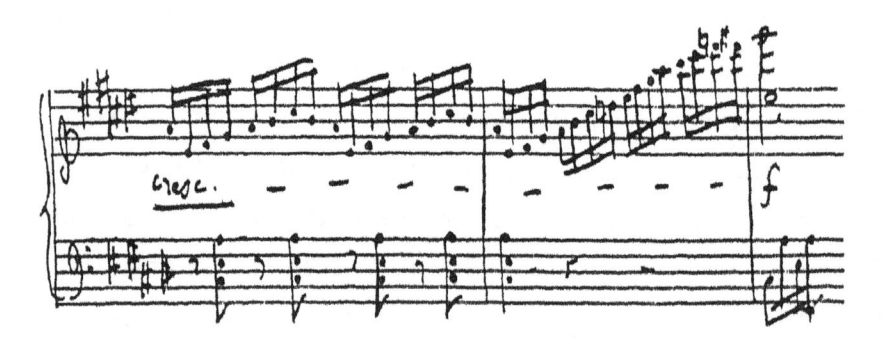

leads to a fresh pelting of the hail, that cuts and shakes the soul :—

until the big phrases of the end of the first part, that dominate the agitation and soar above the torrent :—

As in the antique tragedies, sorrow is subdued by strength of soul.

In the " development " (*Durchführung*) of the sonata there is none of the ordinary musical dialectic, none of the *bravura* of the virtuoso ; all the rules are thrown overboard ; instead of a play of the intellect upon ideas that have been previously set forth, the fragments of the one motive of sorcery are used again and again, come and go at hazard, fall away exhausted,—a faithful image of the interior defeat, the ebbing energies, the wasting of the heart's blood.

Then the wild night-squalls come again,(153) but now with redoubled rage,—a cyclone : fiery arpeggios that surge up from the depths to the heights, frantic convulsions. . . .

And then, as often with Beethoven—almost invariably, indeed—silence. A sudden *adagio* . . . *piano*. . . . With no more strength to cry out, the man is silent, his breath is cut short. And when, after a moment, he recovers it and raises himself again, there is an end to the vain debate, the sobs, the furies. What is said is said, and the soul is empty. In the final bars nothing is left but majestic Strength, mastering, dominating, accepting the torrent.

A gigantic soul-picture, that owes its success much less to the mastery of the artist, who himself is often carried away by the flood, than to the intrinsic quality of this sovereign soul, that even in its convulsions preserves its harmony and its natural nobility.

But this success, due as it is to circumstances too exceptional and too independent of the will, seems to have disquieted Beethoven rather than satisfied him. We cannot insist too strongly on the depth of the shade into which he later throws this masterpiece; and he does so by taking into account the dolorous personal events that had inspired it, and his repugnance to evoke them. He hastens to escape from the grip of these blind forces and write the least passionate of all his sonatas, the happy, sunny *Pastoral* (in D major, Op. 28). And it is then that he makes a remark to Krumpholz that astonishes us: " I am not satisfied . . . I must find another path."

He is not like the God of the Bible; he does not look upon his work and find it good. The builder in him knew no repose of conscience.

HE WAS a born carpenter. For all the exacting hunger of his heart, for all the disorder in the rhythm of it, he had not merely a respect for his trade but a passion for it, an obstinate probity, an almost manual joy in the thing he was shaping, and, after he had attained to mastery, an imperial pride in carrying the technique he had inherited from his masters a stage further, and in perfecting the work they had left to him to do.

I have said what delight his logical mind took in the dialectical play of sonata-form. The dualism of theme harmonised with the dualism of his own nature, wild, rough, loyal, in which reason and passion faced each other as simply as in the heroes of our classical tragedy. The interior dialogue is and becomes more and more the form of his own profound life. The contrasts of motives that he aims at in the sonatas answer to the brusque opposition of his own feelings. He had only to listen to his own preferences to want to give to his musical discourse on the one hand a rigorous plan, rigorously pursued, and on the other hand clear divisions between the various members, the parts, periods and phrases of his harangue. Not that he could express without difficulty, in his ordinary daily life, either in speech or in writing, the disorderly flux of his thought. But under the surface-life his deep subconscious life had an irresistible orientation towards order, clarity, unity. This is certain from the subterranean work revealed in his sketches, that invariably show him to be at first confused, his inspiration merely ordinary, taking days, months, years to dig out his mole-runs, which,—on the faith of some obscure compass or other!—lead him infallibly to the simplest, clearest and best-disposed forms. Thus he could make more free than his predecessors, Mozart and Haydn, with that sonata-form that had been their legacy to him.

If in his first works (such as the sonata in C major, Op. 2, No. 3) he is the solid carpenter rather than the architect, we soon see him take up the pencil in his turn and make draughts of his own, extending the transmitted plan and enlarging the forms with a joyous ease, as in the sonata in E flat major, Op. 7. He shirks no trouble to make himself master of a musical language that shall be beautiful, firm, precise. *Vir bonus dicendi peritus.* The sketches for the first movement of the sonata in D major, Op. 10, No. 3, show how he laboured to purge his thought of vagueness, to eliminate everything superfluous, to seek and find always the most concise and most striking expression. Soon he will feel himself to be master of his instrument,—so much so that for a moment he will be tempted to perform on it like an actor or a virtuoso. The *Pathétique*, as I have said, is a magnificent parade, that certainly deserves its title ; for dramatic pathos, in its best and its worst sense, gushes from it to the heart's content. The piano-tenor ascends the stage and engages with the prima donna in a give-and-take dialogue of swelling melodrama, in the style of *Il Trovatore* ; and both of them indulge in noble gestures and high-flown phrases ornamented after the manner of operatic vocalises. Perhaps, by sheer reaction, I am too severe towards a work that has become rather too famous and has falsified the public judgment of Beethoven. In any case the dramatic—theatrical—elements in the *Pathétique* are undeniable ; and the evidence for them is supported by certain analogies of style and of expression not only with the few works of his, such as the *Prometheus* of 1801, (154) that were written for the stage, but with his great tragic model Gluck, the aria and duet in the second act of whose *Orfeo* remind us pointedly of the furious commencement of the first allegro of the *Pathétique* (155) :—

The success of the *Pathétique*, like the work itself, had something theatrical about it. Moscheles' account shows that people took sides passionately for or against the sonata in a way they usually did only over operatic subjects.

There can be no doubt that Beethoven sought no more victories of this kind because he was disgusted with this one. In the succeeding sonatas he aimed either at greater naturalness (as in the sonata in E major and especially in the G major, Op. 14, Nos. 1 and 2), or at a more impersonal style of construction (as in the sonata in B flat major, Op. 22). Yet to the very end of this period we see him fluctuating between the preoccupations of the architect, obstinately bent on the grand style,(156) and the imperious caprices of a torrential sensibility (157) and a fetterless fancy, both of which demanded satisfaction.

And then, when he turns round on the first height to which he has climbed, and looks back, in 1802, on his first fifteen sonatas, what is it that he sees? A succession of essays that seem to him contradictory and incomplete—architectural sonatas that are abstract in spirit (Op. 2, No. 3; Op. 22); sonatas of feeling (there are many of these) held together by a somewhat feeble logic and filled with the poetic humour of a day; theatrical sonatas that encroach on the territory of the stage; sonatas of passion, such as the *Moonlight,* that are veritable autobiographical confessions (when he reads them again later they annoy him as *Werther* did Goethe; he is ashamed and angry at having let himself go like that!) Taken as a whole, a vortex of dust set whirling by the wind. To-day it is the power of the wind that strikes us; but Beethoven saw only the dust and the confusion.

And this sincere being, whom no one judged with such inconsiderate, pitiless perspicacity as he did, is galled by certain defects in his nature and his art—the bent towards rhetoric to which he has often given way, in spite of his ardent cult of absolute truth ; the danger of emotional softness and romantic effusiveness, which he deems unworthy of a man, but that might become a menace in the world of young women and " little friends " by whom he is surrounded ; the provincial awkwardness, the stiffness of the joints, the insistence of a reasoning faculty that is too anxious to be always right, the somewhat heavy and over-square symmetry against which his art had to struggle to the very end.(158)

All this, of which he alone, perhaps, was conscious in 1802, he speaks of to the most modest and surest of his friends : he must reform himself ! He seeks another route.

But he will not discover the right one at the first attempt. And although he never pauses in his march, for a year or two yet he will lose the track in the thicket : now and then he will have the illusion of lighting again upon the man he used to be, with the same faults, the same confusion, as of old.

E pur si muove ! How far, in reality, he has advanced !

THIS THE G major and D minor sonatas(159) (Op. 31, Nos. 1 and 2) will show us.

At first sight they seem very different the one from the other, hardly to belong to the same period or to have been written by the same man. Who would believe that they figure within fifty pages of each other in the same Sketch-Book, and that it is the second, the more elevated and more fully realised of them, that came into being first? Their immediate succession illustrates that law of alternation I have already pointed out, a law that Beethoven cannot escape from : the necessity to satisfy the two opposite needs of his genius in turn—the pure delight in artistry and the pure expression of personal passion. The G major (Op. 31, No. 1) shows very marked "mimetic" traits,—I am tempted to call them deliberate "imitations" of Italian opera ; for the first movement has the humour, the sallies, the lively dialogue, the waggish style and the burlesque *furia* of a scene from a comic opera.(160) As for the adagio, no one can be in any doubt as to the pre-Rossinian intention to be Rossinian : it is a serenade with guitar accompaniment,(161)—though involuntarily marked in its middle section, it goes without saying, with the heavy, powerful paw of the young bear. But every now and then there comes from it a gleam that anticipates the radiant Serenade of Rossini's *Barbiere*. As for the D minor sonata (Op. 31, No. 2), it is the very antipodes of the other, and one of the most striking examples in all Beethoven's work of direct speech in music. It is he, the man himself!

This dual manifestation no longer surprises us. We are tempted to say that we are already familiar with this sequence of sonatas in two antithetical styles: the *Moonlight*, for example, coming between the worldly fantasy dedicated to Princess Liechtenstein and the *Pastoral*. But when we look a little closer, and no longer at the soul, that is invisible, but at the body (and the body, in truth, is also the soul, but the soul made visible and palpable), at the living substance (and for him who can see to the core, the spirit that governs each organism is inscribed upon it), we soon discover in the body of these two sonatas the transformations the spirit of Beethoven has undergone, and we realise how greatly he has grown.

Two features stand out from the rest—the prodigious enlargement of the form, which will become particularly noticeable in the *Waldstein* (Op. 53); and the novel elasticity of tonality that is evident from the commencement of Op. 31, No. 1.(162)

These two evolutions of the form correspond (as always happens in the case of an artist of genius who is as sincere as Beethoven was) to evolutions of the spirit, —or, to express it more precisely, to untiring efforts to perfect the spirit, to correct its faults and transmute them into virtues. The need for insistence, for repetition, for dwelling upon a point, that we have noted in the temperament of Beethoven, he now converts into an enlargement of the musical members, in a way that enriches the art and gives his sonatas and his symphonies gigantic proportions, without, however, any departure from the harmony of equilibrated numbers. And the massive and powerful unity of his thought is constantly corrected and fertilised by his capacity for sympathy, by the urge of his intelligence to penetrate the forms of other thoughts, those of living beings as well as those of the great dead, by his extensive study of scores,(163)—a study deeper than that of any other great musician from the time of Bach to that of Wagner.

At the same time the methods of pianistic expression undergo a technical transformation under the direct pressure of Becthoven's unsatisfied genius; and this transformation necessarily reacted on his own thought. Reichardt, a shrewd observer who visited him several times during the winter of 1808/9, has left us valuable notes on this revolution wrought by him in the piano : " On the advice and at the desire of Beethoven," he says, " Streicher,(164) discarding the soft touch of the other Viennese instruments, that is depressed too easily and comes back too noisily, has given his pianos more resistance and elasticity : so that the virtuoso who plays with power and meaning has the instrument more under his command as regards the depression and raising of the keys and the prolongation of the tone. He has thus given his instruments a bigger and more varied character; so that any virtuoso who does not merely aim at superficial brilliance in his playing will get more satisfaction out of these than out of any other instrument."(165)

This information, the importance of which for the history of chamber music I need hardly point out, explains why we find, at the core of this great Beethoven epoch, between masterpieces like the *Waldstein* and the *Appassionata*, sonatas such as the F major (Op. 54), in which Beethoven is principally occupied with technical problems, laying small store by the musical or expressive idea; and why the virtuosity—or, if this word offends, for it might imply a mould without a content, and the music of Beethoven, like Nature, abhors a vacuum—why some great works of this period are characterised by a profusion of purely pianistic features, and why even the fine first movement of the *Waldstein* flowered out of some piano exercises.(166)

The man who bore a new order of thought within him had first of all to forge and subdue his own instrument. And Reichardt's remarks, sparing as they are, reveal to us the direction in which Beethoven sought for progress in expression. His first desire is to hold the piano firmly in hand like a horse, the bit held tight.

For what he insists on is not the charm or the brilliancy of the note but exactitude of tone and of line, the obedience of the keys to the will, the subordination of every detail to the Idea that governs the movement. At the same time that he is enlarging the various forms of the movement it is vital to him to increase proportionately his domination of the form in its entirety, of the movement as a whole. The larger and more spirited the team, the stronger must the coachman's wrist be. We shall see the plans become better defined, the horizon lines more clearly marked, in proportion as the landscapes extend.

Unity !

AS IT is impossible for us here to linger over each of the sonatas in turn, we will content ourselves with a summary analysis of the plan of the two greatest works of this transition period between the *Moonlight* and the *Appassionata*,—the recitative sonata in D minor (Op. 31, No. 2) and the *Waldstein* in C major (Op. 53).

The recitative sonata, as we may call it from the character of the first movement, is a chapter from

Beethoven's Confessions. It is also one of the two Shakespearean sonatas.(167) It bears no dedication—a rare thing for a work of this importance. He might have dedicated it to himself. The sketch dates from the winter of 1801/2, and the sonata was finished in the summer of 1802; its place is therefore between the famous letter of the 16th November, 1801, to Wegeler and the Heiligenstadt Testament of the 6th-10th October, 1802. It recalls the proud accents of the one—love, grief, combat, exaltation of living, unconquerable energy(168); and it has premonitory flashes of the sombre heroism and despairing cries of the other.

Never did any work burst so like a thunderclap from Beethoven's brain. There are none of his usual gropings about in the mist; the cloud is torn open at a single stroke, and the Idea breaks forth like Pallas armed. The essentials are projected at once,—the complete themes of the opening (the largo and the allegro), the sequence of the modulations, the angle-pillars, as Nottebohm rightly calls them,(169) and above all, the astounding unaccompanied recitatives of the third part of the first movement, with the tragic pulsations and the febrile shudder that answer them. Let no one talk here of æsthetic detachment, of intellectual labour, ploddingly hatching and multiplying what Vincent d'Indy calls musical "cellules"! Here the whole organism achieves its individuality at birth. From the first sketch, the opening movement of the sonata is a living thing, complete in its evolution.(170)

In the definitive work, Beethoven has only to resume textually the opening of his sketch,—that exceptional form of recitative-introduction :—

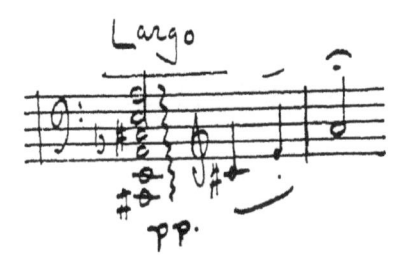

A broad arpeggio chord, pianissimo. A sovereign command; the command that is to dominate the whole tragedy; the " *Es muss sein* " that henceforth will be the eternal leit-motiv of Beethoven's life—eternally contested; for the moment the soul has heard it it is uneasy, it trembles, it tries to escape from it :—

The command is repeated this time with a surprising modulation into C major that gives it a striking calm :—

BEETHOVEN

The spirit is bewitched : it flies and stumbles, unable to free itself from the attraction of the slope that it descends by degrees, trying vainly at each angle to steady itself :—

until it arrives at the bottom, where the Master awaits it. Then it is seized by the current. Not till that moment —at the twenty-first bar !—does the flood attain to the tonic of the D minor tonality :—

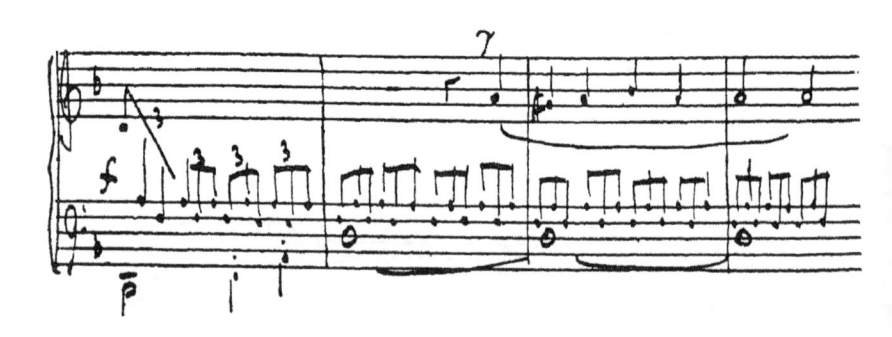

The real drama begins. The broad arpeggio chord of the opening is heard again in the bass, followed by an anguished plaint ; both are swept away by the torrent. *Seven times* the principal motive, the command, is repeated, ascending through all the degrees of the scale, from D to C. At the third time, the plaint of seven notes that is the echo of it is silenced; at the sixth, there is only a cry. At the seventh time, when the command—angry, *fortissimo*, and three times repeated,—ends on a degree higher by a second, the distracted cry also is repeated three times :—

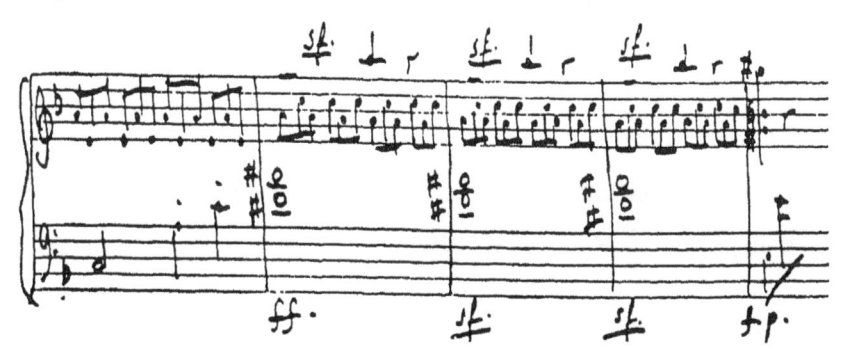

Thus we arrive at the dominant of the chord of the commencement, that is to say, at the key of E. A second motive of terror is heard: it is related to the terrified fall of the commencement; but in place of the syncopated accentuation that betrayed its disorder there, it is now subdued, regularised, even in its sobs. At the extreme point of its fall there enters a new motive of imperious constraint; but it no longer has the implacable character of the opening; it seems to say " Accept ! " A broken dialogue ensues, that might have come from a cantata of Bach. To the Master's injunction :—

the soul reiterates in reply its refusal and its fear :—

At the third time, the Master loses patience. He breaks out abruptly—a *fortissimo* immediately followed by a *piano*. The soul yields :—

and the whole of the end of the first section—the return to the reprise—is in an atmosphere of subdued acceptance :—

The *Durchführung*—the thematic elaboration, that with Beethoven (it is in this that he is great) always corresponds to a psychological elaboration, a process of the soul—begins with the main motive of the opening, in broad arpeggios, the waves mounting *pp* three times, from D to the tonality of F sharp and then to A sharp. Is it the proclamation of peace, attained by acceptance of the Master? No! The struggle must be resumed—but a harder, wilder struggle than before. The motive of command dominates the whole of this portion. Twice the plaint replies: the distance between the two is greater than before: the colour (the tonality) changes incessantly (F sharp, G sharp, A, B natural, C, C sharp, D), first of all every four bars, then every two: then the pace accelerates, becomes a whirlwind of triplets, is hammered out with *sforzati*. There is nothing contrapuntal in the texture, merely the single line; and the contours correspond to each other with symmetrical exactitude. It is a passionate idea expressing itself without artifice, without concealment. At the finish, a pedal bass is masked by the agitation of the parts, that try to check the race, curb it, slow it down, bring back the precipitate heart to the largo of the commencement.

And then, on the threshold of the third part, a unique apparition! The phrase of the largo is immediately followed by an unaccompanied recitative, without any technical link with any of the motives that have been so far employed. It is already the "*Immer simpler!*" of Beethoven. I read in it the interior commentary of the soul on the order that has been imposed on it :—

"*How long, O Lord?*"

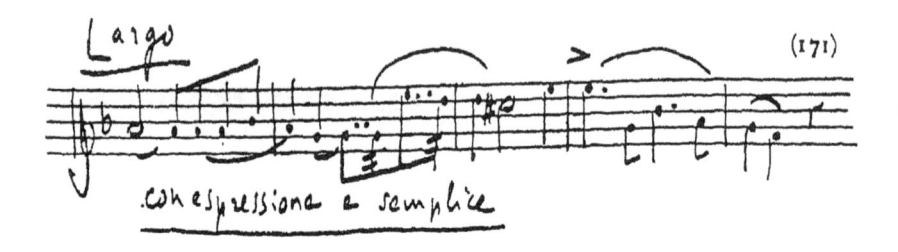

The motive of agitation replies, at first, in the same terms as at the beginning. It is the other part of the soul, that is always in trouble and trembling. . . . The largo repeats its tranquil injunction. The answering recitative becomes more dolorous still, and its personal accent admits of no doubt (172) :—

A confession unique in the art of that epoch! It is the evident forerunner of the Heiligenstadt crisis. The broken soul no longer struggles, no longer has even the strength to respond to the order. It is weary unto death. . . .

The voice of the Master is silent; the opening *allegro* motive of dominating force would be out of place here.

There comes a pause : then some punctuated chords, *pianissimo*, regularly spaced, like heavy, dull pulsations :—

The circulation is restored. Three times these two pairs of chords are repeated,—now harsher, and ascending by unequal steps. A torrent of blood follows in their wake :—

At the third time, the pulsations clash *fortissimo*, and the torrent once more surges through its channel under a voluntarily accepted compulsion, as at the **end of the first part**, with the same dialogue and the final appeasement, that is swallowed up in the *pianissimo* :—

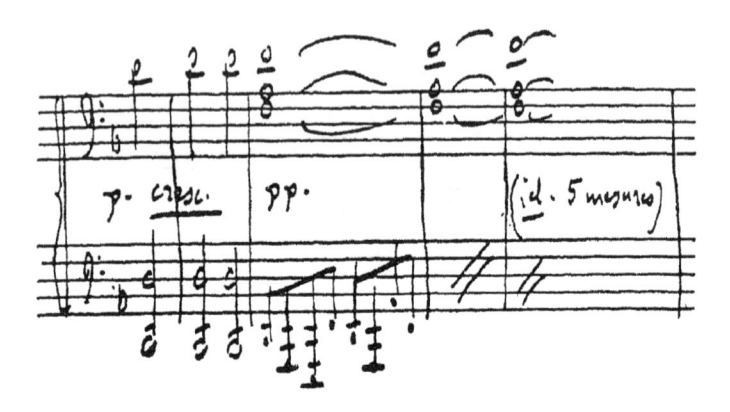

It is the soul that renounces and surrenders itself motionless, into the hands and under the feet of the threatening *Fatum*. And about this acceptation there is an antique grandeur.

I will pass rapidly over the other two movements, though they are of a perfect beauty. This perfection, indeed, is their most marked characteristic. Rarely has Beethoven shown himself more the master of Harmony, not in the more specifically musical but in the essential sense of the word—an equilibrium of art, a divine serenity of the spirit as the Greeks understood it: Ἁρμονία θεμερῶπις, that combines the Elements in the just proportions and binds them together with " nails of love."(173)

The suave adagio, with its Elysian peace, its aerial

balance, goes on feet of velvet, in a half-light that only once or twice rises to a *forte*, seven or eight times to a *sforzando*,—as if with the weary sighs of a breast oppressed with ecstasy—and fades slowly into sleep with a sigh of happiness.

The final allegretto is a *Midsummer Night's Dream* caprice.

But different as the three movements are, they exhibit a constructive art, by turns powerful and delicate, that no other sonata of Beethoven had yet manifested in the same degree. From the architectural point of view one knows not which to admire most, the striking relief of the lines and of the mouldings of the opening recitative movement, in which a deeply sculptured motive of a few notes determines the elevation of the pillars and the vaulting of the whole edifice, or the genius of the fancy that, in a sort of bravado, evolves out of a banal design of four notes, prompted by hazard,(174) an exuberant florescence of ornamental volutes. And nowhere better than here do we appreciate the rôle of the final rondo in the architecture of the sonata. If the first allegro is the great door of the nave, and the adagio the vaulting or the cupola, the final rondo is the steeple.

Yet I would not say, with Nohl, Nagel, and Frimmel, that the ensemble of this sonata constitutes a perfect, or even a complete, organic unity. Even if we do not look to it for a succession of logical ideas or emotions (which it would be very difficult to establish), even if we demand of it only æsthetic unity, the harmonious equilibrium of lights and shadows, and recognise that the artist has ably realised this in the sequence of the movement,(175) it remains true that there is still something lacking in this equilibrium to give the mind full satisfaction. The melodic and psychical substance of the first movement is too heavy, the stuff of the finale is too thin and diaphanous, woven out of gossamer. Lacking counterpoise, the work tends to overbalance. No doubt Beethoven himself was conscious of this. He remedied it in the *Appassionata*.

ALREADY in the *Waldstein* (Op. 53) the equilibrium of the whole is more masterfully assured.

This work, celebrated as it is, is really not well known. The pianistic superabundance that envelopes it in a brilliant network of virtuosity has often stood in the way of the comprehension of its intimacy. One is so accustomed to the tragic face of Beethoven, his imperious gesture, the broad design and sharply defined outlines of his passionate themes, that when he seems to be sauntering over the keyboard with his great agile fingers, as he used to do across the fields with his short legs, one does not suspect the intensity of the dream that sings under this light rain of scales and runs, and the iron will that keeps watch over the dream. This white sonata in C, that flows like clear water, is the most intoxicating ecstasy in nature—an ecstasy controlled by the mind.

We must first of all remember that the sketches for it appear in the Sketch-Book of 1803, shortly after those of the *Eroica*, and a little before the first hints of *Leonora*. It is thus an intermezzo, a flower between two rocks. What helps us to fix the character of it is the appearance, a little earlier, of the first vision of the *Pastoral* symphony.(176) This is at first a mere cutting, in the horticultural sense of that term. But soon its perfume fills the whole room :—

The *Pastoral* having been laid aside for some five years, by reason of the big works that take up all his time, the *Waldstein* for the moment takes its place and deals with the same emotions : it is an earlier *Pastoral*.(177) Moreover, Beethoven occupies his leisure, and seeks distraction from the passionate works that are consuming him,

LB

with researches, to which I have already referred, that have for their aim the perfecting of the piano and of pianistic technique. These two circumstances combined to bring about the unforeseen birth of the *Waldstein*.

He sets out to stir the savourless water of the piano exercise,(178) and his fingers run, fly, while the mind sleeps and dreams. But now lights play upon the surface of the water: the blank mirror becomes alive with glances. The *Dawn* awakes:

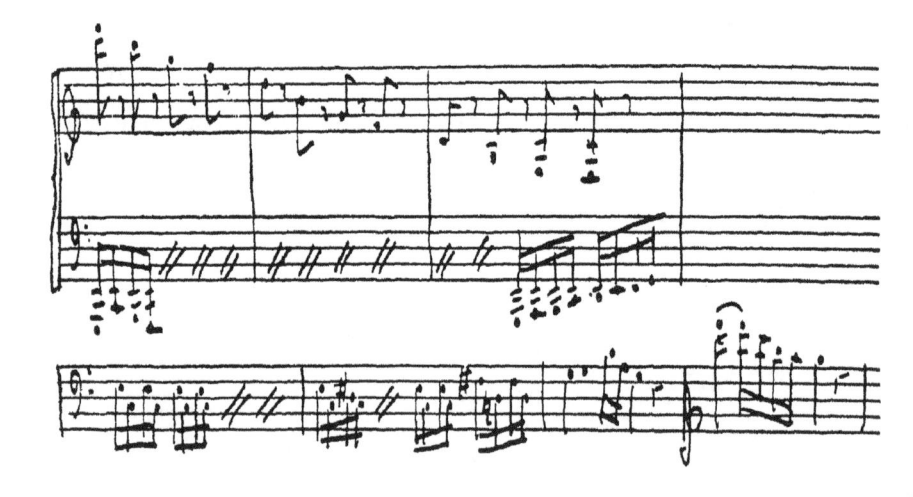

The spirit journeys on. There comes an interior landscape(179)—joy of the open air, of the free flight; and Beethoven is in the fields, filled with a religious emotion. All the chief motives, those of the air, those of the heart, the vibrations of Nature, pious contemplation, are already registered on paper, together with a few of

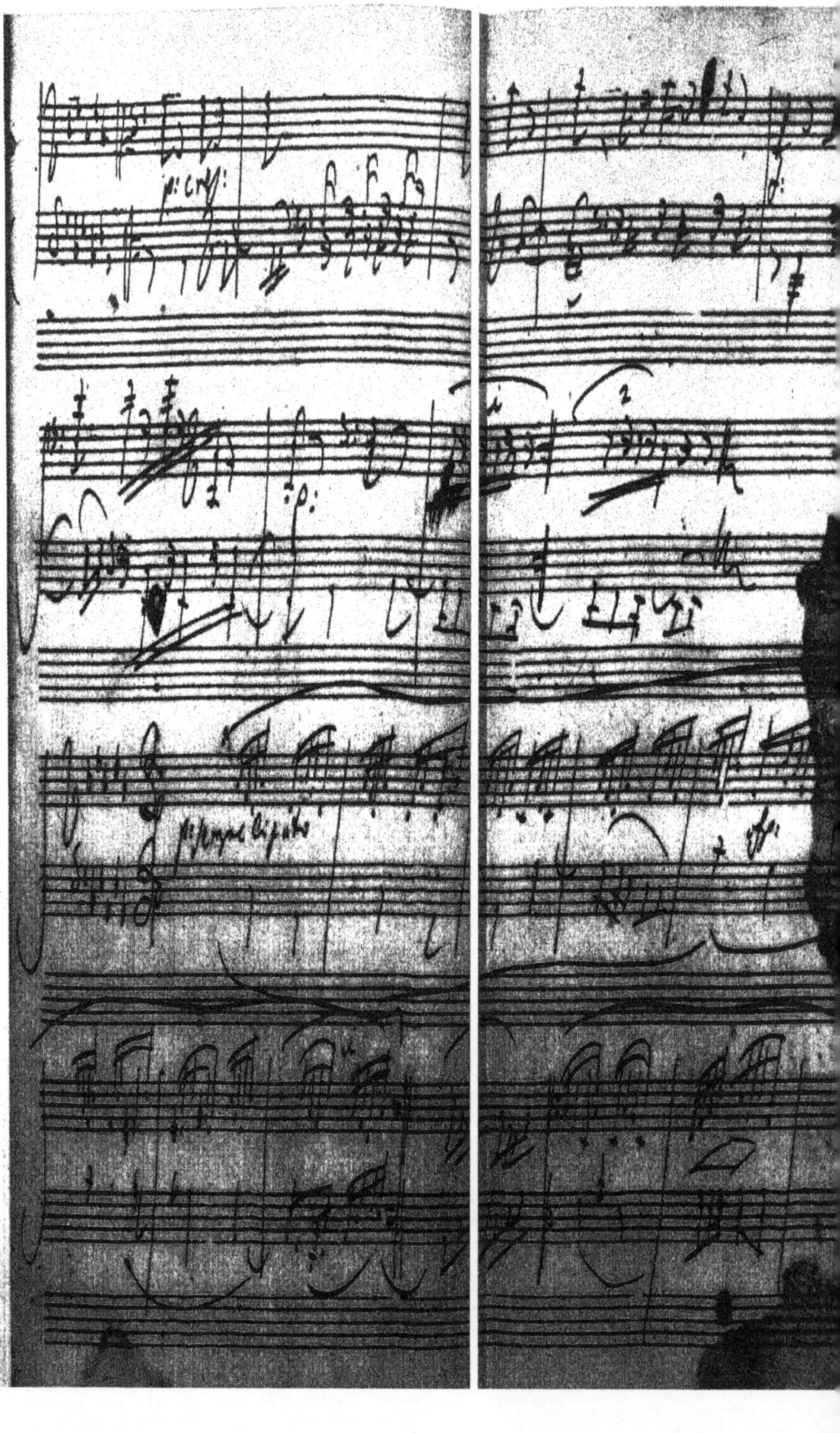

their more delicate modulations. Later it will be the business of the mind to organise them. And, as always, the final reduction will have not only a masterly unity but also, by the Beethovenian miracle, a freshness of touch and a bloom that the first sketches had not. For anyone who can read and savour, it is an exquisite pleasure to follow the development—so natural that one forgets the trouble it has cost—of this poem of sky and earth. Beatings of wings, carollings of birds, flight-tracks through the waves of the limpid air,—these frail motives, transfigured, fill with their humming ornamentation the fine picture the centre and the support of which is the holy joy of the spirit, that swells to a chorale of a whole people in face of the Eternal. Nothing is left to chance : these unusual dimensions, these great periods, the enlarged proportions, the overflowing contents, make no difference to the certainty of the guiding hand : it pilots the bark straight to the goal, from the first rivulet to the open sea,—that coda that hums with the whole life of a day of light, the end of which is the hymn of the universal soul.

But it is the two movements that follow that constitute the main charm of the work ; and it was these that cost him the most time and labour. Happy labour that, with Beethoven, always results in the most spring-like inspirations,—the most spontaneous, one would swear ! We see how, in his art, Beethoven's intelligence was the master of his sensibility,—his perfect taste, his infallible control, and that capacity for sacrifice that does not hesitate to give up a part of the work that has been done, and well done, if there is any danger of the equilibrium of the whole being compromised by it. For he had written for this sonata a long andante to which he was attached.(180) He had worked long and lovingly at it (181); and it was painful to him to feel that the movement had been developed at too great length. As a rule he hardly paid any attention to a reflection of that kind, as he had proved in the case of the immense *Eroica.* There, however, the giant was so perfectly proportioned that the instinct for harmony was satisfied. With the sonata it was not so; the reverie spun itself out until the text was lost to view; it no longer related to the work; it had no longer, like the future *Andante con moto* of the *Pastoral* symphony, its roots washed by the stream; it had escaped from the landscape, and, absorbed in itself, had drawn in front of itself the curtain of its horizon. The worst fault was not that it was too long but that it was out of place. Beethoven cut it out. Between the two vast pictures of the opening allegro and the rondo (that steps out of the customary frame),—in these sunlit expanses—there was needed no more than the shadow of a cloud on the plain, a touch or two of dream. No chatter of the self with itself! The self is swallowed up in Nature.

And so it was after the entire sonata had been sketched that Beethoven arrived at the conception of the *Introduzione, Adagio molto*, that forms the core of the sonata. This immortal half-page is, for me, of a perfect limpidity; it expresses the state of Beethoven's soul in the peace of the fields. The rhythm of the first motive seems to have been inspired by the cry of the quail (*Wachtelschlag*):—

Later the motive of the soul takes up that of the bird and draws quite another meaning from it :—

A gentle lassitude, sighs of resignation, melting away, returning, becoming more sorrowful. But suddenly Nature in its turn takes up the motive; it becomes a livelier appeal, set free from all emotion; the pipings dialogue with each other and multiply like a flock of birds in a grove; the animated mass begins with a *pianissimo* and rapidly dies out in a *decrescendo*: —

Then it is as if the soul again gave the gentlest of sighs, that lightened it of all its cares. Liberated now, it enters into its dream of happiness. . . . Never would one believe that this marvel was embodied in the sonata as an afterthought, so essential a part of it has it become. The finest moment is the transition from the adagio to the rondo, from melancholy to the serenely lighted upper air of dreams :—

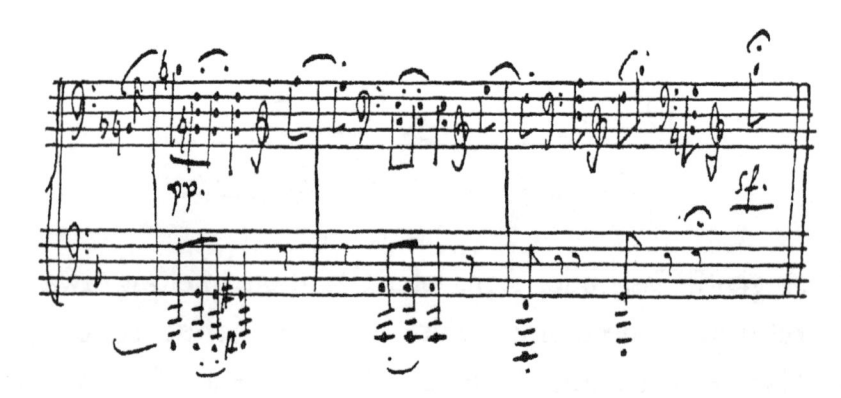

The rondo (allegretto moderato) was not conceived first of all in the form in which it now opens; this is readily understandable, since the adagio that introduced it in the first conception was quite different. It was only in some later sketches (a dozen pages further on in the Sketch-Book) that Beethoven hit upon the now familiar opening motive. But here the discovery of genius is the pedal G :—

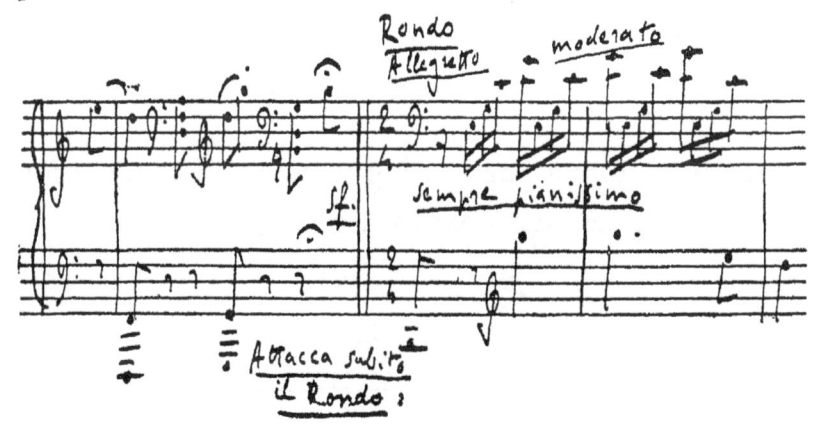

The spirit turns to dream. . . . The immobile reverie of the "Solitary Rambler" merges into the stirring dream of all Nature.

My respected friend Professor Max Friedländer, the undisputed master of the history of the *Lied,* who has inventoried all the popular melodies the blood of which has been transfused into the works of the great composers, believes he has found the main theme of the rondo in a song that, along with *Malbrook,* has been the most popular of Western melodies for three or four centuries —the famous *Grossvaterlied,* that is still sung to-day in

Thuringia, and is principally known to us by the many humorous uses to which Schumann has put it.(182) Beethoven, according to this theory, has taken the second part of the tune, that is frankly comical in intention:—

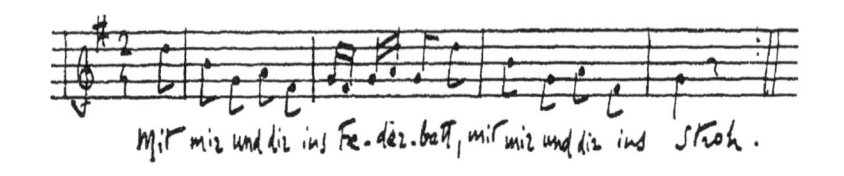

Mit mir und dir ins Fe-der-bett, mit mir und dir ins Stroh.

He noted it on a page dating between 1800 and 1803, accentuating the first note with a *sforzando*: —

Here we come upon the mysterious work of incubation in the genius of Beethoven. The phrase sleeps in his note-book, and doubtless also at the bottom of his thought. When it awakes again, at the moment when he is awaiting Nature's reply to the "Solitary Rambler's" question, it has lost its primitive sense; we can be virtually certain that he has forgotten both the words and the provenance of it; and the accent he has given to the first note now arouses in him no longer the impulse, the heel-stroke of the burlesque dance, but the organ point, the pedal G, that is to set the marvellous reverie free.

In his sketches he writes one after the other :—

Fly, bird ! The cage is open ! The song of the bird of joy fills the air and the fields. Out of the commonest of motives, stylised by art, out of a gross piece of bourgeois gaiety, into which he has brought a radiant smile by the mere displacing of an accent or two, out of the disused form of the rondo, genius has ripened a poetic harvest. The contemplative joy gradually increases in animation. At first the contrasts of tonalities that will later give it its varied brilliance of colour are only hinted at with the greatest delicacy. It runs, it grows; irresistible trills stimulate its ardour; it becomes a whirlwind, a Kermesse, striking the soil with noisy foot. It is interrupted for a moment by an idealised form of the motive of Nature, of contemplation. The round is resumed and becomes still more passionate and coloured. But the heart—but the heart—only takes up again more strongly its hymn of serene joy, in a succession of lovely harmonies the modulations of which were already settled upon in the first sketches (183) :—

There follows that admirable page—one of the jewels of inward music—in which the soul sighs with happiness in the arms of Nature, in the delicate murmurs of the atmosphere, that bathe it in gentle waves that gradually rise, fall, and rise again :—

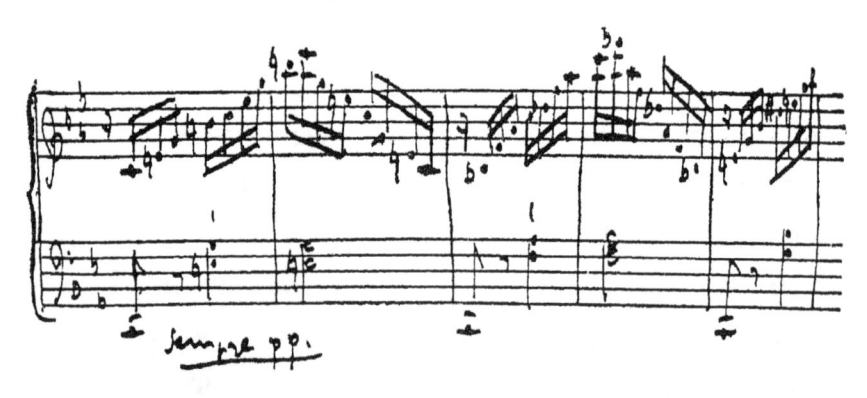

It is as if it were falling asleep ; we feel that the end is coming. And then, with the first theme, everything recommences with a new ardour. The forces gather themselves together, group themselves, and, holding their breath (*pp*, *ppp*), tense, almost immobile, await the signal for the Coda. The irresistible Prestissimo unchains them, sweeps them away like leaves on the wind. Joy overflows. Throughout it all runs the gentle, peaceful motive :—

now enveloped in an almost brutal swirl of force. The sigh of a little while ago has become the pivot around which, in vine-tendrils, in arpeggio-triolets, a graceful, tender design unfolds itself and becomes a round :—

Then the sigh dies away. Nothing remains but Joy. The arpeggio-triolets disappear in the height and re-descend in a rain of octave scales, mounting and falling again. An interminable trill—a distracted laugh—follows them. . . . All the little flutes of the air. . . . And the motive of the commencement, serene Nature, spreads itself joyously over the round and the trills of the birds, that pass through all the modulations of light (C major, A flat major, F minor, C major). The work ends in full sunlight. It is the triumph of Joy.

And now let us take the whole landscape in at a glance! The first thing that strikes us is the extent of it. A vast plain, the horizons bathed in light. Never has Beethoven written so long a rondo (more than five hundred bars!) It is like a summer day: one cannot have too much of it! And yet the composer has not drawn upon the resources of contrapuntal or harmonic construction. As Nagel judiciously remarks, whenever he expresses the fullest force or the highest joy he divests himself of artifices, and his musical speech becomes harmonically very simple. (184) Let us all the more wonder at the fact that, solely by the richness of his patterns, rhythms and accents, he has raised from a grain of *Volkslied*, in the field of the rondo, so abundant a harvest!

The great works we have just analysed, from the *neue Weg* (new path) of 1802, impress me by this new amplitude of constructive (and pianistic) development, and by a fineness of workmanship that (apart from the first movement of Op. 31, No. 2) aim more at toned-down tints and pliable lines than at the clear design and the sharp opposition of light and shade that characterise the normal Beethoven grand style. It would seem (I myself believe it to be so) as if Beethoven himself had been painfully conscious of the externality of his Napoleonic discourses, with their lapidary phrases, cut out of the block with blows of the mallet,—this style as of a Roman inscription, cut straight and square; as if he had tried to loosen the cyclopean rigidity of his limbs, to escape from his own nature. He succeeded in so doing, for many of his commentators have confessed that had not the G major sonata (Op. 31, No. 1) appeared under his name they would not have supposed it to be his; and many of them have been put on the wrong scent by the *Waldstein*. In a sense, we may say that the *Waldstein* (Op. 53), the Op. 31, No. 1, and the final allegretto of Op. 31, No. 2 were just marvellous exercises to acquire suppleness. And it is not only Beethoven but music itself that has here won a new liberty of expression, an ease, a suppleness of the joints, and what August Halm has happily styled " the full and healthy circulation of the blood through the whole organism." Beethoven's instinct appears to have recognised and combated in advance the natural disposition of sonata-form towards arthritism, to a knotting and petrifying of the members—a malady that proved fatal to it in the end.

But the beauty, the grace, the novelty of the works thus far accomplished still do not satisfy him. It is at this moment—the summer of 1804—that he will draw his second bar-line :—

"*God knows why my piano music always makes the worst impression on me, especially when it is badly played.* . . . *Immer simpler!*"

IF, AS has been falsely supposed, he had been of a romantic temperament,(185) he would have emphasised the tendency shown in the preceding works, enlarging the bouquet by adding to it all the flowers of the field and of fancy. But these preceding works are for him only a means towards perfection. His goal is elsewhere; and never has he lost sight of it.

It is, before everything else, Unity. For a character so "entire," a nature so concentrated as his, this is the alpha and the omega. But he desires a *living* unity, one that comes from within, from the heart of the organism; and the organism must be *alive* in all parts, have the *maximum of life*, like that unity that is its principle, its medium, its end. At last he must realise what he has been seeking for since the commencement of his career, the absolute equilibrium of idea and form, of rigour of design and warm suppleness in all the details, of the passionate element and the architectural. Now that he has exercised himself, with a tireless energy, in the practice of the one and the expression of the other, until he has attained perfection, the hour has come for him to enter his forge and achieve the sovereign fusion of the heroic Self and the absolute work. He wishes to create, he does create, like the great Greek sculptors and the masters of Gothic, a new canon of perfect numbers and proportions, a new classical order. He writes the *Appassionata*.

He knew the importance of the work he was constructing; for though he had conceived and projected the grand lines of it with amazing certainty at the first casting,(186) it was two years before he completed it, and three before he gave it to the world. No other of his sonatas shows to the same degree the union of unrestrained passion and rigid logic; we have to go to *Tristan* to find another such torrent of fire in a bed of granite. The work—body and spirit—is an indestructible tissue.

If ever music deserved the name of *Appassionata*—it was not Beethoven, by the way, who gave it this title—it is certainly this. And yet Czerny is not altogether wrong in disputing the title, if we reduce the meaning of the word to that of " amorous passion."(187) But here we have quite another kind of ardour ! A wind of madness blows over the heath of the old Lear ; it is the desperate *lamento* of broken loves, hopes, friendships, ambitions. His situation had worsened since the period—two years before—of the Heiligenstadt Testament, for the unhappy man had been compelled to recognise that his trouble was permanent. The work distinctly bears in its origins the mark of the gloomy summer of 1804 and of the bodily and spiritual sufferings that were heaped upon the Titan after the completion of the *Eroica*.

The moving drama, for him who tries to penetrate to the problem of creation—that vital problem that, without consulting us, Nature is every moment resolving so simply, in us and in others !—is to see the price at which the miraculous conquests of genius are bought. The genius invariably pays for them with his life, his health, the peace of his days. For the peace and the order that, in his art, he imposes on the elements he has evoked are won by an effort of the will so inhuman, so enormous, that when he returns to the life of everyday he is a broken man. Beethoven and Michael Angelo both passed through this shattering experience.(188)

As soon as he has freed himself of the enormous burden of the *Eroica*, Beethoven totters. In that same month of May 1804 in which the work is finished, he falls ill of a serious malady that drags on for months and culminates in an intermittent fever that is long in leaving him. He was living at that time with his boyhood's friend Stephan von Breuning, one of whose letters to their common friend, Wegeler, of the 13th November, 1804, gives us a picture of the ravaged man :—

"You cannot imagine the indescribable (I ought to say frightful) effect that the loss of his hearing has had on him. Picture to yourself the impression that the feeling of misfortune has had on that passionate temperament! He shuts himself up within himself; he often distrusts his best friends. . . . Intercourse with him has become a veritable strain on the mind; one can never let oneself go when talking to him...."

A misunderstanding suddenly breaks out between the two friends, and Beethoven, irritable and exhausted, parts violently from Breuning. In June or July he writes to his young pupil Ries that in the whole world he has never had more than two friends, one of whom is now dead, while the other (Amenda) has been separated from him for six years; Breuning is not a friend, and he will have nothing more to do with him.(189) . . . "And now, an end to friendship!" ("*Und nun auch keine Freundschaft mehr!*")

No more friends!

He might say also, in defiance, "No more public!"

The public, that had already sniffed suspiciously at

the second symphony and the C minor piano concerto,(190) was up in arms against the colossal *Eroica*. It was performed for the first time, in private, at Prince Lobkowitz's house ; and the select audience thought it " of a divine length " (" *göttlichen Länge*"). But at the first public performance, under Beethoven himself, on the 7th April, 1805, the *vox populi* gave its verdict in less euphemistic terms. From the gallery came a cry of " I would give a kreutzer for this to end ! " The journalists gave the scholar a lesson : " The work is wearisome,—interminable and *ill-knit*."(191) And, angry at his having taken no notice of their remarks on the second symphony, they cunningly suggest that the composer should cease his tiresome pretence of originality ! " Let him take his earlier works as models—the Septet [this was their great favourite : we can understand the disgust Beethoven felt for them !], the first two symphonies [already they have forgotten that when the second was given they hurled at him the example of the first !]. If, in spite of their warnings, Beethoven obstinately persists in his bad habits, he will come to a sad end. . . . "

" *That evening neither the public nor Beethoven was satisfied. He refused to respond even by an inclination of the head to the scanty applause.*"

The exasperated composer replies that when he shall have written a symphony that lasts more than an hour they will find his *Eroica* short. Let those follow him who can ! And the misunderstanding on both sides becoming intensified, we see the formation in Vienna of the spiteful cabal that, in the following year (March and April 1806), will break the back of *Leonora*.

Beethoven creates a vacuum around himself. He is too big. He has developed too rapidly. They can no longer recognise him ; he no longer recognises them. The world and he glare defiance at each other, like strangers. Isolation, fever, illness, distraction of the spirit !

It was necessary for me to evoke the storm-charged atmosphere, the black and burning sky under which the *Appassionata* was conceived ; it will help us the better to grasp the meaning of the work, and the sombre fury of the first sketches. The final redaction softened somewhat the infinite tragedy of these. Beethoven, who defines at the first attempt the opening, the main theme, and, after a correction, the whole of the first part of the first movement, adds no indication of the consoling counterpart (in the relative major) of the chief subject :—

There is no slackening of the tension, no attenuation, not a gleam of light : everything is in the opaque minor, a hurricane in the night. It is not until later that there appears, in another sketch, the alluring major. But undoubtedly the soul of the man is perpetually perturbed; which is why the supreme artist cannot bring himself to complete the work just then. He forces himself to wait until calm returns to his soul. And when the light does return he is able not only to dart a tranquillising ray through the clouds, but to dominate the still miry matter of the second part and of the end of the movement, stir the heavy paste of it, knead it, unify it in one molten flood.

AND NOW let us contemplate the monster!

The main theme, that is to dominate the whole movement, is constituted of two elements so closely joined to each other that at first sight they seem to be only one: the first three bars form the first, bars 4 and 5 the second:—

Their duality only becomes apparent in the furious, tornado-like repetition of them that follows bar 17. Two in one: two Selfs in opposition: a wild Self-force, a trembling Self-weakness. At the commencement they come clamped together in the wind that drives them along, *allegro assai*, but *pianissimo*. Then a kettle-drum triplet—as so often in Beethoven; the almost immutable signification of it is the implacable decree of Destiny: "*Thus it is. Obey!*"—gives an impassive threefold answer to the moaning question:—

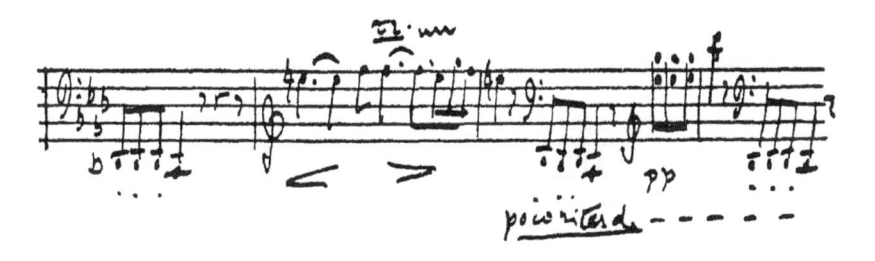

Then the squall bursts, and the all-powerful force surges forward again *fortissimo*, in massive columns, in three crashing ascents. The Self-weakness, in agitation and anguish, supplicates despairingly; we can almost see the clenched hands and the contractions of the heart:—

There is no struggle, no revolt; the suffering soul knows the futility of resistance, and it yields. Then arises the consolatory motive in the major, the virile word, that stoically accepts and will hope in despite of everything. The rhythm of it is the same as that of the motive of brutal force; but the theme is humanised, touched with tenderness, by affectionate inflexions. Instead of :—

we now have :—

To see in this, as Nagel does, "high joy" ("*hohe Freude*"), is to misconceive it. The proof of this is that the motive lacks the strength to maintain its affirmation to the end. When it is repeated, an octave higher, it pauses breathlessly in the middle, and falls exhausted again into the dolorous minor :—

The trills are the trembling of weakness and terror. All this broken energy topples down into the depths of the pit, where a demoniac whirlwind seizes upon it and drives it before it—ascents of the bass in triplets, kettle-drums in C minor, a veritable ride to the abyss, punctuated with laments to which the 4/4 accentuation gives the effect of panting breath, a sort of "*I can no more!*" three times repeated, and falling, octave by octave, into complete exhaustion :—

But the voice of command repeats its injunction :
" Art thou dead ? Arise ! "
And the lament rises once more.

Here, according to the immutable law of sonata-form, the first part ought to terminate and be repeated. But the passionate impulse is too powerful for any return to be possible. So, by a derogation from the rule that is almost unique, Beethoven suppresses the repeat and goes straight into the *Durchführung*.

This " development " is a colossal harmonic and thematic structure. The psychical character of it is much more decided than that of the first part. The second motive of the commencement—the weakness, or the lament—now accepts courageously. To its uneasy interrogation :—

itself supplies the answer,—its " *Yes !* "

Once more the first main motive, " *la forza del destino*," springs forward, but this time in clear tonalities that pass through all degrees of the scale, alternating between high and low. The lament that follows has no longer the former lacerating expression. Above all, the motive of virile consolation is no longer cut short half-way ; it does not yield now, it repeats itself firmly, mounts from sixth to sixth, and affirms its promise with renewed energy :—

And now the tempest can lash!

And the kettle-drums roll!

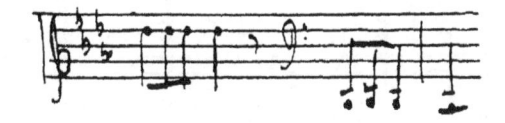

This fantastic hunt terminates the *Durchführung* and links it without a break to the third part. In the whole of this " development " there is not a trace of musical rhetoric external to the subject! The logic of the thematic, harmonic, and rhythmic evolution corresponds to the evolution of the interior drama.

The third part of the movement resumes the motives of the commencement, but this time over the persistent roll of the basses, that for seventeen bars rumble like thunder in the distance, oscillating between the C and the D flat. The contrasts are still more accentuated. When the main theme returns *fortissimo*, with a shattering explosion, it is in the major. For the rest, in the main the combat of the first section is repeated, with its alternatives—subject, of course, to certain variations. And this would be the only contestable point of the action did not a formidable Coda come to renew the form of the sonata, crowning the tragedy of it.

It rises from the depth of the shadows, *pianissimo*, until it defines the motive of confidence, that gradually takes on the aspect of a heroic march :—

This heroism launches the cavalcade, that mounts towards the tempest-lashed heights, striding from top to bottom of the piano in fiery arpeggios, in a frenzy that knows no respite, till it halts abruptly on the dialogue of Destiny :—

—" *Muss es sein?* "—" *Es muss sein!* "—that here takes on an accent of affirmation. " Yes : it must be " . . .

ritardando, then *adagio*, then an organ point . . . first of all acquiescing tranquilly, then, suddenly, with a start of passionate volition :

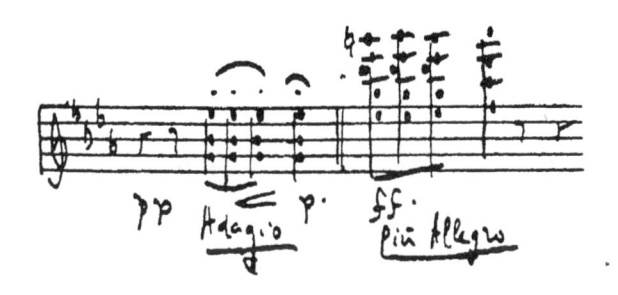

Now the virile motive of confidence has fanfares that suggest the *Marseillaise* :—

Even through the outburst of violence we hear the acquiescence :—

the "*fiat voluntas tua!*"

Finally the principal motive is lost in the distance like a storm in the night.

At this point where the first movement ends—the first act of the drama—the vanquished has won a first victory of the spirit: the *Amor Fati*.

And it is this that explains the impression of liberation given by the seraphic andante con moto.

The simplicity of the design is beyond belief. The theme is almost immobile, the periods are of absolute equivalence. The first eight bars express a divine repose of the soul. In the eight bars that follow, the soul, in its tender religious aspiration, thrice lifts its hands but hardly stirs from its place. The variations of this inward hymn bring no breath of trouble to the paradisiac calm, but simply envelop the theme in their play of light. It is a gentle flight into the golden air. Ariel. . . .

But the truce was only an armistice. When, at the conclusion of the variations, the theme re-enters, the tender urge of the heart has no longer its former perfect peace; the phrase rises by octaves; the harmony becomes troubled. There is no close; an arpeggio of the diminished seventh on the seventh degree of F minor poses a question that at first (*pianissimo*) expresses a hidden anxiety that afterwards leaps up (*fortissimo*) in terror:—

The whirlwind of the finale begins.

We see that this andante—according to the principle already established in the *Waldstein*—has nothing in common with the vast adagio meditations that form the second movements of the earlier sonatas. It is the contrast only of a moment, a fine effect of light between two shadows—here more particularly a zone of anticyclone between two typhoons. And if the first of them merged imperceptibly into it with its *pianissimo* ending, the andante is agglutinated to the second, that clutches it, buries its five fingers in its flesh. . . . The heart of the work is no longer in the middle movement; the whole tragedy is concentrated in the two allegros. The proof of this is that in the sketches the first design for the finale (192) precedes the sketch of the andante.

I have several times evoked the name of Shakespeare—a little while ago, Ariel, *à propos* of the andante; *A Midsummer Night's Dream*, *à propos* of the allegretto of Op. 31, No. 2; and other allusions elsewhere. It was involuntarily; the comparisons leaped of themselves out of the harmonies. But I was careful not to attribute to them an importance other than that of a personal and passing impression. . . . See now how, at this gate of Æolus that opens on the finale of the *Appassionata* to let the tempest through, Shakespeare appears once more; and this time it is not merely from my lips that the name comes, but from the lips of Beethoven. When Schindler asked him the meaning of the two great works the Op. 31, No. 2 and the *Appassionata*, Beethoven answered curtly: " Read Shakespeare's *Tempest!* "

The battle has been joined over this remark; the critics have cut and thrust at each other. Nothing excites them so much as the eternal question of programme music (or music with a subject): " Can a self-respecting piece of music have a programme (or a subject)? "

On the general question I long ago gave my answer: " Music will have, will take, and will do just what it pleases, if it pleases the genius. For musical genius will always write beautiful and well-wrought music, with a programme or without one."

But in the present case why do you dispute, when Beethoven himself has spoken? Does what he has said fail to commend itself to you? So much the worse! (for him or for you); but you have no right to juggle with his words or postulate the inexactitude or lack of intelligence of the man from whom the story comes. Schindler's loyalty and veracity have been established,(193) notwithstanding a few errors that all relate to facts of which he was not the eye-witness and to words he did not hear uttered. But here he is the witness: he heard, and he has recorded. Explain Beethoven's words if and as you like; but accept them you must!

There is no question, of course, of tabulating the precise scenes or personages of the *Tempest* that may have inspired this or that movement. That would be a puerile game. A great musical construction, that is its own self and its own justification, is not a mere vignette for a book: and more energetically than anyone else would the proud Beethoven have asserted the independence of music with regard to the other arts.(194) Imitation is out of the question; but admitting there has been a suggestive influence of this or that scene of the drama on the music, the search for these would be a perhaps not impossible but always problematic task;

we could never be sure enough of our ground to draw conclusions.

But since Beethoven himself has said it, we can be certain of one thing—that he wrote these two works "*under the sign*" of the *Tempest* and in its atmosphere. Now since the two sonatas, that are in other respects so dissimilar, are both of them arresting expressions of the Beethoven soul and the Beethoven passions, in their purest state, the inference is that there is a similarity of *Stimmung* between them and the *Tempest*.

What then is the general *Stimmung* of the *Tempest*?

The unchaining of elementary forces, passions, madnesses of man and of the Elements; also the domination of the Spirit—the magician who at his will can assemble and dissipate illusion.

But is not this also precisely the definition of the art of Beethoven at this stage of his maturity, and particularly in the first Largo allegro of Op. 31, No. 2, and in the whole of the *Appassionata*? . . . The torrent of a wild, implacable Force; the sovereignty of thought, that soars above it all.

For the rest, let anyone who has a mind to do so look for Ariel and Caliban and the duet of the lovers! It may be possible; but all this is mere anecdote, and it has no importance. Even if we were to come upon documents in proof, the true significance of the work would not be altered in the least. With Beethoven, musical illustration is a purely secondary thing—much more so than with Mozart or Handel, or even Bach, to say nothing of the Romantics. His Self is too enormous : he projects over everything his own shadow or his own sun.

But we cannot be indifferent to the reflection that this Self, in the years 1802-1804, had much in common with that of the Shakespeare of the *Tempest*.(195)

We shall see this better now when we raise, with him, the floodgates of the wild finale,—the thirteen furious chords of the diminished seventh that hammer out the first five bars, and, by an unaccustomed transition, pass *ex abrupto* from the second to the third movement :—

The gate opens. The flood bursts out in a cataract, turning again and again on itself before crashing down in foam, at the twentieth bar, on the tonic F minor and the main theme : it is a motion rather than a phrase, a clash of rhythms, a rebound of waves, the visage-less and soul-less hero of the whole movement—the Tempest !

I repeat that I object to seeing in this music a piece
NB

of tone-painting (*Tonmalerei*). But I am bound to recognise that here more than elsewhere the non-human element, strength at its most brutal, most primitive, occupies the chief place, is indeed almost the totality of the finale. Let us admit that Beethoven assimilates himself to it, that he incorporates it into his Self, as he does, in truth, in almost all his great works. But there is this difference, that in nearly all his great works, with the exception of this :—

1. He gives this Force a personal accent ; he anthropomorphises it, establishes a dialogue between it and the man with whom it is in conflict ;

2. The second person of the dialogue, the combatant who suffers and resigns himself—the man,—plays a much more important part and often even ends by monopolising our attention.

Here, in the finale of the *Appassionata*, it is the contrary. The specifically human, individual element hardly finds expression at all in the first part, except in some appealing cries of " Help ! "

that are submerged in the flood ; and in the second part, only in a second motive that is very beautiful, very

THE APPASSIONATA

pathetic, but musically speaking only episodic—a despairing, panting, breathless moan, that also is submerged, drowned, in the full sense of the term :—

In the third part, where the clamour of the tempest mounts to the highest octaves, the voice of distress is heard once more. But it disappears completely; and the Coda shows us only the Ocean unchained.

The whole of the finale is dominated by a single motive—the Elementary—of a fury that rarely ceases, and a richness of combining, clashing, heightening, re-kindling lines and rhythms that complete the picture of this oceanic outburst. In the undulations and the surf of the rhythms :—

in the baying of the accompanying bass :—

in the gallop of the pursuing lines :—

in the polyphony that (as is unusual in these sonatas) in the course of the *Durchführung* adds the tumult of voices to that of the hurricane :—

it is impossible not to see immense sonorous waves tossed up by the wind. In the Coda the mêlée of the howling waves becomes a paroxysm. The design in the bass, that is repeated in each bar in a fury of motion, is like a mass-attack of billows breaking against a cliff :—

until they have beaten it down and submerged it :—

Thus, from one end to another, the principal, the almost unique actor, the hero, is the naked Force of the Elements of Destruction.

If, however, a work of this kind leaves in us no impression of our being beaten down, but on the contrary stimulates us like the breath of the sea, it is by reason of its very inhumanity, its sovereign inhumanity, if I may use that term. There is no longer any question of pitying the man who is the sport of the forces of the Ocean. Man is no longer anything but an atom. The creator has really identified himself with the laws of Nature, the elementary powers, against which he struggled in the first movement. This is a new solution, and one almost unique, I believe, in the work of Beethoven, who does not readily surrender the rights of his unconquerable Self. He must have felt himself in the plenitude of his physical and moral energy thus to be able to abstract himself from his own fate and rejoice in the savage nudity of the Nature that triturates him.

Were it only by reason of the psychical contents of this interior drama, the *Appassionata* would be something exceptional. But it is so also in virtue of the unity of its form—that block from which the hammer of the Cyclopes themselves could not detach a single grain—its never-relaxing tension, its rigorous logic, the athleticism of this body that has no draperies, no ornaments, that is all muscle and solid frame clothed in sound, hard flesh, without a suspicion of fat in it, the violent relief on which a brazen light plays, the monumental phrases that are like a Roman inscription on the pediment of an arch, the fundamental vitality of the style, the character of eternity.

Beethoven has succeeded in constructing in music the imperishable monument of an epoch of humanity, the type of classic art in which is fixed for ever the harmony of one of the great hours of the spirit, the perfect equilibrium of the inner forces, the full consonance of the thought with the matter employed and subdued. The *Appassionata* is worthy to take its place between a fresco of the Sixtine and a tragedy by Corneille : it is of the same family.

AND AS with its sisters, the brilliant victory has been gained, perhaps, at the expense of the morrow. Thus it is with every great human effort ; every victory of the spirit is another line won on the top of the ridge ; one cannot camp there ; after the victory one must descend. The classical masterpiece that the servility of the schools places before us as a model is almost invariably an individual success it would be fatal to attempt to repeat.

The perfection of the *Appassionata* conceals a danger of a double kind. It is characterised by the emprise of reason over the forces let loose. The tumultuous elements are purified, confined within the strict forms of the classic discipline. These forms, indeed, are enlarged to admit of the entry of a whole world of passions. A sea of blood thunders within them : but the sea is closed with the pillars of Hercules. Beethoven, by a tenacious and superhuman tension of the will, has sealed the hinges and put his shoulder to the gate. But woe to those who come after him with neither his fists nor his biceps ! For Beethoven has left in the music of the West certain wild elements that his puissant hand alone could discipline.

The other danger lies at the opposite pole to this. In Beethoven's music everything is on the scale of paroxysm, —not only the fury of the passions but the rigour of the strong-willed reason. And this, applied to sonata-form, that of itself tends to the abuse of the abstract, to excess of oratorical clarity, to the pedantic pleasure of points to be worked out, of divisions and subdivisions, of thesis and antithesis, of the parcelling up of this section and that, runs the risk of ending in a certain ideal of denuded form, a desiccation of the lines, limbs bled white, the neo-classic of the impeccable sonatas of the class-room, that resemble the schema, the algebraic formula of works dead at their birth. Assuredly it goes without saying that the genius of Beethoven never ran these risks ; the super-fullness of its life saved it from that : and Death and Beethoven (to adapt the famous saying) cannot look each other in the face. But already the danger reveals itself in certain celebrated works—perhaps the most celebrated (196)—such as the C minor symphony, where the denudation, in a sense anatomical, of the muscles and tendons of the first allegro turns the beautiful living body into a magnificent " subject " for the dissecting table.(197)

But the hour of the conquest of the summit is not the time to think of the descent. If it is the free spirit's privilege to soar for ever above the present and search the smile on the lips of the coming day, let it leave to the heart the pure joy of drinking to the full of the happiness it has! To-day Beethoven is victor. He knows it. Just as he consecrated the *Eroica* the queen of his first eight symphonies, he awards to the *Appassionata* the first place among his sonatas.(198)

After this, the conqueror does not renew the same combat. It is not in his nature to return on his own traces, after the manner of Haydn and Mozart, who, when a work pleased them, made a whole series of cakes out of the same flour. The end once attained, it interests him no more ; he must look for others.

He forsakes the piano sonata now for five or six years, and does not return to it till 1809/10, with the sonata Op. 78, dedicated to Therese von Brunsvik, that was finished in October 1809 and published in 1810. But in the meanwhile he writes the Rasoumovsky quartets.(199) New demons have ascended from the pit of the soul.

A Page from the *Moonlight* Sonata.

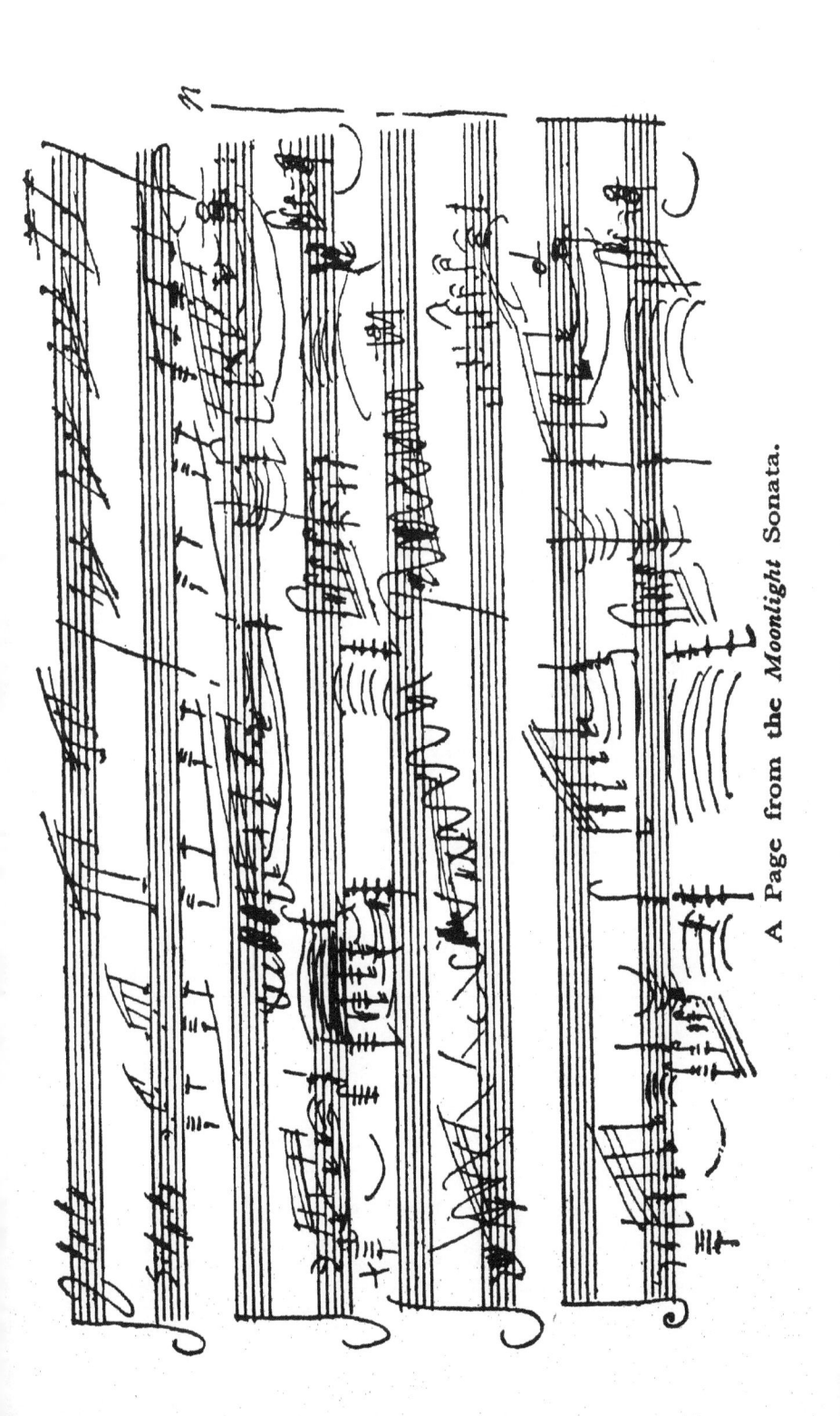

CHAPTER IV
LEONORA

CHAPTER IV

LEONORA

THE *Eroica* and the *Appassionata* were in Beethoven's eyes the culminating peaks of his genius. Speaking generally, the works of this period of three years (1803–1806) remain his favourites until near his death; to him they recall illuminations and tempests whose breath and whose lightnings we still perceive to-day.

Among these privileged works *Leonora* occupies a special position. He placed it on the same height as the others, and he loved it more because it had suffered more.

During the last few weeks before his death, when

giving Schindler the manuscript score, which he had kept hidden under a pile of papers in his room, and the existence of which no one had till then suspected, he said to him : " Of all my children, this is the one that cost me the worst birth-pangs, the one that brought me the most sorrow ; and for that reason it is the one most dear to me. Before all the others I hold it worthy of being preserved and used for the science of art. . . ."(200)

In that life of frenzied labours and struggles, a life in which each work is a combat, in which the musical ideas are conquered and reconquered, wrung out by force, *Leonora* bears the palm ; it was never finished. It was re-written thrice, furnished with four overtures— one masterpiece on top of another—and he wrote a fifth but was still unsatisfied.

Let us first of all look at some of the dates of this ten-years' production.

The sketches for the first five numbers of *Leonora* are found in the Sketch-Book of 1800, after the *Eroica* and the *Waldstein*. Nottebohm, who has analysed them,(201) fixes their date between May 1803 at the earliest and February 1804 at the latest.(202) The later sketches are in a Sketch-Book of 1804.(203) In the interval Beethoven sketched out the first movement of the G major piano concerto and the first and third movements of the C minor symphony. We thus see to what period of maturity of his genius the Prisoners' Chorus and Florestan's aria belong. Nor is this all : immediately after the prison scenes we come upon the sketches for the *Appassionata*, then the ardent duet of Leonora and Florestan, and finally Leonora's great aria in the first act,(204) and the Overture No. 1.

The first *Leonora* grew up in the heart of a forest of masterpieces, and in what an atmosphere of ardent dream and tension of the will ! The man's whole being is at high pressure : the frantic labour of the *Eroica* is nothing in comparison.

Let us recognise that it was a bold venture on which to embark on the morrow of the challenge thrown at the public's head in the *Eroica*. For of all the domains of the art, the theatre was the one in which Beethoven had had least experience. But the very difficulty attracted him ; his pride would dispute the crown with his great dead rivals, Gluck, Handel, and Mozart, in their last bastion.

Perhaps also the theatre seduced him with glittering illusions of fortune, for which some people have not hesitated to reproach him. These virtuous mentors who rebuke Beethoven for having cried aloud his poverty, and smile disdainfully at his perpetual and perpetually vain efforts at economy ! They speak at their ease ! Could there be a more humiliating fate for a Beethoven than to owe his livelihood to the pensions, the good graces, of rich protectors ! Money is independence ;

Beethoven never acquired it. And his independence had to be dearly bought by daily combat.(205)

Before embarking on the struggle, the exhausting futility of which he did not suspect, against the whole world of the theatre—librettists, singers, producers, directors, and, worst of all, the " connoisseurs " (who will be in the right against him in the end, for they are the multitude against the genius)—there is a much harder fight in front of him : the fight against himself, against his inexperience in the art of dramatic music : Cherubini will tell him of it without the least beating about the bush, and send him, for his instruction, " *l'École du Conservatoire de Paris,*" which the proud master of the *Eroica* accepts submissively and gratefully. He will have to check his symphonic temperament, that is always prone to overflow in torrential developments : he must do violence to his nature, which, in the feverish hour of parturition, is like Chaos before the Creation, containing within it the germs of every species of life. The Spirit will achieve the organisation of them only at the cost of terrific struggles, of which the Sketch-Book gives us a glimpse. We seem to see that monstrous age of which Empedocles speaks, in which dim forms feel their way about in the night, seek each other out, coalesce in ill-matched fragments, to form monsters that for long are incapable of life, until the day comes when at last those who were made for each other come together. But here the encounter is the fruit not of a blind destiny but of a furious will, the like of which there has probably never been in that hard ploughed field in which the uninitiated see only the harvests heaped up in the granaries. I refer the curious to the publications that Nottebohm and Otto Jahn have devoted to the Sketch-Book, and to the pages devoted to it in the second volume of Thayer. Words cannot convey an idea of this unheard-of labour. A mere commencement, a fragment of an aria, has been noted down no less than eighteen times, in eighteen different ways. For a single cry, innumerable studies have been necessary. And what is most astounding is the incredible disorder in which these re-touches—(no ! each failure is definitively rejected), these successions of rough drafts, appear. For twenty-two lines of vocal music(206) there are sixteen pages of studies, with the words of the dialogue repeated, mixed up with each other, without head and tail, in a veritable dementia of repetition.(207) We cannot understand how Beethoven could ever find his way about through the mess, how it was his reason did not founder in these bogs ! A mud in flower ! A seething, tormented marsh, pullulating in the sunlight ! . . . And then that splendid garden, designed and planted like the royal groves and classic avenues of a master of Reason and Order in the Grand Siècle !

At last, the complete work. Scarcely has it been born

when it is shown, all red and bleeding, to the public (20th, 21st, 22nd November, 1805). But the temperature of the hall is below zero. The war is on the town,—the defeat, the French occupation : the Viennese aristocracy has fled, the common people have shut themselves up in their homes ; and one cannot precisely see Murat and Lannes going to hear Beethoven ! In this scanty audience the Saxon correspondent of the *Zeitung für die elegante Welt* and the occupant of the next seat to his, a Frenchman, exchange their impressions of boredom. The Frenchman—a Giraudoux of the period, ironical and condescending—shows no surprise ; dramatic composition being, according to him, the highest form of art, it needs an æsthetic " culture " (*Ausbildung*) that naturally no German artist can possess. The Press, that always puts its finger on the spot, says that in this music there is no melodic idea, not a trace of originality, with endless repetitions and a perpetual hubbub in the orchestra, that wanders through all the keys ; the choruses mean absolutely nothing,—particularly the one that describes the joy of the prisoners at once more breathing the free air palpably misses fire (*offenbar misrathen*). (208) The opera had only three performances.

 The few friends of the composer who, in spite of the events of the time, had remained in Vienna set themselves to float the work again ; they tried to persuade Beethoven to revise and shorten it. It was a difficult, indeed, a superhuman task. The tenor Josef August Röckel has left us an account of the scene of December 1805 in the Lichnowsky palace, when the opera was discussed by a small committee. The orchestra is represented by the Princess (at the piano) and the virtuoso Clement, who played all the instrumental soli on his violin. There are only two singers; one of them takes all the high parts, the other all the low ones. The faithful Breuning has undertaken to fuse the three acts of the original version into two; he has re-written the wretched dialogues of the librettist Sonnleithner. For six consecutive hours, from seven in the evening till one in the morning, the devoted little group, whose intentions were superior to their capacity, urged Beethoven to cut down the brushwood here and there. He is as sombre as a storm-cloud; he refuses again and again; suddenly he picks up his score in a rage and swears he would rather destroy it than dishonour it. Then the good Princess almost throws herself on her knees before him; she implores him passionately not to let " his greatest work " perish; she evokes the pathetic memory of his mother. Beethoven is overcome; he bursts into sobs: " I will do everything . . . everything you ask me . . . for you . . . for my mother ! "

Alas, what is it these pious friends have persuaded him to do? Not only has he, with death in his soul, taken out three entire numbers, but here and there, in the remaining numbers, phrases are cut,—nay, whole bars go down before the scissors ; the result of it all is that the continuity is destroyed, the modulations deranged. But, taking his revenge in the symphonic field, Beethoven re-writes his overture—the magnificent Symphony in C major, No. 3. Here he is on his own territory, and he fears no one.

He will soon see! *Leonora*, or rather *Fidelio*,[209] is given again in its mutilated form. This time it receives only two performances (29th March and 10th April 1806).[210] Complete failure! And what displeases most is the overture! Chorus of the pond of critics and " connoisseurs " :—

" *All* impartial connoisseurs are *fully agreed* that never has anything been written so ill-knit, so disagreeable, so confused, so revolting to the ear. The most acid modulations succeed each other in an abominable cacophony (*wirklichen grässliches*)."

To the delicate—and certainly long—ears of these fine connoisseurs, who were deafened by the " shattering din,"[211] disgusted by the " paltriness " of the ideas,[212] the flashing fanfare that cleaves the tragic cloud of the quartet in the prison becomes a " solo for postilion's horn " (*Posthornsolo*)! The oracle who pontifies in Kotzebue's Berlin journal *Der Freimüthige, oder Ernst und Scherz* (11th September, 1806) advises Beethoven to take as his model a magnificent (*herrliche*) overture by

Andreas Romberg—"this lucid beauty without softness, this powerful and yet never excessive use of all the instruments, this fullness of interior life, without factitious over-tension"—which forms an absolute contrast with the obstinate art of Beethoven, that has neither beauty, naturalness, nor facility. Beethoven has an acrimonious argument with the director of the theatre, Baron Braun. The latter wounds him to the quick; he proves to him that at both performances the boxes were full, but not the popular seats, as in the case of Mozart's operas. The enraged composer shouts:

"I do not write for the crowd (*Menge*). I write for musicians (*Gebildeten*)."

"Then don't complain!" is the Baron's dry reply.

Beethoven at once demands his score back, and goes off with it. . . . Silence until a better time shall come! The prison door closes once more on *Leonora*.

There seems hardly any doubt that the work was the victim of a malicious cabal that had been exasperated by not only the art but the personality of Beethoven, and also, it must be confessed, by the tactlessness of his partisans.[213] Breuning says so in so many words.[214] It is the first time the cabal is seen engaging successfully with Beethoven. From this time onward it will pursue its work of hypocritical or violent denigration. We shall meet with it again.[215]

For the moment it has achieved its object; it has

crippled the opera and wounded Beethoven to the heart. Breuning writes on the 2nd June, 1806, that he is dispirited and, in the material sense, ruined by the failure: " nothing has ever caused him such vexation." In vain do the warmly devoted Lichnowskys try to win him a compensation by sending the score to the Queen of Prussia, in the hope that Berlin may avenge him for Vienna's lack of understanding. Berlin remains silent; and for the revenge he has to wait eight years. In 1807 only three detached numbers from the score were published, and these the least characteristic.(216)

At the end of 1813 Beethoven suddenly came in for a noisy temporary popularity, which he owed not to music but to politics. The only one of his works that is unworthy of him, that complete nullity *The Battle of Vittoria*, that celebrates the victory of Wellington, is admired by everyone: even the cabal renders homage, for this time he has come down to its level! *Leonora* profits by this vogue. The Opera directors are looking round for a work that can be put on with the least possible expense for the benefit of three of the singers: they think of Beethoven. He consents to adapt his score to the new exigencies. A practical man of the theatre, the manager and poet Georg Friedrich Treitschke, works over the libretto for the third time; he takes out the first scene in Rocco's house, so that the opera opens in the courtyard of the prison. The characters of Leonora

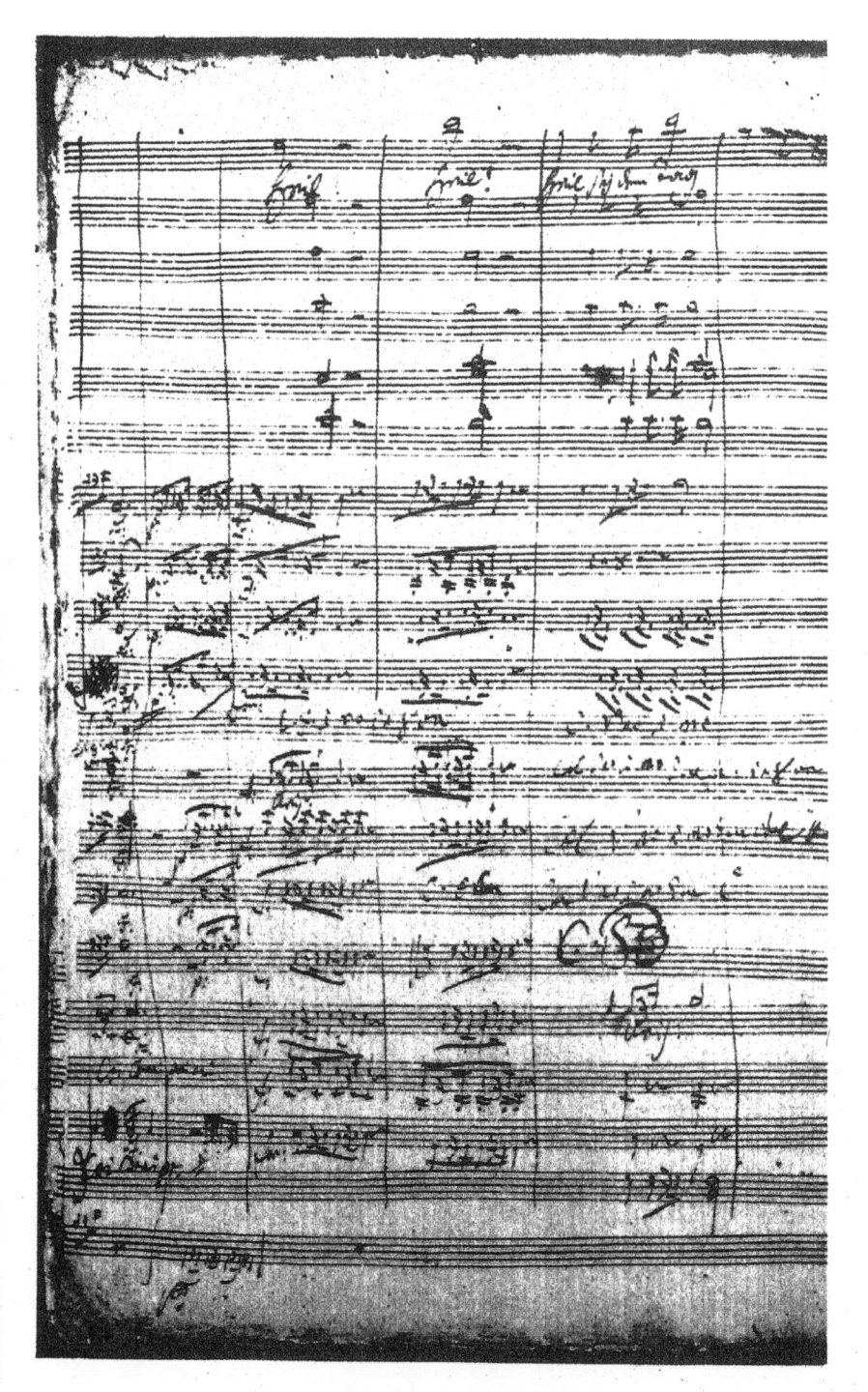

A page of the *Fidelio* manuscript

Portrait of Giulietta Guicciardi, Countess Gallenberg
(probably in 1815)

and Florestan are modified; and Beethoven has to sacrifice some of his finest pages. From the theatrical point of view, however, the work now goes better. But Beethoven can no longer recognise it: he laments that this opera " brings him the crown of martyrdom " ("*erwirbt mir die Märtirerkrone*"). And he writes yet another overture(217)—that of *Fidelio*, No. 4, in E major —that is less inspired than the others, less epic, more on the ordinary theatrical scale. In this form the opera at last succeeds, on the 23rd May, 1814: it is given twenty-two times in Vienna, and afterwards in other towns— at Prague on the 24th November, 1814, under Weber, who learns a good deal from it. Moscheles is commissioned to make the vocal score; and it was in this that Beethoven added, under Moscheles' " Finished with God's help," the famous " O man, help thyself " (" *O Mensch, hilf dir selber* "). He had the right to say so: in fact, he could have given help to God!

But if the performances of 1814 wiped out the insult of 1805 and 1806, it was not until ten years later that an actress of genius, Wilhelmine Schroeder-Devrient, gave the work its crown of glory: she carried the fame of it through Europe to Paris, where it communicated to the young Berlioz a holy emotion that he cherished to the end of his days.(218)

Beethoven died without having seen the rehabilitation of the first version of his work, the integral, uncompromised, and uncompromising *Leonora*; and in his last days he pressed to his heart "*sein liebstes Schmerzenskind,*" as Schindler called it—the dearest child of his sorrow.

WHAT THEN is this work that kept its place in his affections until the last, and of which three successive versions and four (if not five) overtures were insufficient to satisfy his *Sehnsucht*, his passionate desire to realise it? Note the fact that the overtures, with the exception of the fourth, are not simply introductions to the work but separate and independent attempts at the solution of the same problem, fresh desperate efforts to convey the idea of the work by purely symphonic means! Why this pertinacity? Did he see a dramatic-musical problem to resolve? Assuredly, as we shall see, Beethoven brought into the opera house a new form, and his instinct must have made him aware of its difficulties and of the insufficiency of certain realisations of it. But would it not have been simpler, and more consonant with his nature, that took more pleasure in inventing than in re-touching,(219) to approach the problem afresh in a new work instead of obstinately working again and again over the old one? What was there in this work that bound him to it so? What was the unique nature of it? Was it perhaps the subject?

Before examining it more closely, one detail ought to put us on our guard. At the end of the libretto,—which is virtually a translation from the French—Beethoven introduces into the final chorus—*maestoso* for four voices, then *tutti* (220)—these words of Schiller :—

" *Wer ein holdes Weib errungen, stimm' in unseren Jubel ein!* " (" Let him who has won him a dear wife, join us in our joy! ")

Twenty years later he will use these same words again in the hymn to Joy at the end of the Ninth Symphony, so much did the thought mean for him!

That life-long dream of his, that it was never given to him to realise! That idealisation of women and of conjugal fidelity, in which, in spite of all deceptions, he has never ceased to believe! I am not speaking now of the refusals he received, but of the bitter revelations life brought him with regard to the women he had loved,(221) and that made him say to Nanni Giannatasio del Rio in 1817 :—

" I have never known a marriage in which, after a time, one or other of the pair has not regretted the false step. And of the few women the possession of whom would formerly have seemed to me supreme happiness,

I have lived to see that it was a good thing that not one of them became my wife. Ah ! how fortunate it is that often the vows of mortals are not accomplished ! "(222)

No matter ! He is never an apostate to his religious ideal of the betrothed, the wife. He will render her in public a solemn homage, in his two greatest works, the one dramatic, the other choral.

In the same way Goethe, who no doubt had less apparent reason to think himself unfortunate in love, but who, in reality, having known it better had also more reason to know its insufficiency and its bitterness, Goethe, who could not find or keep a companion worthy of him, cannot make his exit from life before he has sung, in the Epilogue to *Faust*, his credo in woman.

Possibly thoughts of this kind seem, to our æsthetes of to-day, to lie outside the circle of art. But since the emperor of art, Goethe, has sealed his greatest work with them, I have some right to note their secret importance in the mind of Beethoven, and the part they played in the enduring attraction that the theme of *Fidelio* had for him.

Let us return to this theme.

It has been much disparaged. The general opinion rather looks down on it, and the wretched performances the work has had during a whole century(223) have confirmed this verdict. It must be confessed that until our time *Fidelio* was played in a way that misrepresented it.(224)

Let us study it more closely. Anyone who has had the good fortune, as I had, to see the centenary performances at Vienna must make his *mea culpa* for the misunderstanding of a century; and one feels the need to share the discovery with others,—the newly-revealed splendour, dramatic and musical, of the entire second act, that unique masterpiece that had no forerunner and has had no successor in the musical theatre. And without a shadow of doubt the grandeur of it is wholly the work of the genius of the musician. Yet the poem has not served him ill; this libretto is a sturdy horse that does not stumble under the weight of its rider. Beethoven did it justice: he maintained *mordicus* that the subject was an excellent one. In 1823, when he was chatting with Weber and joking about the libretti of his younger colleague, and expressing himself scathingly on the incurable mediocrity of the German librettists, he paid the French a compliment and recalled the fact that his *Fidelio* came to him from them.(225)

WHAT CAME to him from them, in *Leonora*, was not merely an anecdote more or less well told but an atmosphere of tragic reality : it was the Revolution.

But the French themselves,—as happens to those who, absorbed in an event, their nose to the detail of the daily round, cannot see the great eternal lines—had been unconscious of the Æschylean breath that came from their tale.(226) Just as in the *Eroica* Beethoven had been the Homer of the Empire, so now, in *Leonora*, he was the Æschylus of the Revolution.

Everyone knows that the story of *Leonora* is taken from Bouilly, who himself was not its inventor, for he had known the heroine of it—a woman of Touraine. He has given an account of her in his memoirs(227) ; but Beethoven knew nothing of these, for they did not appear until after his death ; and *Leonora* came to him in the Spanish costume in which Bouilly, for prudential reasons, had disguised it.(228) There is no Spanish local colour in his music, however ; and his intuition, that pierces to the eternal depths, seems to have divined the proximity of the terrible period he was describing—at no more than ten years' distance from the real drama, and when the actual heroine was still alive.

There is no need for me to tell again the story of the drama, which, in its broad lines, depicts the horrors of a State prison and the devotion of a woman who entered it in disguise to save her husband. The critics have in general insisted only on the improbabilities and incongruities of the libretto, or on the difficulty that Beethoven's symphonic genius had in adapting itself to the dramatic necessities of opera. We are entitled to assume that they have not perceived the true essence either of the poem that Beethoven was setting or of the dramatic Ode he wished to make of it.

To the first of these points some effective answers have recently been made. Hermann W. von Waltershausen (229) has undertaken the defence of the French libretto. He shows that the mixture of styles, that has been so freely criticised—the bourgeois opening that hardly prepares us for the high tragedy that is to come—comes from a view of the subject that is as veracious as it is striking. At the height of the Terror, even in the darkness of this prison in which, it would seem, those who have entered have left all hope behind, the tranquil life of the bourgeois goes on just the same, with its pots of geranium in the window, the young girl's love-dreams, the old gaoler's simple and affectionate calculations of self-interest, his quiproquos and his comic vexations. But the art is in the lightness of the touches, in the imperceptible oncoming of the tragic shadow, that at first just touches these scenes of egoistic tranquillity with the tip of its wing, then reaches further, and at last envelops the whole stage. The French librettist has indicated this. It is not without interest for us that these *poetæ minores* (the word poet is a big one!) of the French bourgeois comedy and opéra-comique did much, according to the German historians, to form that atmosphere of chiaroscuro and mysterious terror in which German musical romanticism found its nourishment. From these *crescendi* of inexplicable anguish and terror, Weber, in *Der Freischütz*, drew effects till then unknown. Our poor French librettists were far enough from these; no doubt these agitations would have frightened them; they had undergone too many of them in the life of the time not to tone them down in their comedies. In the same way some of our writers of to-day who witnessed and were wounded in the bloody catastrophe of the Europe they knew, fly from the representation of it in their art; but in spite of them their æsthetic diversions bear the agitated imprint of it. The obscure source of the tragic perturbation that was so much to the liking of romanticism was the social agitation,—the terror during the Terror—of the preceding generation. What that generation had been able only to stammer forth, a Beethoven expresses in its naked truth, without any beating about the bush, out of the plenitude of a great heart and with the mastery of genius. His *Leonora* is a monument of the anguish of the period, of the oppressed soul and its appeal to liberty,—a formidable *crescendo* swelling from suffering to joy, traversing the road of hope and combat—an ascent from the abyss **to the clear sky.**

This filiation between a robust junior and the elder members of a noble race—these, however, a trifle debilitated and overborne by the rigours of the time,—is not confined merely to vague moral resemblances. It is clearly marked in the music, with a precision that permits of no doubt.(230) The symphonic style of *Leonora* derives in essentials from that of Méhul and Cherubini. Here again it has been able to ripen the rather green and dry fruit, to press out the whole of the juice of it where they were content with a few drops.

We have to remember that in the *Leonora* period Beethoven, who could still hear, enjoyed the French operas that were the delight of Vienna (231) ; and for him no living master could compare with Cherubini. Among the *Fidelio* sketches we find, in Beethoven's writing, passages from *Le Porteur d'eau*. Seyfried and Schindler bear testimony to his unceasing admiration for the composer of *Medea* ; and we know that Beethoven himself, at the height of his genius (in 1823), wrote to Cherubini paying humble homage to this work.

It is not surprising, then, that traces of this influence should be found in his own music. Even during his lifetime E. T. A. Hoffmann, who always saw more deeply than his contemporaries, had been struck by the community of race between Cherubini's overtures and the *Coriolan*. Since that time Wagner and the German critics of our own day have pointed out several resemblances between them. The question has recently been elucidated, so far as the Beethoven overtures are concerned, by Arnold Schmitz (1925). The examples he gives, the similarities he notes, show clearly that Beethoven derived a good deal from the French composers of the Revolution; but they prove also the magnificent use he made of his booty. If some of the analogues may be explained on the theory of a common source—Gluck (for example, the mighty unisons with which all Beethoven's tragic overtures open)(232)—the majority of the others bear witness to the moral contagion of the France that had as yet barely emerged from the Revolution and still felt the shock of it; a whole family of characteristic effects or motives in the operas of Méhul and Cherubini exhibits the nervous fever, the uneasy agitation, the painful excess of excitement of which I spoke a moment ago in connection with the poems; the composers may not have been clearly conscious of it, but for long enough afterwards it ran shuddering beneath their skin, like the periodic attacks of an old malaria. Schmitz has drawn up a remarkable inventory of them: the obstinate use of certain stereotyped formulæ for effect, such as the boil and swirl of the unison strings in the coda of the *Leonora No. 3*, the source of which is Cherubini's *Elisa* overture; " alarm " effects; brusque repetitive figures that seem to keep clashing with each other between two walls; sequences of syncopated chords (here the resemblance is striking) employed at the same moment and in the same place in the coda of the *Leonora No. 2* and in that of *Elisa* (233); unquestionable analogies of complementary rhythms in the *Leonora No. 1*, the *Fidelio No. 4*, the *Coriolan* on the one hand and Cherubini's *Elisa* and Méhul's *Stratonice* on the other (234); resemblances between certain themes in Méhul's overtures and in those of Beethoven; and so on. Lastly, the idea of the tremendous trumpet fanfare in the *Leonora No. 2* and *Leonora No. 3* came from Méhul's overture to *Hélène*!

But here we become more than ever conscious of the magic power of genius. It is nothing to have ideas: the thing is to realise them. And for the realisation of them neither intelligence, nor a fine sense of art, nor skill in form, necessary as all these are, is enough; these are only the portico. Enter the building and erect the vault! Each of the really remarkable suggestions of Méhul or Cherubini is merely the invitation to proceed along a certain path; they draw back at the first step, but Beethoven presses on. Passion does not merely suggest; it demands the complete embrace! Cherubini recoils; he is too intelligent not to know what he is letting slip from his grasp, but he doubts his own strength; he turns away from the lovely form, and is satisfied to sketch a noble intellectual portrait of it. His themes lack blood, his melodies are abstract: he has formulated **the rules of the game** clearly enough, but he will not risk the hazard of it. Beethoven throws the whole of himself into it. And into this inferno of the soul—passions, combats, sufferings—that the musicians of the Revolution have indeed known but have not dared to enter, Beethoven, following in their track, boldly penetrates, and, leaving them on the threshold, descends to the depths.

THE DESCENT into the abyss and the subsequent ascent out of the night into full sunlight : this is the dominant impression produced by *Leonora*. The tragic contrast and the *crescendo* of light are realised with perfect mastery, however, only in the second part of the first act—after Leonora's famous aria. Until then Beethoven has been hesitating, searching ; as yet he has caught only a glimpse of his true subject. And when suddenly it dawns upon him : " *Ach! brich noch nicht, du mattes Herz!* "(235) he is overwhelmed, transported into a completely different world of music. It is too late now to re-establish the transition from Singspiel to opera, from the comedy of everyday life to high tragedy ! Certainly that task was not an easy one : but it was not above the capacity of a Beethoven. Mozart had accomplished it, and even Gluck, whose *Iphigenia in Aulis* and *Orfeo* are a harmonious blend of the highest lyrical forms and the simplest, the most popular.

But *Leonora* was for Beethoven a first essay; when he began it he was entering a *terra ignota*. And his natural mistake was that, for lack of power to take in the whole of this new continent with one of those eagle glances that, in the *Eroica* or the C minor, survey the whole field of battle, he prudently set himself to begin at the beginning. He followed the order of the "numbers" with exemplary patience and unexampled tenacity,(236) constraining his herculean muscles to turn the spinning-wheel of the little Marcellina, to copy Mozart in the familiar domestic scenes, to array his giant music in the hoods of the puppets of the little song-plays of Leipzig or Paris.

It goes without saying that a labour of this kind cannot be absolutely in vain in the case of a Beethoven; and these introductory numbers are distinguished by some fine details of orchestration, some delicate expressions of feeling. Particularly successful are the quartet in canon,—the vocalised evolution of which was not lost on the young Berlioz of *Benvenuto Cellini*—and the duet between Marcellina and Leonora, with its innocent tenderness and its charming orchestral ornamentation.(237)

But it is evident that Beethoven's heart is not in his work as yet, that he is writing like a pupil of the Singspiel elegants. The whole of this first part of the first act, this half-way house in which Mozart was thoroughly at home, is cold, and imitative not of nature but of books. Even in the second half of the act the scenes and characters that do not lie close to the thoughts and passions of Beethoven are only half-successful. Pizarro is a traitor of melodrama, not lacking in savage grandeur (Weber did not forget him), but with a touch of the ridiculous about him. And in the first version of the end of the first act (Pizarro, Rocco, Leonora: Pizarro and his bodyguard) some fairly new and moving pages are combined with the heavy conventions of pompous declamatory opera,—a sort of Meyerbeer *avant la lettre*.(238) It is the revenge, we might almost say the punishment, of sincerity. Beethoven cannot lie : an artistic nature like his is completely unable to simulate emotions it has not experienced. By the very nature of his being he must love, hate, believe, take fire. Nothing by halves : everything in extremes.

He might have made a frank plunge into the very centre of the drama with Leonora's aria and the Prisoners' scene ; but to do that he would have needed the support of some great librettist formed in the school of Gluck. He had around him none but mediocrities, hangers-on of the theatre, who were nowhere so much at their ease as in the insipid conventions that had been manipulated a thousand times already. Being a newcomer in the theatre, he lacked the authority to assail them as Gluck would have done. Still less had he Gluck's robust health, his weight of manner, that would have made it possible for him to ascend the stage and give battle with fist and tongue to this crew of routineers and liars, the actors, the singers, the chorus, the instrumentalists, the librettist, the producer! He was a sick man; he heard only half of what was going on; he ran the risk of having it said, "Why do you interfere? You are deaf." And so he accepted what was given him; he began with the established conventions.

But what we have to consider is not the point of departure but the point of arrival. These conventions that he so meekly and unwillingly endorses, this formal frock-coat in which his great chest suffocates during the first ten numbers—see him burst them and tear them in pieces with a single stroke!

LEONORA has spoken: she speaks with the tongue of immortal Hope. . . .

"*O Hoffnung!* . . . *Hoffnung!* . . ."

At that time Hope was Beethoven's good goddess. He was still young—no more than thirty-five; none of his wounds was incurable; he was still far from the sad Resignation that twelve years later will be his frozen muse.(239) Hope has deceived him; but still he goes on hoping. In the very middle of the sketches for *Leonora* he makes five big sketches for the song *To Hope*.(240) The melody is beautiful, ample, tranquil; but how pale it appears beside the aria of Leonora! Here hope rises from the depth of suffering, from the depth of the bleeding heart.

I recommend all lovers of Beethoven to procure the first version of *Leonora*.(241) The score that most people know has been enriched with new beauties, of which the finest is the second Prisoners' Chorus at the end of the first act—"*Leb wohl, du warmes Sonnenlicht!*" and the whole work is better balanced. But it has lost some unique pages, the disappearance of which leaves us inconsolable. The original version gave us Beethoven's emotion in the purity of its first welling, for the immediacy of which not even the most perfect re-touching by art can be a compensation. It was so, for example, with Leonora's aria. The new recitative that introduces it is no doubt more dramatic; and the *adagio* of remembrance with its mystic vision in the high thin notes of the violins :—

The Kohlmarkt, Vienna, in Beethoven's time

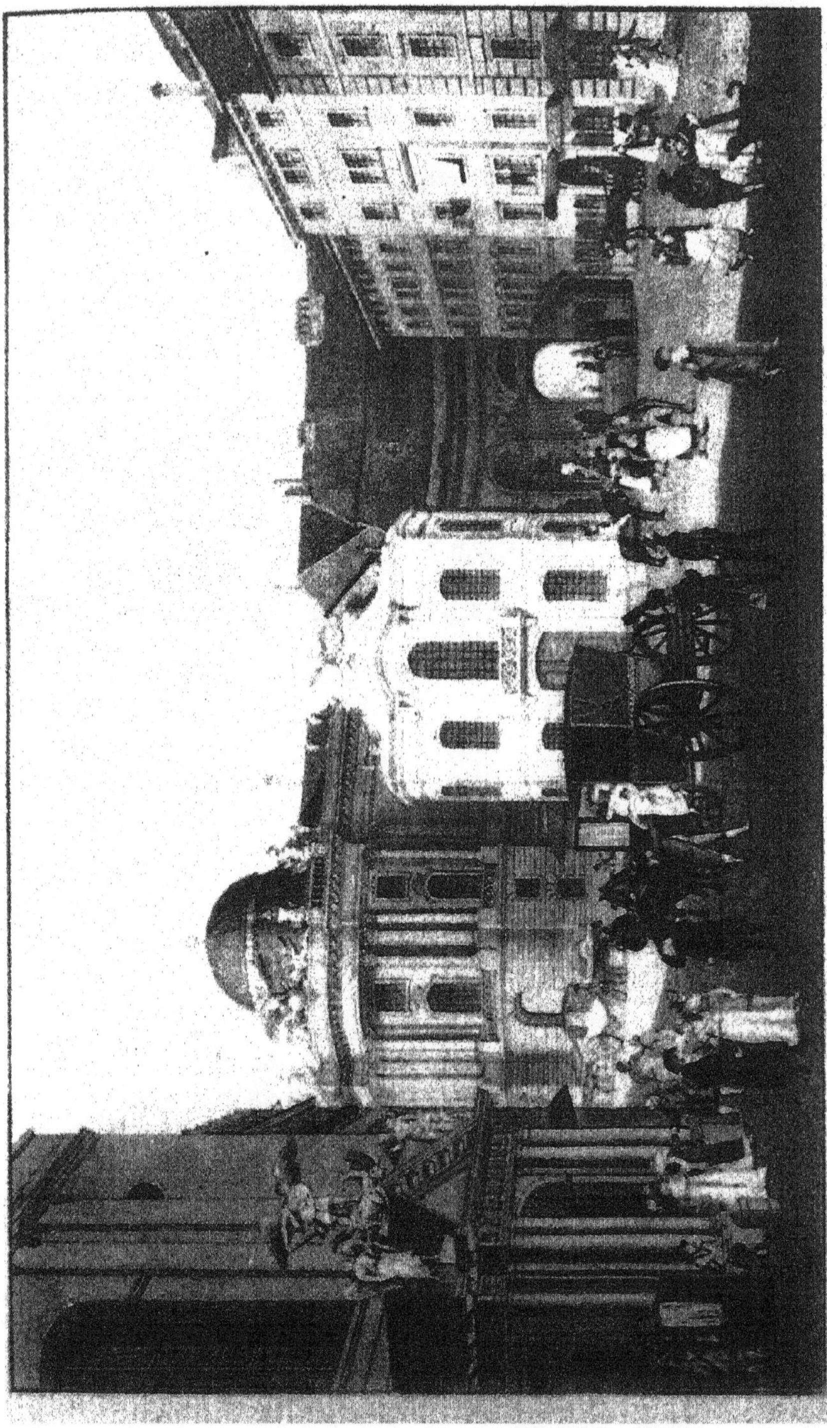

—that rainbow in sound—has a beauty as pure as it is novel. And yet I regret the loss of the first appeal to Hope in the original version:

"*O Hoffnung! ... O komm! ... Hoffnung! ... O komm! ...*"

that almost spoken(242) sigh, to which the song of Hope already replies in advance in the orchestra, in the deep horns and bassoons:—

It is as if we saw Hope approaching in the clouds.... She stretches out her arms to the unhappy one.... And then begins the august song, the hymn of hope in affliction, that prayer of all wounded hearts, that none of them will ever be able to sing or hear without a gush of hidden tears. It is our Beethoven, whom no other musician—and how many others are dear to us!—can ever replace in our confidence; for he touches with a pious hand the solitary soul's most sacred strings.

The ample melody unfolds its tenderness and its plaint, rhythmed by the pulsations of the orchestra, that is like a heart oppressed. The first version does not, as the second did for purely material reasons of economy of time, link this orison on to the cry of heroic action with the horn fanfares : "*Ich folg' dem innern Triebe!*" It went by way of a natural and moving transition, by the thought of "*him for whom* the faithful wife *endures this suffering*"; and the scene ended, in accordance with the logic of the emotion, with the aria di bravura (in the literal sense of the term), the fire of which, the epic accent and the modulations gleaming like sunlight, pre-announce the finales of Weber.

But the gem of the act is the scene that follows—the Prisoners' Chorus. They come out from the shadows, feeling their way. Timid and hungry, they sip the daylight drop by drop. Where before had this trembling joy found expression, these quivers of the heart, this fear of happiness ? They hardly dare speak their joy. These Beethoven *pianissimi* ! What a part they play in the work ! They have been too little noticed.(243) These men, cut off from Joy, scarcely dare touch her with the tips of their fingers when she appears to them. And Joy hesitates to draw near to them, for, like them, she is wounded. Their emotion finds a religious expression. God indeed is in it. . . . " *Gottes Hülfe.* . . . " The trembling hearts are lighted up by her presence. . . ." *O Hoffnung ! Rettung ! . . . O Freiheit, kehrst du zurück. . . .* " Then fear takes possession of them again ; they whisper to each other ; they enjoin on each other silence, prudence. . . . But about this shuddering mass and its timid murmurs the orchestra sings the happiness of daylight, the delight of air in the lungs ; and the imprisoned soul seems to escape in the liberating lines of the flutes, clarinets, and violins.(244)

In the first version of the poem, Beethoven, in order to finish the act, had to accept, in place of the re-descent of the prisoners into the darkness, a melodramatic scene in the manner of Monsieur Scribe : the traitor Pizarro bids his sbirri be vigilant, and these, in a docile ensemble, protest their devotion like a chorus in *Les Huguenots*. The musician has put himself to extreme trouble to translate into music these words and this situation, of the silliness of which he was conscious ; and as he was quite sincere, the first ideas that involuntarily came to him were comic.(245) He put his pen through them and began again ; then, in despair, he broke off to write a sonata, a triple concerto, and some other pages of *Leonora*. In vain ! He could not take fire from the unfortunate scene ; he had to resign himself to an empty and turgid finale that weighed on his conscience. Luckily, when they came to re-cast the work in 1814, the intelligence of Treitschke provided him with the means to get rid of this absurd ending, which he replaced by the divine chorus and quintet that now terminate the act. This second Prisoners' Chorus forms a pendant to the other, a perfect contrast and perfect harmony with it ; after the ascent from the tomb, the re-descent into it—the unutterable melancholy of regret for the sunlight they are leaving, the hope that beats its wings and dies.

This time Beethoven takes us by the hand and does not let us go until the end. We descend with Orpheus into the depths of the kingdom of Affliction. But here the situation is reversed : it is Eurydice who goes to save her Orpheus.

The entire third act of the first version (i.e., the second act of the *Fidelio* that is performed to-day) is a sublime religious Mystery, a Holy Sepulchre in which the soul agonises and comes to life again. Where in all opera, since *Alceste*, had accents like these been heard ? But the great heart of Gluck did not possess these means of symphonic expression. These mighty, pillar-like harmonies,(246) these resonances from the heights, these basses that sigh like a Prometheus Bound, these syncopations, these stemmings of the blood, these pulsations in cross rhythms,—and above them, always, the great sweeping flood of the development, and on this unresisting suffering the consecration of an infinite goodness ! . . . Ah ! now Beethoven is at home again ! No more of the theatre ! The public is forgotten : he is the king in his castle of Solitude. He is filled with his immense Self. And the whole world, and each of us, recognise ourselves in him—like him, alone and infinite. . . .

After the orchestra has created the abyss around us,

the voice of the soul sings in the silence the desert in which it is perishing:

"*Oed' ist es um mich her; nichts lebet ausser mir....*"

But it does not struggle: it resigns itself. And the religious grief of the lovely *adagio cantabile* in A flat major recalls the vanished happiness. In certain aspects of it we recognise the tremulous Beethovenian affirmation of truth:

"*... Wahrheit, wagt' ich kühn zu sagen....*"
and the heroism of the acceptance of suffering in the consciousness of duty done:

"*Süsser Trost in meinem Herzen, meine Pflicht hab' ich gethan....*"

In the first version this stoical character persisted to the end. An *andante un poco agitato* in F minor, virile and melancholy, controlled in its very agitation, prefigures certain great songs of Schubert and of Berlioz, affirms the "*Do thy duty, come what may!*"

"*Florestan hat recht gethan....*"

This seems to me more in conformity with the truth and energy of the character than the somewhat factitious hallucination that has been substituted for it in *Fidelio*, —the *poco allegro* in F major:

"*... Und spür' ich nicht linde, sanft saüselnde Luft?...*"
in which Florestan believes he sees the walls of his prison opening: it is a quite different atmosphere, lit by dreams, bloodless and discoloured. It has, however, its dramatic

beauty, that made Berlioz faint with emotion; he has described " this sobbing melody, these orchestral palpitations, the long-spun song of the oboe that follows Florestan's song like the voice of his wife. . . ." Both versions end in an exhausted *pianissimo*.

The same mute is maintained during the dramatic scenes that follow; and in his markings Beethoven insists on this effect. At the head of the tragic duet of the grave-diggers that succeeds the " melodrama "—that epic elegy—over a Schubert-like accompaniment (veiled trombones, horns, basses, contra-bassoon) that surrounds the plaint of the oboes and clarinets with the monotonous rumble of its waves, he has written:

" This number must be played very softly from start to finish; the *sforzandi* and *forti* must not be made to stand out too much."(247)

From the commencement of the act, the action has been in the epic key, and rightly so. The individual drama has become Destiny. Even the lament of Leonora, digging the grave of the man who is about to die—she cannot yet know if it is her Florestan—keeps clear of the too romantic, the too subjective; it rises to the majesty of the story; her pain is transmuted into a universal pity.

" *Wer du auch seist, ich will dich retten . . .* "

For a single moment—(" *Ich will, du Armer, dich befrein* ")—the accent surges to a *sforzando crescendo* without, however, going beyond the *mezzo forte*; and this is the culminating point of the scene: it is the ecstasy of the genius of liberty. Rocco begins to wonder at this young man who is talking to himself; then the work is taken up again, and once more the scene ends *pianissimo*.

There are the same half-tints in the trio (Florestan, Leonora, and Rocco). The *crescendi* pass from *piano* to *piano*, taking in their course a short *sforzando* that is almost immediately followed by *piano* (the *sf p* that is so characteristic of Beethoven). The melody of pity, sorrow, gratitude always maintains its broad calm line, in which there is no trace of romanticism. The *più mosso* at the end (248) is still *piano*, and it dies away in a *pianissimo*.

Here, then, are three great scenes (four if we include the Prisoners' Chorus that terminates the first act) that are played out in a chiaroscuro, with a delicacy of means, a reticence of emotion, that are in complete contrast with the conception of the plumed, emphatic Beethoven entertained by those who do not know him.

They are in equal contrast with the declamatory routine of the opera stage. Berlioz observed that the public of his day was disconcerted by them; it greeted each of these *piano* endings with " a rigorous silence." Not that silence is here an evil! We do not ask for applause in the theatre: we ask that not the **hands** but the heart shall speak. I wish that every musician who seeks to fathom the art of Beethoven could have under his eyes, as I have had, the manuscript score of *Leonora*, with his own corrections. On a single page (249) they would see

"*sempre più piano ppmo*"

written seven times in pencil between the staves, and again at the top and the bottom of the page, in big letters, the same injunction :

"*sempre più piano ppmo.*"

When I come to analyse the works of his last period I will point out the omissions of which the editors have too often been guilty in the last sonatas, in which the *ff* had been indicated by Beethoven with the utmost discretion. The " big notes " are as revolting, in a performance of *Leonora*, as the big, vociferous, ill-shaped women who don Fidelio's hose. We need to be reminded of what we are too prone to forget—that Beethoven is a master not only of energy and overwhelming dynamic effects but of chiaroscuro and the half-tint. If, as we shall see later in connection with the peroration of *Leonora*, his light at its fullest flashes and burns, that is precisely because of the drastic economy with which he employs his sunlight during the greater part of the work.

Here we have the most striking dramatic example of this. The long self-collection of the first three prison scenes, in which grief wraps itself in shadow and expresses itself in half-tones, is succeeded without transition by the fury of Pizarro hurling himself on his victim. But here again what a difference between the fury of a Beethoven and that of a Wagner ! How much less persistently it is maintained on the colossal scale of violence, how much more nuanced it is, and always in motion like a flood ! Pizarro begins *f*, not *ff*. His rage rises from *pp* (250) to *più cresc.—fp—cresc. sempre—più cresc.—il forte sempre più f*—and finally *ff* for the delirium of revenge,(251) to which the horns, trumpets, and drums give echo.(252) Leonora's intervention is signalised not by a *ff* but by a *fp* :—

" *Zurück !* " (" Stand back ! ")

followed by a sudden *p*. The *ff* does not return until Leonora, unmasking herself, cries :—

" *First kill his wife !* "

And the veil falls instantaneously again : *decrescendo piano*, with a wood-wind accompaniment.

When the agitation is at its height,—at the moment of the launching of the defiance of Pizarro, who gradually recovers from his fear—the movement does not rush headlong on as the crude popular taste would expect ; just where we might read beneath the words a torrent in flood :—

" *Shall I tremble before a woman ?* "

" *Death to you !* "

Beethoven writes: "*più lento.*" Thus the line of the two adversaries fronting each other, and their gesture, with its great outline that is more orchestral than vocal, assume the amplitude of antique tragedy.(253) And the trumpet fanfare that at this moment falls from the tempest-racked sky has the disturbing effect of a lightning flash. It cleaves at a stroke through the agitation of the four characters; the shock stifles their cry; and the miraculous liberation is expressed not by an outburst of transport but by a retiring inward upon themselves, a prayer. It is only after the second fanfare, and when the troubled spirit begins to discern the truth of the situation, that the opposing passions find their explosion. And the scene ends—for the first time in the whole act—in a *fortissimo*, and in an agitation so immense that the music does not finish but (in the first version) remains poised on a suspended chord:—

Here we come upon one of the most regrettable of the *Fidelio* suppressions. Beethoven had taken the utmost care not to pass *ex abrupto* from this musical turmoil to the love duet; and he had avoided employing the spoken word during the paroxysm. He had written a long and poignant accompanied recitative, *allegro ma non troppo*. Pizarro has made a hurried exit before the entry of the Minister. Rocco has run to spread the news in the prison. Husband and wife are alone. Leonora, broken with emotion, has fainted; and Florestan, standing in chains in the shadow, does not understand what has happened; he scarcely dares believe in the reality of it all; he struggles with his fetters, he calls upon his wife. The lovely appeal of the oboe: "O Leonora! Leonora!" is answered by the tender lamentation of the clarinets and bassoons:

It is Leonora who, still unconscious, speaks to the beloved. Florestan gives a cry; he sees her lying prone; he would go to her, but cannot. Once more the clarinets exhale their panting sigh. Leonora comes to her senses; and the melody of the oboe is like the light dawning again within her:—

She rises, totters, supports herself against the wall, runs to Florestan:—

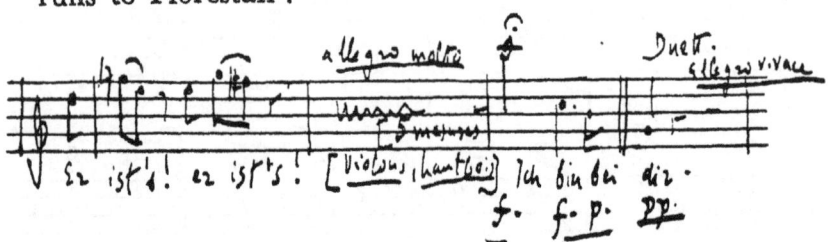

Her cry is accentuated with a *f*, not a *ff*, and at once dies out in a *pp*. And then, and not till then, begins the duet of wild passion.... " What love ! What transport ! " says Berlioz. " What embraces ! How madly these two souls embrace each other ! How they stammer under the stress of their passion ! " The jubilant sweep of the violins is broken by the most profoundly moving *adagio* arrestations of the ecstasy :—

" *Nach unnennbaren Leiden. . . . Mein Mann an meiner Brust. . . .* "

Needless to say, it was this passage that the distinguished amateurs of the day criticised most sharply. This " wild joy " struck them as being in bad taste ; they reminded Beethoven that " silent, profound, and melancholy sentiment " would have been " more in keeping with the situation."(254)

It is curious that Beethoven should here have taken one or two effects from Mozart's palette. But it suffices for his own passion to be fused with them to make them no longer the same. The rapturous duet, that stifles, recovers itself, rises to a new exaltation and falls again, with a surprising rhythmical freedom, has in the second version an orchestral ending filled with a joy of love that inspired Wagner to the aria in which Elisabeth expresses her childlike happiness at the commencement of the second act of *Tannhäuser*.

Joy has made her entry ; and Beethoven flings the

great doors wide open to her in the monumental scene that terminates *Fidelio*.

He did not reach his goal at the first attempt. In the first *Leonora* the duet of husband and wife was followed by a chorus of prisoners crying vengeance in the interior of the prison. They are heard in the distance, and Florestan reassures the anxious Leonora. The clamour draws nearer; the avenging band pours upon the stage. Then comes the Minister, bringing with him liberty. The whole of this animated scene was dramatically good and striking. But the great musical poet, the epic bard, renounced it; and he was right. He knew that after the intoxication of the duet no more could be endured than the great final cry of the chorus and orchestra, the festival of a whole people. For a similar reason he suppressed, in the succeeding scenes, an episode that was excellent for the drama but stemmed the tide of joy—the intervention of Leonora and Florestan, begging the Minister to spare their enemy the punishment of the *lex talionis*, imprisonment in the very dungeon that Florestan had just quitted. . . .

"*The punishment,*" they say, "*would be too terrible for Pizarro, who would not have, like Florestan, his conscience to sustain him.*"

We may be sure that it was a wrench for Beethoven to sacrifice this passage, that corresponded so to his own sentiments, his own lofty humanity. But as against the moralist the artist had the last word (255); and so the great choral Ode is launched on the sun-bathed sea, every sail spread to the wind.

First of all comes Leonora's religious joy as she frees Florestan from his chains :—

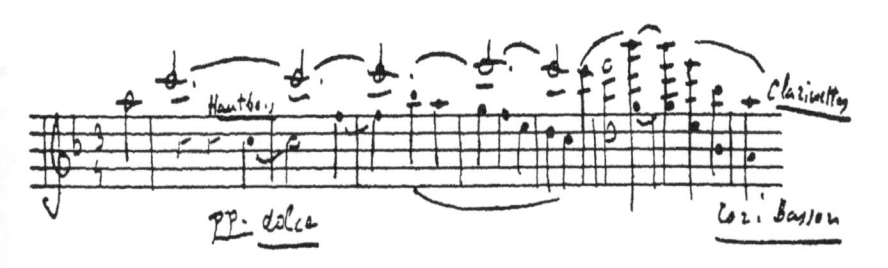

—the fine melody that Beethoven adapted from the principal work of his youth, the *Cantata for the Death of Joseph II*, that remained unpublished until our own day. The phrase is given out by the five solo voices, accompanied by flute, oboe, clarinet, horn, and bassoon, and then taken up by the chorus, that gives it its whole fullness of calm and serenity. It dies away in a *pianissimo*.(256) Immediately afterwards arises the triumphal hymn to Fidelity, the canticle to Woman :—

" *Wer ein holdes Weib errungen,—stimm' in unsern Jubel ein!* "

Sung at first, in the original *Leonora*, by the solo quartet, it was marked *maestoso*; it calls, then, for a less impetuous tempo than is given it to-day. The chorus repeats it; a tender phrase sung by Florestan and Leonora in duet glides into it like a branch in flower.

St. Peter's and Vatican, Rome

Vue de la Ville de Vigone et de ses Environs.

The acclamations of the chorus *ff* are followed by a sudden *pp*, in the orchestra—pizzicati triplets in the strings, with the horns sustaining. Above the quivering silence of the throng, Florestan intones the *Jubellied*, the song of joy, beginning with the high G and leaping an octave, in the style of the tenor who, in the Ninth Symphony, introduces the march of Heroic Joy :—

The solo quartet and the chorus accompany in subdued tones.

Finally the choral mass breaks out in full splendour—*ff sempre ff*. In the second version Beethoven adds the voice of Leonora, hovering above her own apotheosis. Then the final Victory, with its brass, its drums, its triumphant clamours, its floods of white light—an orgy in C major.

[AND NOW

AND NOW, is all said? Is the work finished?

No. The principal thing is yet to be said. Beethoven writes the overture.

The *overtures*. The case is unique in the whole history of music: four overtures for one dramatic subject! A genius that struggles desperately for ten years, amid the torrent of his passions and of his manifold other works, to capture in these symphonies for an opera . . . what realisation that flies from him? What idea possesses him, that, for ever incapable of satisfaction, for ever calls out for expression? (257)

It was indeed a problem that tormented Beethoven: the problem of the overture in general. He was obsessed by it at a certain stage in his career; and in spite of the admirable and diverse replies he gave to it we cannot say that he ever arrived at a definitive solution. Rather do we get the impression that at a certain point he became discouraged; at any rate he abandons these explorations of genius into a new territory, that was to be traversed after him by the masters of the symphonic poem and the Wagnerian drama.

On the one hand he had to meet the exigencies of the stage of that epoch, that accommodated itself ill to his epic manner; and on the other hand the contradictory exigencies of his own genius, in which, his whole life through (as we have seen when studying the sonatas), two sovereign and equally imperious instincts were at war with each other—the instinct of profound and vital expression and the instinct of beautiful, ample, solid construction : emotion and form. The real problem (and in the four *Leonora* overtures Beethoven has posed and tested it through all its length and breadth) was this :—

" Shall expression govern the form, or form the expression ? "

In any case it has to be understood that, with a Beethoven, the form must always have its rights. Whoever sacrifices this is no artist ; but he who sees and wills form alone is only a small artist. We reserve our admiration for him who is possessed by both exigencies and strives to harmonise them. But this can be done in either of two ways : by handing over the direction of the work either to the master builder or to the poet in the grip of his passionate idea. This double response was given by Beethoven in the *Leonora No. 3* and the *Leonora No. 2*.

These alone matter. The No. 1 is only an uncertain essay, that failed to satisfy Beethoven but led him to the splendid discoveries of the two later overtures. The No. 4 is an abdication in face of the necessities of the theatre. For the moment let us put it aside.

The three overtures in C major,—the rough draft that is No. 1 as well as the No. 2 and No. 3, that are masterpieces of different kinds—have one feature in common : Beethoven's music has signed them not " Leonora " but " Florestan." The prisoner's song appears in all three; but whereas in No. 1 it is merely pinned on like a quotation, it becomes the very breath of the being of No. 2 and No. 3: in No. 2 especially it is alive and palpitating, a veritable leit-motiv that develops and is transformed in nine different ways, traversing the whole gamut of the action and the passions of the drama, in turn "pathetic, lyrical, and martial."

This unprecedented artistic innovation, that was to meet in the nineteenth century with the fortune we know, at the same time illuminates for us the interior vision of Beethoven. The subject of his song in the *Leonora* overtures is the solitary, immured, persecuted man,—Beethoven himself; and this is his dream of happiness and victory. It is not a mere matter of the personification of a musical theme: into the No. 2 Beethoven brings the essence of the dramatic atmosphere and of the action. In the very first bars the magician evokes before us the walls of the prison, the half-light, the lament of the unhappy captive. With what expressive audacity he modulates this last! The daring and the subtlety of the final sequences of harmonies in the adagio introduction were never again achieved by Beethoven. He was too much in advance of his time; these were pearls cast before swine. Cherubini himself became lost in this "medley of modulations," and confessed that he could not recognise the principal tonality of the *Leonora No. 3*.—The flood of the action bursts forth in the allegro. In the course of this feverish stream, Florestan's melody recurs in various episodic forms expressive of grief and despair. To the *Durchführung* (the intermediary section of the allegro) is confided the rôle that belongs to it by nature,—that of bringing the opposing elements of the drama into conflict with each other and throwing their contrasts as well as their antagonism into high relief. Here Beethoven was in his element, on the musical battlefield that he himself had just created in the *Durchführung* of the *Eroica*. But here nothing can be left in doubt; his intentions must be precisely defined. At the end of the *Durchführung* the tragic action culminates; the violence of the passions that have been interlacing like a knot of serpents is now, as in the tragedy itself, severed at a single stroke, by the trumpet fanfare; and the decisiveness of the dramatic intention is increased by this fanfare coming, in the No. 2, not from the orchestra but from behind the scenes and from a distance. This appearance of the *Deus ex machina* to resolve the tragedy is answered, in the No. 2, by the voice of Florestan, now, however, bathed in a new light, clothed in new harmonies: the prisoner is no longer immured in darkness; his suffering is drawing to an end; happiness is on the way,—is come.... And the melody explodes in a chorus of overflowing joy and energy—the dazzling Coda. In order to express this logical development of the action and its triumphal termination, Beethoven has deliberately cut out the *reprise* of the allegro that tradition insisted on in the symphonic form of that time.(258)

The innovation was not understood ; the orthodoxy of the leaders of taste and opinion was up in arms against this heresy. Beethoven, finding himself unsupported by a single intelligent voice, racked by the problem of form, and, as I have said, obsessed by the exigencies of the great architect in him, was assailed with doubts in the face of his own superb audacity. He renounced his conquest ; with rare abnegation he cast aside the work of genius that, but for a happy chance, would have been lost to us for ever, and with a vigour that was rarer still he set himself to write a new overture that, without resembling the other, should equal it.

This overture—the No. 3,—by refining the design, equilibrating the masses, restoring the *reprise*, and freeing the symphony from the primacy of the poetic element (which in the No. 2 had held the reins of the music), was a return to the classic lines of the traditional sonata-form,—but a return of a kind possible only to a Beethoven, the lines being given an imperial amplitude and energy. Who does not remember the great crescendo at the end, that is like a mountain torrent, swollen by the rains of many storms, pouring down in an inundation ?

And now make your choice between the two masterpieces if you can ! The one is symphonic drama, the other is dramatic ode. We may, as Schumann did (and as the school of Wagner and Liszt ought to have done),(259) prefer the No. 2 ; or, with the orthodox, we may prefer the No. 3. Let us rather prefer them both ! They are two complementary worlds, evoked from the void by a genius who was his own peer. In the one the drama governs the lyricism ; in the other, lyricism is supreme.

Evidently neither of them is suitable as an Introduction to the opera. They are both too gigantic : they crush the earlier scenes ; how can we descend from these epics to the babblings of the gaoler's family ?

The No. 4, in E major, is more complaisant ; it introduces us into Florestan's prison by the service stairs. It is intended for the bourgeois first act, but without contradicting the general sense of the opera ; Beethoven the lion has donned the skin of the Singspiel. But do what he will we recognise him beneath it, though spectators whose hearts are not of the stoutest need not be scared by the sight. The drama to which they are to be introduced is just hinted at discreetly, in the most attenuated form—a few adagio bars of meditation, of prayer (that have no touch of anguish about them, no tragic shadow) at the commencement and at the end, immediately before the Coda. Then a brilliant, scintillating presto, that is almost a rondo *à la* **Weber**. Without irreverence I recall Bottom about to play the lion :—

" *I will roar you as gently as any sucking dove.*"

Here the lion plays the nightingale.

Let us accept this Introduction, but without enthusiasm. The drama being what it is—Beethoven not having been able to set it sufficiently free of the too long bourgeois comedy of the first act—this is the only one possible.

But what are we to do with the two great overtures in C major? Must they be sacrificed? Shall we consign them to the concert room?

As regards the No. 2 I fear we must resign ourselves to this; it is too complete a drama in itself; it would only be a duplication of the other drama; it suffices by and for itself.

But the No. 3 is another matter. This is not, like the No. 2, a summary of the action: it is its lyrical efflorescence, its transposition to an inward stage; or, to employ a metaphor that is the antithesis of this and is perhaps more exact, it is the roots of the drama in the universal soul. To fill this rôle the ancients had the tragic Chorus; but they lacked the superhuman means of the modern symphony, — those Choruses without words, those Oceanides of the orchestra that send their waves beating upon Prometheus' rock.

All his life Beethoven was obscurely tormented by this problem of the introduction of this new lyric form into the musical-dramatic. Just as we shall see him, in the Ninth Symphony, endlessly hesitating and groping before he can decide in which form and at what precise moment the voice shall rise, like the Ionian goddess, from the instrumental sea, so in *Leonora* we find him, in obedience to a powerful instinct that has no precedent to guide it, searching for the roads that lead, in the inverse sense, to the sung dialogue at the core of the symphony. But if he himself realises this, for his own delight, how can he impose it on a Vienna theatre where Routine stands in massed battalions? He is too far in advance, too solitary; and in the end strength of conviction fails him. He gives up the idea of integrating his symphony in the opera, of which it is at once the chorus and the core.[1]

It is our business to replace it there! I know that this innovation still meets with much opposition. All the traditions of the opera house are against this new monster —an overture in the body of an act. Even a connoisseur as enlightened as Hermann W. von Waltershausen describes the performance of the No. 3 after the prison scene as " a dramatic catastrophe," not to mention the

---

[1] *Translator's Note* :—In the original : " dont elle est—sans jeu de mots—le chœur, et le cœur."

fact that it sates the ear with a banquet in C major before the C major orgy of the finale.(260) I should have been of the same opinion if I had not had a direct experience of it. But after having, with the rest of the audience at the centenary performances in Vienna, realised the tremendous effect of the symphonic No. 3 spreading itself out like a triumphal arch between the love-duet in the prison and the final choral and popular apotheosis in the broad daylight, I bowed myself under the vault of this sonorous Sixtine, and I grasped the genius in Beethoven's conception. Placed there, the overture reveals the veritable drama that Beethoven wished to write, and, in spite of his epoch, has written.

We have seen him ascend from the first to the second act, from the bourgeois comedy of the eighteenth century to the grand musical tragedy of which Gluck had dreamed, but daring to free it of the antique draperies that, with their noble convention, impede its movements. We have even seen him pass, at times, beyond the limits of the subject and the tragic character—Florestan in chains—to penetrate to the depths of that Solitude that is in the souls of all living beings. Yet the drama holds him fast until the end of the prison scene; he drains all its rivers of grief, of hatred, of fury, and of love. With the duet the drama ends.

Then there is added to the tragedy the creation that is truly Beethoven—the lyrical conclusion, the universal

Ode, the symphony No. 3 and the choral scene. Leonora and Florestan disappear; in the final apotheosis they are nothing more than the coryphei of the People. It is no longer the adventure of a human pair that is being sung: it is Liberty and Love. . . . An immense choral symphony to which there is nothing comparable in all music with the exception of the finale of the Ninth, but that is, I venture to say, more beautiful than that, more perfect, overflowing with youth, radiating happiness; for it is the vigorous branch in flower of the tree of life in the hour of the full sap, at the apogee of the Year.

AND NOW we perceive the unique significance of *Leonora*, that king-oak of the forest. I do not know another that is like it. It has had no successor; certainly not among Wagner and his posterity. Wagner is a cutting from the Beethoven symphony, not from the Beethoven choral tragedy. That he could not grasp; he was too encumbered with metaphysic, stamped with the gigantism of thought that developed in the growing Germany of the nineteenth century—that adolescent that grew up too quickly, ill-proportioned, long-armed, long-legged, a sex and a brain, with little heart, or that a libertine one.

The grand and classic humanity of *Leonora*—that had its roots in the *Alceste* and *Orfeo* of Gluck and in certain of Mozart's scenes—remains as the monument of a better Europe of which, on the threshold of the nineteenth century, Goethe and Beethoven had a glimpse, and that a hundred years of subsequent torment have not been able to realise.

AFTER THE disaster of the crushing of *Fidelio* by indifference and cabal in 1806, Breuning wrote on the 2nd June that Beethoven, wounded to the heart, " had lost his joy in work."

Even the fraternal friend himself did not know the heroic reserves of his friend ! At the moment when Breuning wrote those lines, Beethoven had already taken up work again. And what was the work ? From the 26th May he had been engaged on the three Rasoumovsky quartets, Op. 59.[261]

At this point of my journey I pause ; for we have arrived at a turning-point in Beethoven's art and his interior life. I perceive in these quartets, for the first time perhaps in Beethoven's music, " demoniac " elements that will become more pronounced later. The hinges of the soul are grating : at the bronze gate of the Roman monument a strange Visitor has knocked.

For our part let us close here the gates of this book ! It is consecrated to the will to order and the classic reason, to the imperial master-workman who dominates all the peoples of Dream, defeated and conquered. In the succeeding chapters we shall see stage by stage the Wars of Independence, the revenge of the Dream.

October 1927.

TO THE READER

THE REASON why the author has not included in this volume the chapter devoted to the first quartets and trios is that, following the plan adopted for the sonata, he has preferred to embrace the ensemble of the mountain range from the peaks that dominate it ; and these peaks, in his opinion, are the Rasoumovsky quartets, Op. 59, and the Erdödy trios, Op. 70.(262) He accordingly defers the description of these to another volume.

So again with the concertos, which I shall contemplate from their cloud-piercing peak, the fourth concerto, in G major.

If, on the other hand, I am asked why these Beethoven studies begin with the thirtieth year of the composer, in 1800, I reply that it was no part of my plan to write here the biography of Beethoven and trace the whole development of his being from infancy to death. My plan was to limit myself to the exploration of the great

Epochs of his creation, to those mighty crises of his being in which he seems to be perishing and then renews himself. In truth my work presents itself, in accordance with the rhythm of the unfolding of the man's life itself, like an Oratorio of the Seasons. But I begin at the moment that is half-Spring, half-Summer; and I shall end with the snow-capped summits of the last quartets—with the primrose thrusting its way upward through the frozen ground.

Let me add that, in the present stage of Beethoven research,[263] we lack sufficiently definite information as to the early days of the composer. For this we must wait.

And may I also add, finally, that I look upon the present Essay only as the first state of an as yet very imperfect engraving, that will have to be retouched more than once in the light of my own researches.

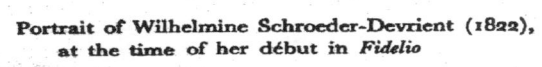

Portrait of Wilhelmine Schroeder-Devrient (1822), at the time of her début in *Fidelio*

The Vienna Theatre in which *Fidelio* was first performed

DIE METROPOLITAN KIRCHE ST. STEPHAN IN WIEN. — L'ÉGLISE CATHÉDRALE DE ST. ÉTIENNE A VIENNE.

NOTE I

BEETHOVEN'S DEAFNESS

NOTE I

BEETHOVEN'S DEAFNESS

IN THE tragic Heiligenstadt Testament of 1802 Beethoven begged his doctor, Professor Schmidt, to "describe his malady immediately after his death," and to add to "the history of his malady" the sorrowful avowals he himself had made,—"so that the world, as much as possible, may be reconciled with me at least after my death."(264)

This request was fulfilled not by Professor Schmidt, who died long before him, but by Dr. Joh. Wagner, assistant at the Vienna Pathological Museum, who, on the morrow of the composer's death (27th March, 1827), performed the autopsy in the presence of Dr. Professor

Wawruch, who had been Beethoven's medical attendant during his last illness.

The report of the autopsy (265) and the confidences, oral and written, of Beethoven himself to some of his friends,(266) are the only solid bases for an explanation of the mysterious malady. Many doctors and many musicologists have attempted this; there is a whole literature on the subject.(267) Yet the light we have on the subject is not yet quite complete. Opinions differ, and no one can yet explain precisely by what miracle of genius the perfection and the power of Beethoven's musical imagination were not more affected by the disaster that, as we shall see later, ravaged the auditory centres to the point of making him completely insensible to external sounds.(268)

All these discussions, however, have not been in vain. By a process of elimination the field of the enigma has been narrowed down; and quite recently a paper read by Dr. Marage before the *Académie des Sciences* (269) has directed research towards an explanation that, if not indubitably certain, seems to me to come very near it. I have found in it a confirmation by medical science of the results at which I myself had arrived by psychological intuition and the analysis of musical phenomena. But before I state the conclusions at which I have arrived and summarise the correspondence between Dr. Marage and myself that enabled us to compare our respective diagnoses and confirm the one by the other, I must put the reader in possession of the essential documents.

I. BEETHOVEN's letter to Amenda (June 1801):—

"... Know that the noblest part of me, my hearing, has become very bad. Even in the days when you were with me I felt traces of this, but I kept silence about it. Since then it has been getting worse and worse."(270)

Now Amenda came to Vienna in 1796 and left it in 1799. His life in common with Beethoven belongs to 1798/9.

II. Beethoven's letter to Wegeler (29th June, 1801):—

"... For the last three years [therefore since 1798] my hearing has been getting weaker and weaker, and the cause must have been [the condition of] my bowels, which, as you know, was already at that time wretched, but has got worse, for I have a continual diarrhœa that has made me extraordinarily weak. . . ." (271)

He adds that in spite of fortifying medicines the trouble became worse until the autumn of the year just past (1800), when he was often reduced to despair.(272) He was ordered cold baths, that did him harm, and warm baths, that improved his general condition but not his hearing. The winter of 1800-1801 was "truly wretched; frightful colics."(273) He became as ill as ever, until the last four weeks (i.e., May 1801) when the surgeon Vering succeeded in ameliorating these crises somewhat by means of further warm baths, pills for the stomach, and an infusion for the ear.(274) Beethoven became stronger; but the noises in his ears continued day and night.(275)

For the last two years (i.e., since 1799), he says, he has avoided all society in order to conceal his deafness. At the theatre he has to sit close to the orchestra to follow the actors. "The higher notes of instruments and voices I cannot hear if I am a little distance away from them. . . . Often if a man speaks softly I scarcely hear him,—the tones, yes, but not the words; and yet if anyone shrieks it is insupportable. . . ."(276)

III. Beethoven's letter to Wegeler (16th November, 1801).

Vering is applying vesicatories to both arms, and this is painful for him, as each time it is done he is deprived of the use of his arms for a couple of days.

He agrees that "the whistling and humming" is not so bad as it was, "especially in the left ear, which is the one in which the trouble began.(277) But the hearing is certainly no better." He dares not even "say definitely whether it has not become weaker." But at any rate the bowels are better.(278)

Later,(279) however, he speaks of the feeling he has of increasing vitality:—

"My youth—yes, I feel it—is just beginning.... For some time now my bodily strength has been increasing, also my powers of mind. Each day I get nearer the goal of which I am conscious but that I cannot describe.... Oh, it is so beautiful to live life a thousand times!"(280)

IV. The Heiligenstadt Testament (6th October, 1802).

"... Think! six years ago [therefore in 1796] I fell into an incurable condition, that has been made worse by ignorant doctors...."(281)

It is the first time we find Beethoven date the origin of his trouble so far back. But it has to be observed that by "this incurable condition" he does not mean the trouble with his hearing. If we turn to the letter of 29th June, 1801, and to Wegeler's notes (in the *Biographische Notizen*) on the friend of his youth, we see that what had originated in 1796 was "the bowel trouble, that [according to Wegeler's diagnosis] was the principal cause of his infirmity—of the deafness and of the dropsy that carried him off." The question of deafness does not arise until 1798 at the earliest ("*seit drei Jahren,*" 1801).

But at the time when Beethoven is writing the Testament he has been "half a year in the country" on the advice of his doctor, who has advised him "to spare his hearing as much as possible." And it was a little while before this, during a walk in the summer of 1802, that the painful scene described by Ries occurred. Ries has been imprudent enough to draw his attention to a flute that was being played in the fields. Beethoven has not heard it, and he is crushed. The shock must have been overwhelming, for he speaks of it in the Testament some months later.(282) It was perhaps not so serious to be deprived of the society of human beings; but at the thought that the voice of his best friend, Nature, should be lost to him he gave way to despair. It would not have taken much, he says, to have made him put an end to himself. By God's grace the creative energy was too imperious in him! In this very hour of his deepest distress it overflowed. It was it, and it alone, as he says, that made him go on living.(283) Let us not forget that it was precisely at this moment that the demon of the *Eroica* cried out within him, "Forward!" It was a magnificent illustration of the all-might of the spirit, that carries the body over the abyss, like the apostle Peter walking on the waves!

Four years more, and Beethoven hardens himself to a proud denial of his infirmity in face of the world. His friends have to be very careful not to let him see that they have remarked it, for that infuriates him. And so it goes on, until at last, defeated, but grander still in his defeat, he writes in 1806 on a page of sketches for the finale of the third Rasoumovsky quartet (Op. 59, No. 3):—

"*Let thy deafness be no longer a secret, even in thy art!*"(284)

In my later volumes I will follow step by step "the light that failed."

LET US now investigate the causes of it.

First of all we must look at Beethoven's account of them, and the accounts of his friends.

We have seen that, for Wegeler and for Beethoven (letter of 29th June, 1801), the root-cause was enteritis.

For Breuning, it was a case of articular inflammation, due to the excessive use of ice-cold ablutions.

SB

This hypothesis resembles that of the Fischhoff manuscript, in which we read of an imprudence on Beethoven's part. On a summer day in 1796 or 1797 he had stood naked, in a high perspiration, in a cold draught at the open window, and so contracted " a dangerous malady " (" *gefährliche Krankheit* ").

Beethoven himself gives more precise details of this in a conversation he had in 1814 with the surgeon Aloys Wissenbach,—a reliable witness ; he was his intimate friend and a medical man of high professional standing. The origin of his troubles was " a terrible typhus."[285] What was the date of this typhus, of which no mention occurs in any letter? Perhaps in the summer of 1797, on his return from his journey as a virtuoso to Berlin ; for between May and October 1797 there is a lacuna in his biography.

Lastly, in a conversation of 1815 with Charles Neate, whose testimony is equally above suspicion, he finds another cause—a heavy fall on his back ; being at work in his room one day, he hears someone coming whom he cannot endure ; he turns round impetuously, loses his balance, and falls full length " as they do in the theatre. . . . When I got up again, I found I was deaf, and I remained so. The doctors say there was a lesion of the nerve." (" *Die Aerzte sagen, der Nerv sei verletzt* ").

But it is important to observe that this accident could

hardly have happened before 1801; for Beethoven said to Neate :—

"I was at work at an opera at the time."

"*Fidelio?*"

"No, it was not *Fidelio.*"

The importunate person to whom the story relates was the first tenor, who had already made him re-write an aria three times to the same words, and who had come a fourth time. Now this can relate only to *The Mount of Olives*, on which Beethoven was engaged between 1801 and the year of its production, 1803. The accident might therefore have happened in 1802, shortly before the Heiligenstadt Testament; and thus we should have the explanation not of the origin of the malady but of its aggravation and the crisis of despair.

To sum up : none of the alleged causes—neither the chill, nor the (later) fall, nor even an organic intoxication by some infectious malady—seems to modern science sufficient to have *of itself* produced the deafness, though anyone of them may well have *contributed* to bring it on or to aggravate it.

I now turn to the diagnosis of Dr. Marage, who has specialised for thirty years in the study of hearing and its variations, and, since 1900, has observed thousands of cases of deafness.(286) In a recent communication to the *Académie des Sciences*, basing himself on the main facts related by Beethoven in the letters to Wegeler already cited,(287) he begins by ruling out various forms of otitis that have been regarded as causes :—

"This is not a case," he says, "of a deafness due to middle-ear otitis with suppuration, for in this kind of deafness the first tones to disappear are the higher and the lower, the medium tones continuing to be audible. Nor is it a case of otosclerosis, for in these affections the deep notes disappear first, the higher tones being often audible in an exaggerated form at the commencement of the malady (288); and with Beethoven the contrary is the case. But when the deafness begins with the higher tones, and especially when it is preceded by hummings, whistlings, and exaggerated sensitiveness to shrieks, there must be a lesion of the inner ear,—including in this term the labyrinth and the cerebral centres, from which the various branches of the acoustic nerve proceed. . . . From 1798 onwards the trouble is not otosclerosis but labyrinthitis. Later, in 1801, the deafness increases and follows the normal evolution of these cases. He still hears words, but he does not understand them; what really happens is that he no longer hears anything but the vowels; the consonants have disappeared, for these are of short duration—often only one-twentieth as long as the vowels. At last, in 1816, the deafness is complete for all tones."

In his note to the Académie, Dr. Marage had been

APPENDICES

content to define the nature of Beethoven's deafness without settling its cause or causes. I took the liberty of questioning him on this point; he placed his vast and generous knowledge at my service; we interchanged many letters on the subject; and it may be useful for me to state the results to which our correspondence seems to lead :—

First of all, proceeding by elimination, Dr. Marage rejects the following explanations of Beethoven's deafness :—

(*a*) Catarrh or otosclerosis of the middle ear; for these produce a different kind of deafness;

(*b*) Typhus affecting the auditory centres; for after that malady the deafness would have developed to the full;

(*c*) Chills and acute influenza; these would have produced serious middle-ear otitis, traces of which would have been revealed by the autopsy;

(*d*) The heavy fall on the back, and the cerebral disturbance resulting from it; for in this case the deafness would not have been preceded by buzzing noises (289);

(*e*) Syphilis, which has sometimes been regarded as the cause; this produces an absolutely different order and development of deafness.

There remains a labyrinthitis, that may have been produced by two main causes, one of them cerebral, the other intestinal.

The consensus of our information points to a pseudo-membranous enteritis, of old standing, and chronic.(290) Beethoven, who had neither the wisdom nor the leisure to attend to it in time, must have been generating toxins for years; and this auto-intoxication spread to the auditory centres.(291) The ground was thus prepared for deafness.

But the true cause, direct and deep-lying, must be sought for in the brain itself of Beethoven. Here Dr. Marage's observations are in striking agreement with mine:—

"The subjects," he says, "who develop the form of deafness that begins with the loss of the higher sounds are generally over-strained intellectuals.... All the functions are normal until the moment of the appearance of the buzzings and the deafness. Until then, Beethoven's hearing had been remarkably fine. Now an organ that is hypersensitive is the more easily attacked by a malady.... Beethoven's inner ear and auditory centres, that were hypersensitive, subjected to intensive labour, and overwrought, became congested...."

Now I myself, when studying the essence of Beethoven's creative genius, had been struck by the "furious concentration" that is the characteristic mark of it, and that distinguishes him from all the composers of his epoch. I had insisted on this point in **my commemoration address at Vienna**(292):—

" In no other musician has this grapple with thought been more violent, more continuous, more invincible than in Beethoven. . . . All his music bears the imprint of an extraordinary passion for unity. . . . The whole of his work is stamped with the seal of a will of iron; we feel that the man's glance is sunk in the idea with a terrific fixity. *And it is not merely a case, as might be thought, of the solitary immured in himself by deafness, who is untroubled by any sound from the outer world. Long before the deafness the same characteristic is observable. . . .* (293) It is a natural disposition. From infancy Beethoven is absorbed in his interior vision, that eyeless vision that is at once of the whole body and of the whole spirit. When an idea occurred to him, in the crowded street, in the course of a walk or of a conversation, he had, as he used to say, a *raptus*; he no longer belonged to himself but to the idea; he never looses his hold on it until he has made it his. Nothing will distract him from the pursuit. He described this frantic chase to Bettina in the language of hallucination: ' I pursue it, I grasp it, I see it fly from me and lose itself in the seething mass. I seize it again with renewed passion, I can no longer separate myself from it; I have to multiply it in a spasm of ecstasy, in all its modulations.' This passionate pursuit, this multiplication of the idea that has been seized upon, bent to his will, subdued, and is imposed on the hearer by the hammering of the rhythm, the hallucinatory repetitions, the sensuous heat of the orchestral colour and the modulations, produces on simple and sincere natures that yield themselves up to it an *effect of hypnosis, a Yoga. Like the Indian Yoga, once one has attained to it one carries it about with one everywhere, when walking, talking, working, in every act of the daily life. It is subjacent; it is like an aromatic oil injected under the skin. . . .*"

It was not at hazard that I employed this word Yoga three, four, or five times in the course of my Study. During the course of the present year my labours have brought me into contact with some of the greatest of the contemporary Indian minds that have practised Yoga, notably the extraordinary Ramakrishna, that incomparable master of religious contemplation, and his great disciple Vivekananda.(294) I had read their strangely precise description of all the degrees of this Yogist concentration, and of the physiological and moral effects of what they call the rising, in the canals of the body, of the *Kundalini Sakti* (the essence of energy). But they know the dangers of it, through having, like Ramakrishna, escaped them by a miracle; and they warn their disciples of these dangers. They forbid them to surrender themselves to Yoga at hazard and without an inward necessity; they know well that these exercises in passionate and boundless concentration always conduct to the brink of cerebral apoplexy or of mental alienation. Some of these adepts have come out of their spells of Yoga with eyes red and bleeding, " as if eaten by ants."

All these images recurred to my mind when I was thinking of the congestions that Beethoven used to extinguish brutally with ice-cold ablutions. And when I read Dr. Marage's diagnosis I communicated to him, on the 4th February, 1928, the passage I have just quoted, and I asked him if there were not points of analogy between the state of Yogist concentration and Beethoven's violent, tenacious, continuous, absolute absorption in the fixed idea. Could not the otitis have been brought on by this cerebral régime, in truth that of a genius, but a murderous régime, the natural psycho-physiological dispositions thus provoking the catastrophe? And could this, in its turn, have reinforced tenfold the dispositions of Nature?

Dr. Marage agreed wholly with my suggestion. " The cause of Beethoven's deafness," he replied on the 6th February, " seems to me to have been the congestion of the inner ear and the auditory centres—a congestion due to the overworking of the organ by his furious concentration, his terrific fixity of idea, as you so well express it. Your comparison with the Indian Yoga appears to me to be very exact. . . . " In a further letter he adds : " The vesicatories on the arms that Dr. Vering ordered in 1801 were indicated : they acted as eliminating doors for the toxins : they are analogous to our fixation abscesses. The result would be an immediate amelioration of the buzzings."

The conclusion one thus seems driven to by the force of the facts is one that is tragic in a different way from everything that this glorious misfortune has suggested to our imagination and our pity : the cause of the misfortune was in Beethoven, *was* Beethoven. It was his destiny ; it was himself who, like Œdipus, brought about the catastrophe. It was inscribed in his nature from the beginning, as it were a law of his genius.

BEETHOVEN's genius (I ought to say his " demon ") produced his deafness. Did not the deafness, in its turn, make the genius, or at all events aid it ?

This is the counterpart of the question ; Dr. Marage has stated it clearly, but without resolving it. For the answer—if there be one—cannot be given without the assistance of the musicians ; while these in their turn should take counsel from the data of the medical specialist.

The most important fact here is not so much the *deafness* as the *hummings* :—

" If Beethoven," says Dr. Marage, " had suffered from an otosclerosis, if, that is to say, he had been plunged into the night of non-hearing, *intus et extra*, as early as 1801, it is probable, not to say certain, that he would not have written any of his works.(295) But his deafness, which had its origin in the labyrinth, had this peculiarity, that if it cut him off from the outer world it had the advantage of maintaining his auditory. centres in a state of constant excitement, producing musical vibrations and hummings that he sometimes perceived with the utmost intensity. . . . If it suppressed the external vibrations it augmented the internal. . . ."

It may be then that the deafness endowed his palette with new colours and gave him an auditory exaltation that must indeed have often been painful, tyrannical, besetting, but that also may often have been accompanied by euphoria.(296)

Let us then examine the medical data.(297) Subjects attacked by labyrinthitis frequently hear, according to Dr. Marage, lovely instrumental and vocal melodies that fill them with light, but which, try as they will to fix them, they cannot retain. (Do we not recognise Beethoven chasing his hallucinations across the fields and through the streets?)

But apart from this intoxication, which, indeed, we often meet with in his works (sometimes it amounts to frenzy), are there any characteristic traits in his music that we can attribute to these excitations? And if so, dating from when?

Dr. Marage would place the hummings as early as 1796. I will not venture on a discussion of his medical argument,(298) although the Beethoven letters that I have cited do not seem to me to carry us any further back than 1798. But *musically* it is very difficult for me to detect any change in his sensibility. In any case it does not appear to have affected his harmonic invention and modulation before 1802 at the earliest. These are much less complex and "dissonant," in the school sense of that term, than those of Haydn and Mozart, not to mention, of course, those of Bach. There is very little music that is more resolutely consonant; and no other master, with the exception of Handel, has shown so immoderate a partiality for the common chord. But did the pathological influence manifest itself precisely in this uniformity, this insistence of affirmation, the squareness of phrase to which I have already drawn attention,(299) the occasional stiffness, as it were, of "l'homme armé"? In that case it is hardly possible to separate it from the very being of Beethoven; and an inquiry on these lines would have little interest. As a matter of fact I can trace, in the period preliminary to the catastrophe of 1802/3, an effect of his malady only on the soul of Beethoven, not on his technique—that is to say, his convulsiveness of movement and his melancholy. Even during the period of sovereign exaltation that has been the object of my study in this volume, the reason and the will maintain constant control and absolute mastery of all the elements furnished him by his senses; nothing is left to chance; and the most unexpected acoustic collisions, such as the famous entry of the horn before the reprise in the first movement of the *Eroica*, if they had their source in a hallucination of hearing, had also, as we have seen, been coolly calculated, willed and insisted on throughout the long labour on the movement. It is only when we reach the period of the Rasoumovsky quartets (1806) that I can distinguish clearly an upheaval in the house and the abrupt intrusion of certain strange elements that have forced the door.

But I do not in the least deny that they may have surreptitiously glided in ten years earlier. It is the mark of genius to bend to its service everything that constitutes or deforms its nature, its powers as well as its weaknesses, even its maladies. The master in this line was Goethe; and if some day I have the leisure to paint the portrait I owe him, I will show how he succeeded in forming from the morbid elements that abounded in him a principle of spiritual richness and strength.

Beethoven, who was much less conscious of himself but more powerful by instinct, managed, by the mere current of his vital energy, to sweep every obstacle away in his own torrent, and to bray them all in the rich lime brought to him on the flood of his substance. When we see enumerated,(300) among the abnormal vibrations that assailed the damaged hearing of the man, the rhythmic obsessions of passing regiments, the heavy hammering steps of a crowd, the rumbling of carriages in the distance at night, the repeated blows of the hammer on a bar of iron, the teuf-teuf of two vehicles held up in a torrential rain, the furious psalmody of an excited mob—or, in a different order of impressions, fanfares, bells,(301) an immense aviary in which the birds are singing *in tune*, and so on—can we help being reminded of his music, that is as full of birds as a May day, those incessant military march rhythms of his, the heavy cavalcades, the bolides that fly past us in the *Appassionata*, the heaving Ocean, the roaring nations, and—why not—the furious blows of Fate knocking at the door?

Yes, all this is possible; but no one can prove it. In any case what matters is not that these sounds should have been perceived by him but *how* they were perceived. The miracle is that they should have been transformed by the spirit into works of art. Any one of us can hear, in nights of insomnia and fever, the humming of his blood in his arteries. But only to a Beethoven is it given to set the peoples of his symphonies marching to these rhythms. There is the genius—out of chaos to create a world.

It may be as well for me to give here the text of the autopsy report.

Report of the Autopsy on Beethoven

of Dr. Joh. Wagner,

Assistant at the Vienna Pathological Museum. (302)

". . . Der Ohrknorpel zeigte sich gross und regelmässig geformt, die kahnförmige Vertiefung, besonders aber die Muschel desselben war sehr geräumig und um die Hälfte tiefer als gewöhnlich ; die verschiedenen Ecken und Windungen waren bedeutend erhaben. Der äussere Gehörgang erschien, besonders gegen das verdeckte Trommelfell, mit glänzenden Hautschuppen belegt. Die Eustachische Ohrtrompete war sehr verdickt, ihre Schleimhaut angewulstet und gegen die knöchernen Theil etwas verengert. Vor deren Ausmündung und gegen die Mandeln bemerkte man narbige Grübchen. Die ansehnlichen Zellen des grossen und mit keinem Einschnitte bezeichneten Warzenfortsatzes waren von einer blutreichen Schleimhaut ausgekleidet. Einen ähnlichen Blutreichthum zeigte auch die sämmtliche, von ansehnlichen Gefässzweigen durchzogene Substanz des Felsenbeines, insbesondere in der Gegend der Schnecke, deren häutiges Spiralblatt leicht geröthet erschien. Die Antlitznerven waren von bedeutender Dicke; die Hörnerven dagegen zusammengeschrumpft und marklos, die längs derselben verlaufenden Gehörschlagadern waren über eine Rabenfederspule ausgedehnt und Knorpelicht. Der linke viel dünnere Hörnerve entsprang mit drei sehr dünnen graulichen, der rechte mit einem stärkeren hellweissen Streifen aus der in diesem Umfang viel consistenteren und blutreicheren Substanz der vierten Gehirnkammer. Die Windungen des sonst viel weicheren und wasserhältigen Gehirns erschienen nochmal so tief und (geräumiger) zahlreicher als gewöhnlich. Das Schädelgewölbe zeigte durchgehends grosse Dichtheit und eine gegen einen halben Zoll betragende Dicke...."

(*Translation.*)(303)

"... The cartilage of the ear was extensive and of regular form; the scaphoid cavity, and more particularly the muscle of this, was very large and about half as deep again as usual; the various angles and turns were strongly marked. The meatus contained glistening epithelial scales, especially in the region of the tympanum, which was hidden by them. The Eustachian tube was much thickened, its mucous membrane swollen and slightly drawn back towards the bony part. In front of the tubal orifice and towards the tonsils were little cicatrised pockets. The mastoid process was large and showed no groove; its cells were large and lined with a hyperæmic mucous membrane. There were traces of the same hyperæmia in the whole substance of the petrous bone, which was traversed by prominent blood vessels; this was notably the case in the region of the cochlea, the membranous spiral tract of which was slightly reddened.

"The facial nerves were particularly thick; the acoustic nerves, on the other hand, were atrophied and devoid of myelin. The accompanying acoustic arteries were dilated to the extent of being wider than a crow's quill; and they were of cartilaginous consistency. The left acoustic nerve, that was much thinner than the right, sprang from three very slender grey threads proceeding from the fourth ventricle; the right nerve was a single root, stronger, and clear white in colour. Their (304) origins from the fourth ventricle of the brain showed cerebral matter that was much firmer and more hyperæmic than the surrounding matter.

"The brain proper was of much firmer consistence and contained a smaller proportion of water than is normal. The convolutions seemed to be of double depth and more numerous than ordinarily.(305)

TB

" The cranial vault was throughout of great density and about half an inch thick." (306)[1]

---

[1] *Translator's Note :*—M. Rolland makes use of a French translation by Dr. Emile Wennagel, who points out the difficulty of a literal translation of the German, the meaning of which is not always absolutely clear. See Notes 303, 304, 305. In making my translation I have had both versions in mind. It was necessary in some places to follow Dr. Wennagel's phraseology, because M. Rolland refers to this in his notes.

NOTE II

A BEETHOVEN SKETCH-BOOK OF 1800

NOTE II

A BEETHOVEN SKETCH-BOOK OF 1800

THE Sketch-Book F 91 that is in the Prussian State Library (Berlin) is a perfect mirror of the Beethoven of 1800. We are able to consult it at first hand; for not only has Nottebohm given a very good summary of it in his *Zweite Beethoveniana* (307) but there has recently been published a complete reproduction of it in the ordinary notation.(308) It is the only one of the Sketch-Books that has been made available in its entirety to the general public.(309)

Nottebohm gives between the end of 1799 and the commencement of 1801(310) as the time-limits of the volume. I should say it was completed before the mournful writer of 1800/1.

The greater part of it is taken up with the *Prometheus*;

but it might be said that the violin sonata Op. 24 (the *Spring*) gives the tone to it and embraces it with its tendrils. For the Sketch-Book opens with the first phrase of the last movement of this; the sketches for the four movements multiply and spread their boughs over the whole book; in particular the delicious melodic evolution of the first movement keeps recurring everywhere, evoking and drawing along with it many designs for other works,—and this even down to the final page.

Interspersed with this work are: the violin sonata Op. 23; the second symphony, the furious labour upon which will continue for a long time yet; the first sketches for the *sonata quasi una fantasia*, Op. 27, No. 1, with all its social grace; and the piano sonata Op. 26, the last movement of which, the Scherzo and the Funeral March,(311) keep cropping up everywhere.

There are also fugitive hints of some passages in the first quartet, Op. 18, No. 1 (that was probably intended for Amenda and written in the preceding year, though Beethoven recast it in 1800); the first two bars of the *grave* introduction to the *Pathétique*, Op. 13 (that appeared in 1799), an imperious reminiscence of which bursts into the first movement of the second symphony, where it is submerged—it is as if Beethoven had wanted to renew his energy in it; and the first idea of the *Bagatelle* for piano, Op. 33, No. 7. I say nothing of the large number of sketches for works that were never written—sonatas, a symphony, a *Scena stromentale,* and so on. The pre-figurings of some of these are very fine.

Taking the Sketch-Book as a whole, the dominant note is of the theatre, the salon, the free play of the musical faculty. Notwithstanding the Funeral March, that has a wholly external and theatrical character, the tragic muse makes her appearance only as a personage of the ballet, in a sketch for *Prometheus;* and even melancholy no longer finds the moving accents it had had two years earlier in the largo of the sonata Op. 10, No. 3. It was a year of happy activity: the young genius feels his wings growing, and plans a higher flight.(312)

NOTE III

**THE BRUNSVIK SISTERS AND THEIR
COUSIN OF THE "MOONLIGHT"**

NOTE III

THE BRUNSVIK SISTERS AND THEIR COUSIN OF THE "MOONLIGHT"

I HAVE spoken of Beethoven's good fortune in the matter of women's friendship, especially in the period of his youthful glory in Vienna, between 1799 and 1806. This " wild man " (which he was in spite of himself) met with an affectionate understanding on the part of the women of the aristocracy, many of whom were gifted musically and were remarkable interpreters of his music.(313) Several of them showed a tender attachment to him.

But in no household did he find a purer and more faithful, a more truly fraternal, friendship than in that of the Brunsviks. Whatever solution the future may yield of the enigma of the " Immortal Beloved," the name of Brunsvik will remain eternally linked with that of Beethoven, who himself inscribed it at the head of two of his finest works. The brother and the three sisters contended with each other to show him affection and respect; and two of the sisters, who loved him and whom he loved, were beings very much above the ordinary, the most charming and loftiest souls of their epoch.(314)

The one who dominates the group,—Therese—does not acquire the eminent position she occupies for posterity until a later period of Beethoven's life than that we are studying in the present volume. It is only when she is nearing her thirty-fifth year, after hard experiences—confessed or hidden, but in the end surmounted—that she becomes conscious of that religious and humanitarian mission that made her the equal, in heart and intelligence, of her noble friend Beethoven and of the most saintly feminine souls that have ever been on earth. At the appropriate time I shall consecrate to her, in another volume, the altar of gratitude that is her due.(315) Here I propose only to indicate her place in Beethoven's intimate circle. But during these years her sister Josephine also occupies a post of honour near him.

I will confine myself, then, to a rapid sketch of the lives of the four Brunsviks (the brother and the three sisters) so far as these touch upon Beethoven's life in the years between the *Moonlight* sonata and the *Appassionata*.

And by the side of the Brunsviks their cousin Giulietta is entitled to a place.(316)

THE HUNGARIAN Brunsviks traced their origin to a Duke of Braunschweig, Henry the Lion, who went to the crusades in the twelfth century with his sons. One of these, on his return, settled in Hungary and founded the family. In 1775 the *Hofkanzleireferendar* (a high functionary of the court) Anton I of Brunsvik, lord of Korompa, was created a Count by Marie Theresa under the name—borne by all his line—of " Brunsvik of Korompa." He was the grandfather of Beethoven's friends.

A remarkable " characteriological "(317) study of Theresa von Brunsvik, by Dr. Margit Révésy, traces her many gifts to her rich heredity. On the paternal side—the Brunsvik—there was an abundant culture and a refined taste, a love of the arts and sciences, and a special interest in pedagogy, which subject was a preoccupation with the enlightened aristocracy of the time, that had been brushed by the wing of Liberty. From the maternal side—the Barons Seeberg—there came a tenacious and well-controlled energy that acted as a counterpoise to the Brunsvik mobility of spirit.

The eldest of the four children,(318) Therese, who was the Empress's god-daughter, was her father's favourite and the confidante of his thought. He was an enthusiast for the cause of American Independence, and for liberty in his own country. " I was brought up," says Therese, " with the names of Washington and Benjamin Franklin." The father adored music; and Therese, who began to learn the piano at the age of three, was able, at six, to play in public before the Budapest nobility a concerto of Rosetti to an orchestral accompaniment. " I remember," she says, " being lifted up and put on the piano stool and playing without the least nervousness." She developed so rapidly that she soon outdistanced her teacher. She returned to him the task he had set her, with the remark that it was too easy: " *Etwas Schwereres !* "

For the rest there was no regular plan of education; the four children grew up like little wild flowers. For eight months of the year they lived at their estate of Martonvásár, which their grandfather had founded on the Hungarian Puszta, that had been occupied and ravaged for a century and half by the Turks. It was a marshy desert, an immense stretch of bare country, a fever-centre: but no one troubled about that.(319) For the children it was a wild paradise of unlimited freedom. The father was always away in Vienna, engaged in his official occupations, to which, however, he gave scant attention, for he was a man of the world, amorous and beloved. The mother was always on horseback in the fields, roughly ordering everything, directing with an iron hand the work of cultivation, canalisation and tree-planting that was ultimately to make a model property of Martonvásár; she corresponded with the high officials of the estate in Latin. The last thing she gave any thought to was the education of her children.(320) Intelligent and ardent, they read everything that came into their hands—novels, Latin books brought home from school by their brother, borrowed volumes of poetry that intoxicated them.(321) It was a free and delightful but dangerous development. There was stored up in them a mass of energy for which they had no outlet; they were without a guide, without a model. The four children were inseparable companions and passionately fond of each other; Therese was later to be made the victim of this love by her younger sister, Josephine, who took advantage of it. When they were of the ages of about eleven to fourteen they very seriously constituted a small republic. "To this day," Therese wrote near the end of her life, "I know nothing better or happier."

Her father died in 1793, when she was eighteen; the tragedies of Europe, the troubles in the Low Countries, the death of Joseph II, the French Revolution, the unfortunate war with the Turks, had broken his already weak health. Therese felt the sorrow more deeply than the others of the family; and melancholy developed the religious side of her nature. But in this daughter of an active mother even contemplation took on an active character; and her faith in the divine was (in all humility) a faith in herself, the instinct of a future mission. In her little garden in the centre of the great park she had had constructed a mound surmounted by a pyramid of red marble, dedicated to the memory of her father. There she would sit for hours; and there one day she solemnly consecrated herself, after the emphatic-heroic manner of the time, " Priestess of Truth." She kept her vow, without emphasis, all her life; she was the proud servant, bruised but never wearied, of the True.

THE DAY came when these wild colts of the Puszta, intoxicated with air and space, were taken, without the least preparation, to the big town to be trained. It was brief and brutal. " Our mother took us from the children's room (322) to Vienna. We were there eighteen days and three hours, and in that time everything was decided. From that time onward the bitterest days and the most tragic experiences were our lot."

But these days had for prelude a final fortnight of care-free happiness, that commenced with the visit of Beethoven.

From what we have seen already we can imagine how they got on with him. For the free son of the free Rhine, the untamed one who always suffocated within the walls of a town, it must have been a great joy to see these little dryads, bearing with them the odour of the forests and plains, bring him their young enthusiasm. But to find him they had to climb to his third story in the St. Peter Platz. Beethoven never put himself out to pay a call on any Excellency whatever—unless she happened to be young and pretty; he awaited them on his Mount Ida. Their Excellencies Tesi (Therese), Pepi (Josephine) and their mother cheerfully climbed his steep staircase.

Therese has left us so charming an account of this excursion that I cannot deny myself the pleasure of quoting it :—

" I entered with my Beethoven sonata with violin and 'cello accompaniment (323) under my arm, like a little girl going to her lesson. The dear immortal Ludwig van Beethoven was very amiable, and as polite as he could be. After a few remarks *de part et d'autre* (324) he placed me at his out-of-tune piano, and I began at once; I played valiantly, and sang the accompaniment for 'cello and violin. He was so delighted that he promised to come each day to our hotel, the *Griffon d'or*. This was in May of the last year of the last century [May 1799]. He kept his word; but instead of staying for an hour after midday he would stay four and five; he was never tired of lifting and bending my fingers, which I had the habit of holding straight and stiff when lifting them.(325) The noble being [*der Edle*] must have been quite satisfied with me, for he did not fail us once during sixteen days. It was five o'clock in the afternoon before we realised we were hungry. Our good mother fasted with us; but the hotel people were angry.

"It was then that there sprang up between Beethoven and us the intimate friendship, the friendship of the heart, that endured to the end of his days. He came to us at Ofen, at Martonvásár; he was received into our social republic of distinguished people. In the park there was a circular space planted with magnificent lime trees, to each of which had been given the name of a member of our society; so that even when we were sadly separated from these we could still commune with their symbols (*Sinnenbildern*) and they with us. Very often in the morning, after our "Good-day!", I would ask the tree this and that that I wished to know; and never did it refuse to answer! . . .

"In the eighteen days at Vienna we had not a moment's leisure. Our mother took us to the studios and the notable buildings; we saw everything that was to be seen. Aunt Finta, a lady of fashion with four daughters, arranged our promenades—the Prater, the Augarten, the Luscigarten at Dornbach; and everywhere we enjoyed ourselves. We went to the theatre. In the evenings we danced; and on our way back to our hotel, between ten and eleven, we had ices in the Graben, and laughed and joked. At four o'clock in the morning we were up and dressed, to run about the fields at five. . . . Ah! that was a life! And Beethoven, who was in every one of the parties, must have been pleased with it! That was a passion! [*Das war eine Passion!*] Then at night we had to practise [the piano]! The neighbours fled in horror. We were young, fresh, childlike, simple. Whoever saw us loved us. Admirers were not lacking. . . ."

Beethoven, who remained ever afterwards in touch with them, dedicated to them (326) on their departure the four-hand variations on the song *Ich denke dein* (" I think of thee ").

Alas! a few weeks later one of them, the youngest and prettiest, Josephine, was married, in spite of her tears, to a man of fifty whom she did not love, at the bidding of an imperious mother who had little judgment and who was indifferent to the desires of her daughters.(327)

Music and Beethoven were a consolation to her while waiting for the children whom she adored; they were not long in coming. During the autumn and winter of 1800 Beethoven visits Pepi regularly; he comes every three days to give her lessons, and he is "*scharmant.*"(328) They felt all the more drawn to each other because poor Josephine, though married to an authentic Count, found herself put in quarantine with him by the aristocracy. A long time previously the Count had been compelled, as the result of an unfortunate duel, to seek obscurity under a plebeian name; and now that he had resumed his title his peers refused to recognise him. So the pair lived in isolation. For this the Count found an easy consolation in his pretty wife; but she had not the same reasons for being contented with his society. That of Beethoven was dearer to her; and the aristocratic young woman, who was later to reproach her sister Therese so harshly for her bourgeois manners and tastes, took no offence at the bourgeois origin of the distinguished friend who avenged her for her isolation—and profited by it. But they were both too honest to entertain the idea of an amorous liaison while the husband was alive; and if an attachment dawns between them they never confess it to each other.

BUT AT the end of 1800 Giulietta Guicciardi appears on the scene. She came from Italy.(329) She was hardly any older than Shakespeare's Juliet, and no less seductive. But she was not fitted by nature for the tragic, for the proof of which we have only to look at the charming miniature of her of this date,(330) with the mischievous little face, the animated eyes, so sure of their power, the lovely, avid mouth, the delicately plump figure that she holds so straight. She knows she has only to show herself in the Vienna salons to create a sensation. Certain little remarks, not devoid of malice, of her cousins Brunsvik lead us to think that " la belle Guicciardi," as she is called from the beginning in Vienna, is putting them in the shade.(331) Beethoven takes fire at once. The ardent stage of this passion seems to extend from the spring to the autumn of 1801(332) ; it no doubt came to its climax, and to a confession, at Korompa during the summer of that year, in the house of her uncle Brunsvik, who had gathered around him and his daughters his young and pretty Brunsvik and Guicciardi nieces.(333)

That the passion was encouraged we can hardly doubt, even though in after years Giulietta and her family denied that they had ever been aware of it.(334) But a drawing by Giulietta herself(335) betrays the *Vergognosa* who conceals herself in order to see better : it represents Beethoven—young, fashionable, bewhiskered,(336) in an elegant frock-coat pinched in at the waist—leaning on his elbow, his chin in his hand, on the garden balustrade and devouring with his eyes Giulietta's window on the ground-floor; while she, hiding behind the curtains, peeps out on this odd Romeo.

In any case Beethoven had no doubt that she returned his affection; his letter of November 1801 to Wegeler says explicitly, " She loves me and I love her."(337) And in 1823, talking with Schindler, he writes in his Conversation Book these categorical words : " I was greatly loved by her and more than ever her husband was " (" J'étais bien aimé d'elle et plus que jamais son époux ").(338) He even accused her of having in later days taken advantage of her passion for him and exploited it.(339) These cruel words, that I am compelled to quote, for they have passed into history, have weighed on the memory of the gracious woman ; and every Beethovenian has read the worst into them. It is probable that had Beethoven been able to foresee this he would have been the first to regret his remarks. Observe that he had taken the precaution to write them in French, so that they should be unintelligible to any of his associates but Schindler, whose malicious gossip had called them forth (Schindler was the type of good friend who believes it to be his duty to report faithfully to his friend whatever is likely to annoy or distress him). What was Giulietta's crime ? Not to have loved him whom perhaps she had encouraged to love her ? Not much effort on her part was necessary for that ! It needed only her eyes. She was the *Primavera* ; she does not love, but she is loved ; and it is justly so, and one should be grateful to her. Beethoven, like every deceived lover, was unjust ; and the bitterness of his rancour after twenty years only proves the depth of his wound. A further testimony to it is the fact that until his death he preserved, in his secret sanctuary, the portrait of *La Giovinetta*.

For the moment, in 1801, he is giving her lessons ; and as he refuses to take money from her she makes him a present of a dozen shirts sewn by her own lovely hand. She was a good musician, though perhaps not so truly an artist as Therese, for Beethoven often gets angry, throws the pages on the ground, and stamps about in his rage. But she is clever enough to play very prettily,(340) and the Guicciardi pride themselves on having the master at their soirées. It is during the winter of 1801/2 that he dedicates to the " *Damigella Contessa* " the *Moonlight* sonata, which is published at the beginning of March 1802.

Disillusionment has already come. From the first months of 1802 Giulietta openly shows her preference for the young Count Gallenberg, who was hardly a year older than herself, and had been an intimate friend of hers since her arrival in Vienna.(341) On the 6th October, 1802, Beethoven writes the Heiligenstadt Testament ; but this tragic letter indicates the summit of the passionate crisis (the curve falls after this) rather than the commencement of his despair. Moreover, in this grief of his, flouted love holds only the second place; the true tragedy is the state of his health, which he now knows to be incurable.

He had not failed to see the difficulties, if not the impossibility, of a marriage with Giulietta, even in the days when he believed himself to be loved by her.(342) The revelation that she preferred Gallenberg to him, bitter as it was, could not be, for a man still young and overflowing with energy, such a catastrophe as the forced renunciation, ten or twelve years later, of the "Immortal Beloved,"—his last harbour of refuge. He was sufficiently master of his feelings not to break off social relations with Giulietta; the decisive proof of this is a letter of Giulietta to Therese, dated 2nd August, 1803,(343) in which we see Beethoven visiting Giulietta in the year after the Heiligenstadt Testament, and the little coquette, too sure of her charms, boasting that she has given him a scolding.(344) Beethoven's visits to the Guicciardi house are confirmed by a letter of Josephine Brunsvik, written during the course of the same summer. His visits probably lasted almost until the eve of the marriage with Gallenberg (3rd November, 1803) and the departure of the couple for Rome.

Portrait of Josephine Brunsvik, Countess Deym
(Miniature)

Portrait of Giulietta Guicciardi, Countess Gallenberg

PEPI (Josephine) regained for a time the place in Beethoven's heart of which Giulietta had for a moment deprived her. "*Der göttliche Beethoven*," as she called him, enchanted her with his music, his quartets, his septet, his sonatas, his "divine variations." And it was she who played the sonata that had been written for Giulietta.(345) Each of the new sonatas that at this time "opened a new path," as Beethoven himself had said, —after the two sonatas *quasi una fantasia*, the *Pastoral*, and the first two of Op. 31 (that appeared in August 1802)—were taken at once to Josephine, who read them with delight and wrote to Therese: "These works annul everything he has written until now."(346)

We can understand Beethoven being more and more attracted by this woman who understood him so well, —this good, beautiful, intelligent, artistic creature, full of grace and wit, whose charm had conquered Vienna. Her seductive power was all the more irresistible because of its innocence; according to one of her passionate admirers, "She had not the least idea of it!"(347)

Beethoven's correspondence shows him eager for her society, exigent, imperious.(348) As yet there is no question of anything but music; or at all events music is the pretext.

But at the end of 1803 the husband Deym disappears from the scene; a pneumonia, contracted on a journey to Prague, carries him off in a few days. He leaves his young wife with four children; his financial affairs are in disorder, and she can make nothing of them.(349) From this date Josephine's health is broken; she suffers from nervous fevers of which she never gets rid.(350) Grief at her husband's death and the confusion of his affairs, and the aristocratic fragility of this hot-house plant that a rough breath can kill, deliver her over to the hazards of feeling; and Beethoven, from whom she is no longer separated by the barrier of conjugal honour, at once sees the door of hope swing open. His passion increases. In the summer of 1804 he is Pepi's neighbour in the country, and he sees her frequently.(351) But it is during the winter that his assiduity becomes so ardent that it disquiets Pepi's sisters; and they occupy themselves with the problem not of how to put an end to it —for everyone in the Brunsvik family loves him—but of how to keep it within bounds. The danger is not only in the excitement of Beethoven, whom the Brunsviks know, but in the weakness of Pepi, who, as the future was to show, was of the type that is the victim less of its own heart than of that of others, for it knows not how to say No.

It is easy to follow this romantic story by means of Charlotte's letters to Therese and Franz in November-December 1804 (352) :—

"Beethoven is extraordinarily amiable (*äusserst liebenswürdig*); he comes every other day, and stays with Pepi for hours" (20th November). Pepi is the first to become aware of his most secret thoughts, the first to whom he plays "several magnificent numbers" from the opera he is writing; and it is not a matter of indifference to us to learn that this feminine image was associated with the first inspirations of *Leonora*.

A month later "this is becoming a little dangerous."(353) On the 24th December Charlotte writes to Franz: " Beethoven is here almost every day: he gives Pipschen lessons—*you understand me, my dear!* "(354) At the commencement of January 1805, again: " He comes almost every day, and is infinitely amiable (*unendlich liebenswürdig*). He has written a song for Pepi." But Pepi insists that no one else shall see it : it is a secret !

On the 20th January Therese can no longer conceal her apprehension:

" But tell me, what is going to happen with Pepi and Beethoven? (*Was soll daraus werden?*) She must look out. (*Sie soll auf ihrer Hut sein!*) I suppose it is with reference to her that you have underlined these words in the score you send me : ' *Ihr Herz muss die Kraft haben nein zu sagen.*' (' Your heart must have the strength to say No.') A sad duty, if not the saddest of all ! "

It is impossible to be more explicit. There is no need to search for reasons why Therese and Charlotte should regard a marriage as impossible. They were plentiful enough—class feeling in the first place, though Josephine, at a later date, will say sadly to Therese that " very rarely is it permitted to a certain class to choose a companion after one's own heart . . ." (355), but above everything, incompatibility of temper. The Brunsviks knew Beethoven too well not to be aware of the intractable character of their great intimate, and of the crushing menace of that developing deafness the cloud of which already cast its shadow over his future. Pepi's two sisters had the best of reasons for warning her against such a union. A fragile work of art like the exquisite Josephine, elegant and invalid, rising from her sofa only to receive company or to play the piano, unskilled in practical life,—could one imagine her in the hands of a Beethoven? These two different worlds, these two sick beings,—what would they have made of each other?

Later, however, Therese reproaches herself for having helped to separate them. In her unpublished *Journal*, which Mlle. Dr. Marianne de Czeke has been good enough to allow me to see, she gives voice forty years later to a moving expression of regret that sounds like remorse. Long after both Josephine and Beethoven are dead, in March 1847, she writes : " Beethoven . . . he who was so very like her in spirit ! . . . Josephine's friend in house and heart! They were born for each other, and (356) . . . [here I give the German words, for they may bear a double meaning] . . . *und lebten beiden noch, hätten sie sich vereint!* " This phrase would be striking enough if we were to translate it : " If they were still living, they would be united." But in the opinion of Mlle. de Czeke and certain linguistic authorities whom I have consulted, Therese's general style and the Viennese idiom of the day (in which the " *und* " carries a hypothetical meaning), would authorise us to read : " Had they been united, they would be living now ! "

The sisters, then, had their part in the responsibility for Josephine's decision ; but in any case this decision could not be condemned ; we can imagine that Josephine herself believed it to be necessary ; and " her heart had the strength to say No." I will not go so far as to believe, with La Mara, that it cost her a great deal ; but even if her inclination had not been strong, her natural goodness of heart must have made her suffer by the thought that she was causing suffering. And these inward questionings and uncertainties were a torment to her. Her health gave way under them ; we see her, in January, a prey once more to her nervous crises, to cruel headaches, to a profound melancholy from which music alone could rouse her. I fancy that, in the months that followed, Beethoven was warned in some way or other ; for when, in September 1805, the song that had been written for Pepi and was dedicated to her appeared,(357) the dedication was suppressed.

If there was any explanation between them it was affectionate, without the least hint of a quarrel. At the end of March, Josephine still speaks with the old warm interest of "the good Beethoven."(358) During the summer of 1805 they are neighbours again at Hetzendorf(359); then they become separated, and meet again only at rare intervals. In the winter of 1805/6 Josephine, at her mother's house in Ofen, is a queen of beauty and wit in the festivities arranged by the Grand Duke of Tuscany: she kindles ardent passions among the aristocracy. After that time her life drifts away from that of Beethoven; and in the summer of 1808 she comes under the sway of Baron Stackelberg, whom she marries in February 1810. Soon she is overwhelmed with domestic and financial anxieties; and when, in 1811, Therese speaks to her of Beethoven and asks of her a little service in connection with her old friend, Josephine does not reply. The past is dead: the painful present occupies all her thoughts.(360)

AS YET I have spoken only incidentally of Therese; during this period she occupies only a secondary place in Beethoven's life. For one thing, she has much fewer opportunities than her sisters of meeting him. She is the least favoured; she is generally living far from Vienna, at Martonvásár or at Ofen, with her mother, from whose domineering character and narrowness of mind she suffers a good deal. Further, at this period she is apt to be isolated by her extremely delicate health. All these circumstances undoubtedly contributed to the formation of her strongly-marked individuality.(361)

All who have spoken of her, until an acquaintance with first of all her *Memoirs*, then her *Journal*, restored the true picture of her, have been inaccurate in their representation of her. The general mistake has been to attribute to the young Therese the characteristics of the mature Therese. No man and no woman can be painted in a single portrait that will summarise the totality of the life; and the more vital they are the falser is the summary, for the more will they have changed with the years. Those who will not admit the possibility that Therese and Beethoven, who had known each other since 1799, should have waited ten years before they drew near to each other,(362) merely prove that they have been spared—it is not altogether an advantage !—the vicissitudes of life. It never occurs to them that the Beethoven of the years after 1810 may have been a different man from the Beethoven of 1800. Nor was the Therese of before 1809 the Therese of the *Journal* that was written after she was thirty-five. Life is a hard school; and poor Therese had, like Beethoven, to go through some painful experiences before she could attain, again like him, to a religious concentration on herself and to a virile *Ergebenheit*. . . . " Resignation. . . . Oh, hard combat ! "(363) sighs Beethoven. And Therese cries : " Suffer and renounce ! "(364)

Her intimate jottings, which I have been privileged to read, at last tear away the veils that hid the " hard combat " of her heart, and the crisis—or rather the succession of crises—that wholly transformed her.

The first revelation brought us by the *Journal* (of which I must speak only with the utmost discretion, out of respect for the wishes of the depositaries of it) (365) is the absolute sincerity of this soul. Many men and women in the France and Germany of the bygone time have gazed into their mirror and described themselves courageously. But it is rarely that self-esteem has not played its part in the description ; and, as with the Impenitent of Geneva, certain ugly features are only avowed out of a pride in the public confession of them— or else, after the fashion of the coquettes of the seventeenth and eighteenth centuries, care is taken that the faults are a mere spot on the face, their piquancy heightened by the shadows of the portrait. There is nothing of this kind in Therese. She writes neither for the public nor for her own vanity ; she is making her confession in the true sense of the term, the religious examination of her conscience (366) ; and she does not spare herself, for she is alone with God. She pardons herself nothing ; she overlooks nothing in herself.(367)

And this lucidity of gaze, that penetrates without the least weakness into the crevices of her thought, is allied with an inward flame, an unbridled imagination,(368) that seem incompatible with this absolute need for truth. It is because she knows the weakness and the perils of them that, when alone with herself, she furiously pursues and denounces them. But warned though she may be, again and again she falls, and these descents to earth, these combats, these revolts give to the interior life of this young girl, who, for the rest, is only imperfectly endowed to express them,(369) a hidden pathos that will later attain to grandeur, and, by flashes, to the sublime. Ah ! how little do those who pronounce her intellectual and frigid know her as she really was !

Let them read her letters to her sisters in 1805,(370) in which she tells them of the passion she feels for a young officer,(371) and especially her letter to her mother of 29th September, 1805, in which, the man she loves having been killed, it is said, in a battle with the French, she fancies she sees him, bleeding, in a dream :—

"Nothing matters to me now; I have only one desire—to avenge myself on the French ! To kill him who killed my beloved !"

It is possible that this passion is deceived in its object, that, as her sisters fear (372) and as she herself will later be the first to recognise and to reproach herself for it, it is only illusory ; but is not this the nature of passion,

WB

that intoxication of the senses and the imagination, that fog-enwrapped vertigo that blurs the lines of distinction between others and one's self? If I could only publish certain extracts from the *Journal* of 1810 that have been confided to me, in which the terrified Therese finds herself on the edge of a moral abyss towards which she has been driven by an unexpected, overwhelming squall of passion, and becomes aware of the wild forces, the culpable thoughts that have been passing subconsciously through her! (373) This frail girl (yet with such powers of resistance! she survived all her family and lived to be eighty-six!), this chaste woman who knew no other little arms around her neck than those of the children of other women, the thousands of little orphans whom she adopted, was and always ran the risk of being the prey of the powers of the unknown in the soul, and being delivered over to the hazards of their gales. And she knew it, knew it in shame and terror. She was built to understand the tragedy of the *Appassionata*, that had been dedicated to her brother, and that she was the first to hear and perhaps to play.

For the rest, she had a sound intelligence, and a taste that guided her by instinct to the loftiest and most beautiful. When, in January 1805, she is sending her sisters Schiller's *William Tell*, which she has just discovered, she writes: " Truly, as long as Schiller and Beethoven are creating one ought not to wish to die ! "

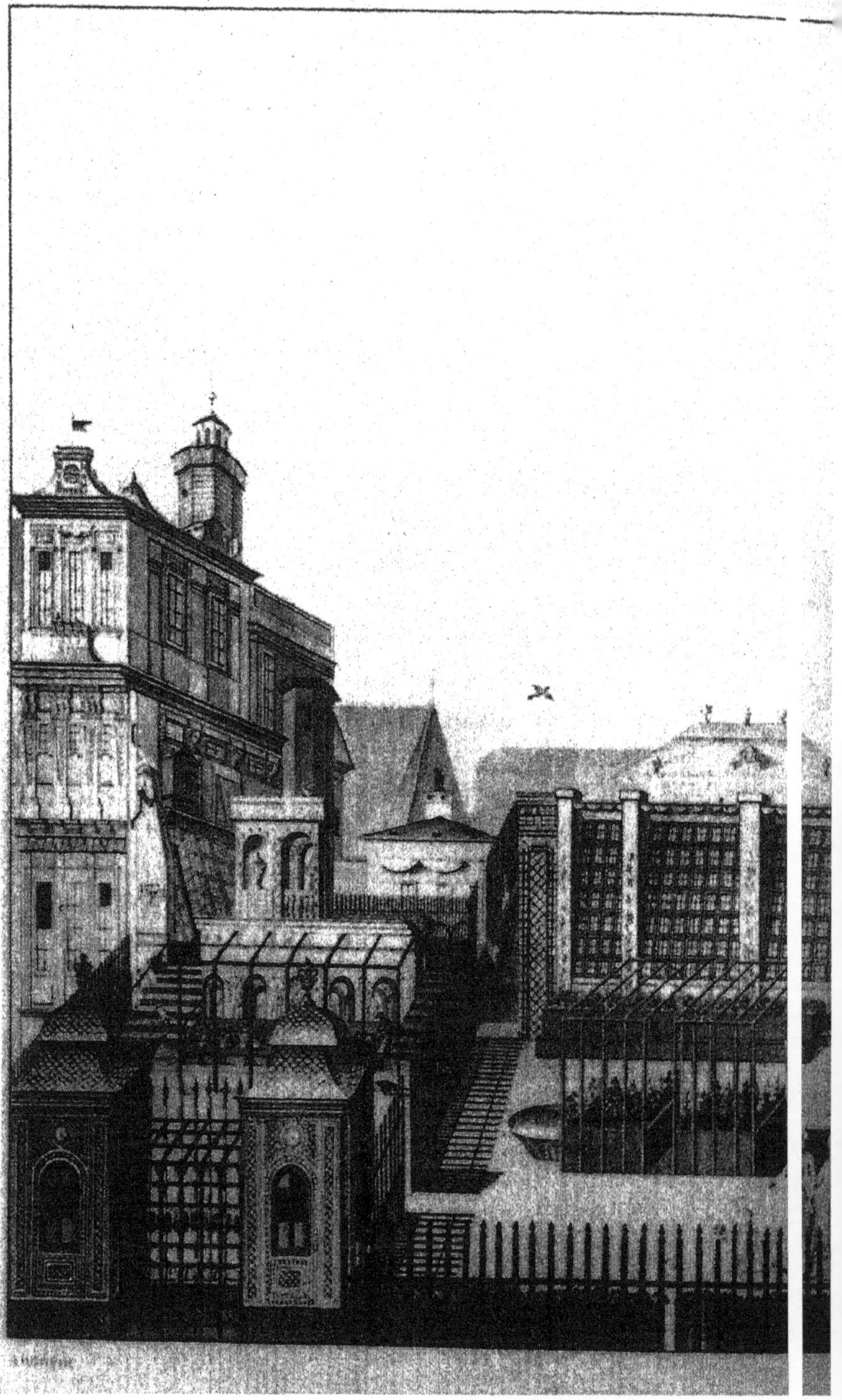

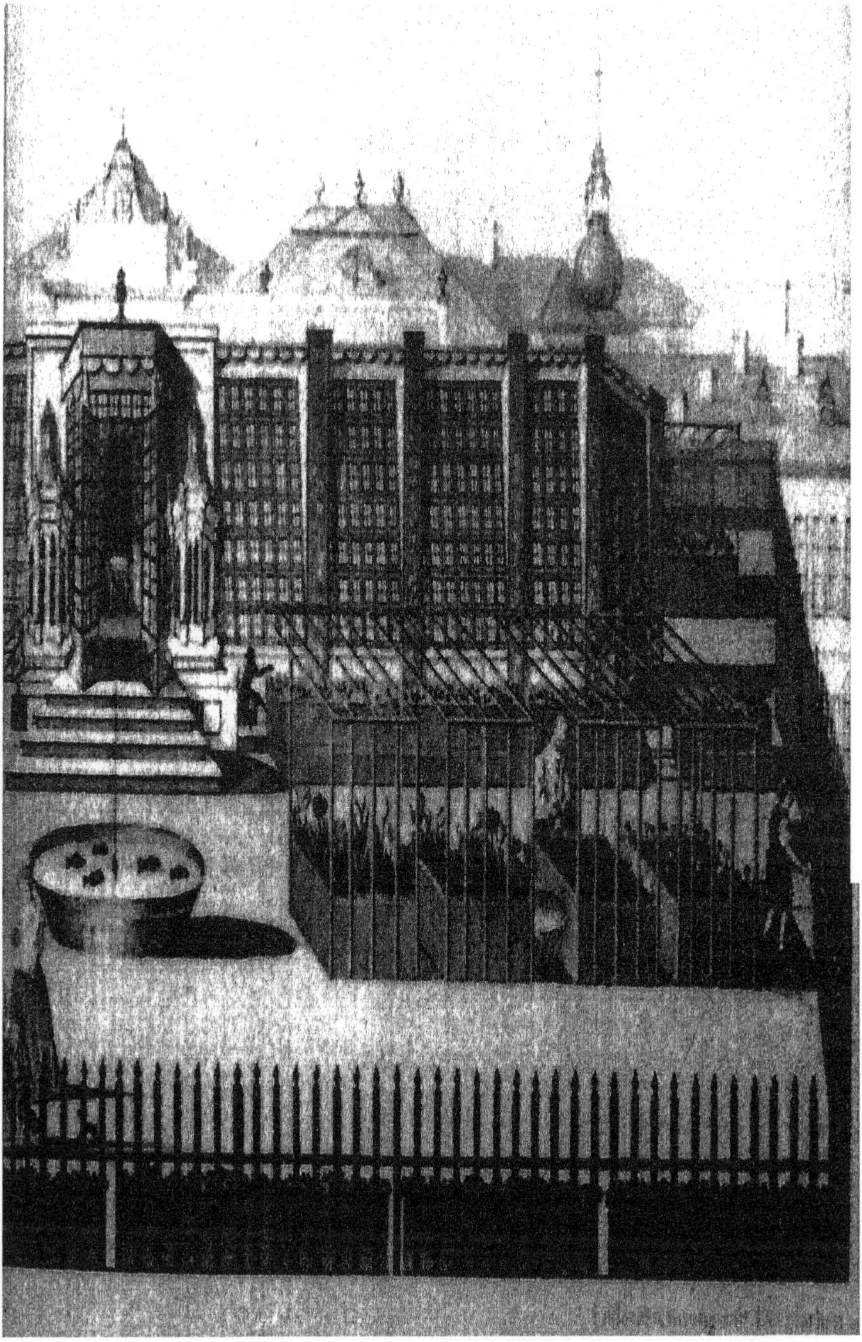

And this remark of the young girl about Beethoven links up, after more than half a century, with that of the old woman evoking the memory of the great vanished friend and comparing him with Christ.(374) In spirit she was of the secret company of genius, and she knew it when, in this same year 1805, she wrote, not without a pride for which she reproached herself harshly later: "Immediately after the geniuses come those who know how to prize them."(375)

Her musical talent was considerable. A friend who used to go to the best concerts said in 1805 that he would give them all "to hear Therese play a single Beethoven sonata." Another letter, in 1808, speaks of her "charming fingers, that play Beethoven's sonatas in a style that turns the master's and his disciples' heads."(376) She was not only a pianist; before taking lessons from Beethoven she had studied harmony and counterpoint with an organist; and in 1805/6, during the musical festival organised at Ofen for the Grand Duke of Tuscany, Therese's knowledge and authority were sufficient to enable her to assume for several months the co-direction of the symphony concerts(377) with the composer Spech, besides taking a contralto part excellently. Her chief successes were in poetic and lyric declamation. She drew and painted. Her intelligence was equally attracted by the sciences, and in later years she urged the claim of women to study these.(378)

The richness of her nature is thus sufficiently indicated. And yet, without the rude shocks and the moral crises that, between her thirty-third and fortieth year, ploughed up her very soul and brought about in her a second, a veritable birth, she might have lost herself, like the majority of aristocratic women, in the thousand futilities of a life of happy and useless idleness.

This painful birth to a high destiny is shown without the least concealment in her *Journal*. The more intimate portions of this cannot yet be published; but at any rate I can assure my readers that I have not found in it a line, a confession, that does not increase one's respect for the memory of Therese. I can understand perfectly the mistrust of the depositaries of these papers of the section of the public that leaves its finger-marks on the secrets of the heart. I will therefore confine myself to a sketch of the moral evolution of this feminine soul during the early years of the century.

The brilliant young girl who found Beethoven in the spring of 1799 was careless enough of the future; existence seemed to her a happy dream. Life began by separating the three sisters who were so passionately devoted to each other. After Josephine's marriage Therese remained isolated in her mother's castle. She was of a lively sensibility, with an excess of imagination that was fed by her reading and her dreams. She was a great dreamer: her retired and idle life, that alternated for several years with spells of fashionable and empty pleasures, encouraged at the same time this fever of the spirit and a tendency to fly from anything like regular activity or even physical effort. Her health suffered by it,—all the more because the tendency was contrary to her true nature. This becomes plainly evident later: the heroism of action was her normal temperature; and the damming of this need threatened to pervert her whole being. In the exaltation of this delicious somnambulism she formed, as she herself confesses, too high an opinion of herself, and conceived a wounding disdain of others. This attitude was not calculated to win her sympathy; and her character became bitter in consequence. She showed herself domineering, of a rough and crushing frankness (379) that brought her into conflict with the rest of the family, even with Josephine, whom she adored. And here we can detect, under the pen of Therese, the curious ascendancy of the younger girl. Pepi, a widow with four children at the age of twenty-five, dominated the elder sister by means of the superiority of her experience and the certitude that she was loved. Therese became passionate only over Josephine, and could not refrain from falling foul of her; into everything she brought disquiet and tempest. Josephine, who had just lost her husband and was shaken to the depths, had need of all her strength to maintain her moral equilibrium; she showed no indulgence and cut herself off from this tormented and tormenting sister of hers. " I still feel," Therese writes, " all the bitterness, the pain and the despair that took possession of me, when, after several attempts [to live together], she told me for the last time that she could not keep me with her, that I dragged her down, that I hindered her from advancing, and that, in her sick state, with four children and a big house to look after, it was impossible for her to have the influence on me that she would have liked. . . . I went away, and thought I was separated from her for ever."

This was during the summer of 1804, at the very time when Beethoven, their neighbour in the country, was listening to the thunder in him of the tempest of the *Appassionata*.

Another tempest was devastating Therese's heart. She had the feeling that she had lost everything,—both friendship and love. It was complete night within her : she lived through months of despair, during which she could not help comparing her own total abandonment with the happiness of others—Josephine surrounded by children, admired, flattered by society, courted by Beethoven ; the youngest sister, Charlotte, betrothed and soon afterwards married. After having consumed herself in solitude for months, her energy revolted ; she would at all costs regain the esteem and the love she could not do without. But into the achievement of her purpose she put the old violence. First of all, from November 1804 to November 1805, there is that passion, of which I have already spoken, for a young officer (Toni) whom, it seems, she loved ; but the others opposed the union. Then, in the winter of 1805/6, at Ofen, she is seized with a mania for amusements and fêtes in which she wants to play, and does play, the leading part,—a striking illustration of the demoniac force that is engendering in this abrupt, wild creature, taciturn, violent and just a little deformed. She is determined to make herself loved, admired, sought after, courted. She succeeds magnificently. She is, and becomes still more so, beautiful, gay, witty, lively, amusing ; she has every talent ; she is an admirable musician, "queen of declamation," dramatic and lyric, "frivolous of speech, with a thousand trinkets and an infinite number of dresses" that bring her "incredible successes." She is the princess of the salons, sought after and loved ; even the Grand Duke of Tuscany is smitten with her.(380) Happiness transfigures her ; and, with its coming, there return to her serenity, sweetness, affectionate thoughts. She dreams of marriage ; but, as she says, to this apparent victory there corresponded no victory within herself. An ordinary woman would have been content ; but in Therese, as in her sister Josephine, there was a foundation of moral seriousness and above all (much more in Therese than in Josephine) of intrepid truth, that permitted of no illusion as to the emptiness of the soul and could not remain satisfied with that.

This was in 1807. Josephine, who had long been separated from Therese, wrote to ask her to return and help her in the education of her girls. Therese, proud of this change of heart in the sister she loved, burning with desire to run and throw herself in her arms, still cannot rid herself of all the rancour the offence of old had bred in her; and her new successes in the social world make her shrink from accepting the life of humble affection and domestic devotion that Pepi offers her. She replies evasively, postpones her decision, and goes to Karlsbad. Later she regrets bitterly having let go by this last chance to attach the heart of Josephine to her for ever; for Josephine, who once more draws away from her, meets in the following year the man whom she is to marry and who is to prove the misfortune of her life. And Therese, without explaining herself in her confession of 1809, lets us see that for her also "the misfortune of my whole life" was decided in those two years.

What had happened between 1807 and 1809?

Without trying to elucidate the mystery here, and without seeing any connection between these unknown troubles and the presence of Beethoven, it can be shown that it is at this moment he becomes part of Therese's most intimate circle. She had never ceased to feel an interest in him as an artist; and Beethoven, when he

Portrait of Countess Therese von Brunsvik. (Original portrait by Kallhofer, hitherto known only in the mediocre reproduction by J. B. Lampi, engraved by W. Unger, and in the copy, made by Therese herself, that is now in the Beethoven House in Bonn)

saw Josephine or Charlotte, never failed to wish Therese, through her, "*alles Schöne und Liebe*" (381) ("all loveliness and love"). But these amiabilities did not go beyond the formulæ of ordinary courtesy. They take on a more intimate tone in 1807, when Beethoven asks Franz to embrace his sister Therese for him, and teasingly reminds her that she had promised to paint his portrait.(382)

Franz was the intermediary: the brother and the eldest sister had been drawn closer together by the fact that neither of them had married.(383) And Franz was a passionate admirer of Beethoven's music. It might even be said that music was his sole passion; for until his forties, when love took its revenge, this weak and ailing, gifted and inactive young man showed an indifference towards women that laid him open to pleasantries. His sisters called him "the ice-cold Knight" ("*der eiskalte Ritter*"). There is something comical in the fact that this piece of frigidity should have had the honour of the dedication of the *Appassionata* (or was it really dedicated to him, or only to others through him?). But for the one and only Beethoven he was and remained enthusiastic. Beethoven sent him the manuscripts of his works as soon as they were finished.(384) He took refuge with him in Hungary; and it was in Franz's castle that he seems to have completed the *Appassionata* during the summer of 1806. He was treated by the young Count as one of the family; and between 1807 and 1812 their friendship took on quite a fraternal character. . . . " Brother! dear brother!" wrote Beethoven, who, indeed, in a letter of 1802, vowed that Franz was his only brother,—more brother to him than those of his own blood.(385)

We can believe, then, that a stream of affectionate interest circulated regularly, by way of Franz, between Beethoven and Therese; and the jovial commission of the 11th May, 1807, reached its address. We shall see later that Beethoven received from Therese not only " his fine portrait " but an allegorical drawing in which she represented him under the form of an eagle gazing at the sun.(386) This, however, belongs to a later period, which I reserve for a further volume, together with the problem of the famous letter to " The Immortal Beloved,"—the date of which is now settled as 1812.

During the period with which we are at present occupied, Beethoven and Therese discover themselves to each other only slowly. Therese, indeed, has hardly begun to discover her own self. The years 1807 and 1808, the summers of which she passed at Karlsbad, are for her a period—and the last—of fashionable pleasures and agitations. Her health has been restored; and her mother, in order to assure her a way of life that shall be independent and worthy of her name, has had built for her, it is said, a house at Egra.(387) She sees

Beethoven often enough in these years; but it would seem that the memory of Josephine's affection for him is still uppermost in him. The name of the one sister calls up in his mind that of the other.(388)

Everything changes in the course of the year 1808,—not only Josephine's life but that of Therese and the direction of her thought. During the summer Josephine comes to Karlsbad to take her sister to Switzerland. They visit Pestalozzi, at Yverdon. Josephine is preoccupied with the education of her children; but it is Therese who receives the moral radiance of the apostle —" an indescribably ugly little man," she says, " but of a heavenly goodness, with a gigantic energy that dominates from above whatever is common." Pestalozzi kindles in her a spark of the divine flame (389) that, after having developed in silence for some years, will now consume her utterly; she becomes the passionate genius of that work of education and social action the magnificent creation of which—the love of poor and abandoned children, a sort of universal maternity—Hungary celebrated in 1928.

Josephine contributes to this evolution,—not without a certain egoism, for she shifts to Therese's shoulders the heavy burden of the education of her many children. For at Pestalozzi's she has met Baron Stackelberg, to whom she has taken a fancy and who will become her second husband. Her preoccupations enclose her within the circle of her own house and people; and into the service of these she draws and sacrifices the devotion of Therese. The latter's grandeur consists in the fact that she will love the sacrifice to the point of converting it into a source of new life and happiness, though not without passing through a period of passionate meditation to which the *Journal* bears witness: she was not free from doubts and sorrows. I should say that it is psychologically possible and natural that at this time, more than at any other, Beethoven and Therese should have come near to understanding each other and uniting their destinies; though I do not venture to say that it was so.(390) I shall go into this question later. Let it suffice here to say that these years (1809-1813, that lie outside the limit of the present volume) are for each of them the period of the great crisis, of trials, deceptions, and inward unsettlement.(391) The true Therese is born: the young Beethoven dies.

REFERENCES

REFERENCES

1. One of the last songs of the old Goethe, in the Second Part of *Faust*.

2. And this first volume is the chronicle only of the first campaigns, from Marengo to Wagram.

3. I must confess that, a very few works excepted, I do not care to hear him played by women. He himself, however, had no objection to this—when the woman was attractive to him!

4. "*Löwenstimme... Die Nase viereckig wie die eines Löwen ... Das Haar dick, in die Höhe'stehend ... Stirne und Schädel wunderbar breit gewölbt und hoch wie ein Tempel ... Bis an die Augen ging sein erschrecklich starker Bart...*" For all these details see Ries, Röckel, and particularly Benedict, who, seeing Beethoven with Weber, was struck by the contrast between the two men.

5. Röckel (1806), Reichardt (1808), Müller (1820), Benedict (1823), Stumpff (1824).

6. His nephew, whom he loved as a son, tried to commit suicide.

7. The comparison was made by some of his visitors. Stumpff says of him, " He is of medium height, strong of frame like Napoleon, the neck short, the shoulders broad, the head large and round."

8. " Unfortunately I have to give up too much time to it ! " (Letter to Wegeler, November 1801.)

9. Nothing hurt him so much as this, for these evil reports came even to his ears. On his death-bed he heard that some people attributed his dropsy to over-indulgence in drink ; and the poor man begged Breuning and Schindler to defend his memory against the charge. Let me quote some moving passages from a little-known letter from Schindler to Wegeler of the 6th July, 1827, published in Stephan Ley's fine book *Beethoven als Freund der Familie Wegeler-Breuning* (Bonn, 1927) : the letter comes from the rich Wegeler-Beethoven archives— " Beethoven, in the last weeks of his illness, often spoke to Breuning and myself of the vexatious talk there would be about his moral character if he died of this malady. . . . It grieved him exceedingly, all the more because these calumnies were spread abroad by men whom he had received at his table. He implored us to preserve for him after his death the love and friendship we had shown him during his life, and to see that at any rate his moral life was not besmirched " (*und zu wachen, das wenigstens sein moralisches Leben nicht befleckt wurde*).

10. But we must mistrust here the testimony of Schindler, who hated Holz for having ousted him.

11. His two pretty "sorceresses," Unger and Sontag, who sang in the "Hymn to Joy" in the Ninth Symphony, were very ill after a dinner he gave them.

12. Also a discreet allusion of his doctor Bertolini, to whom his weaknesses were known. (When Bertolini was ill with cholera, in 1831, and believed himself to be dying, he ordered all the intimate Beethoven papers in his possession to be burned.)

13. An excess of scrupulosity prevents the publication of certain documents that exist in a Berlin collection,—sketches sent by Beethoven to his doctor, that had to do with a malady that must have dated from the first years of his residence in Vienna, the nature of which Beethoven himself did not understand exactly. See the articles of Dr. Leo Jacobssohn, head physician of the Städl. Krankenhaus Moabit-Berlin, in the *Deutsche Medizinische Wochenschrift* (Sonderabdruck, No. 27), and in the Berlin *Der Tag*, No. 276, 1919.

14. See the letter of June 1801 to Wegeler,—later, be it noted, than the onset of his malady, which must have had profound repercussions on his character.

15. Such as his servants, to whom he was both insulting and violent. See the Hogarthian scene narrated by Ries.

16. "*Kraft ist die Moral der Menschen, die sich vor Anderen auszeichnen, und sie ist auch die meinige.*" (Letter to Zmeskall, about 1800.)

17. "*Unser Zeitalter bedarf kräftiger Geister die diese kleinsüchtigen heimtückischen elenden Schuften von Menschenseelen geisseln.*"

18. "Never since my childhood has my zeal to serve poor suffering humanity relaxed. . . . Never have I accepted any reward for this; I need no other than the feeling of well-being that always accompanies a good action." (December 1811.) This passion for charity increases later, after the man has known suffering—notably in the period 1811-1812. For the moment it is in the shade.

19. "*Ich will dem Schicksal in den Rachen greifen*": Beethoven to Wegeler, 16th November, 1801.

20. Karl Nef, *Beethovens Beziehungen zur Politik* (*Sonntagsblatt der Basler Nachrichten*, 1st, 8th, and 15th July, 1923). In this same year 1790 the first big work of Beethoven, the cantata on the death of Joseph II, for solo, chorus and orchestra, celebrates, in the melodramatic style of the Revolution but still not without grandeur, the herculean struggle of the man who brought "the monster Fanaticism" to the ground.

21. The story is told by Frau von Bernhard. Cf. Nohl and Kalischer.

22. The story comes from the tenor Röckel, who was present.

23. Yet he loved them; and some words of his show that in his heart he preserved his gratitude to them. But this

gratitude gave no one whatever rights over his liberty. Let me add that he paid his protectors royally: to Prince Lichnowsky he dedicated the three Trios (Op. 1), the *Pathétique* sonata (Op. 13), the Funeral March sonata (Op. 26), and the second symphony; to Princess Lichnowsky the piano arrangement of the *Prometheus* ballet; to the princess's mother, Countess von Thun, the B flat trio (Op. 11), etc.

24. See the account of the prince's physician, Dr. Weiser, in Frimmel, *Beethoven* (1903); also Thayer (Eng. ed., II. 69). The scene was much more violent than the accounts indicate; but Beethoven's friends tried to hush the affair up. In an intimate letter of the 28th December, 1837, from Ries to Wegeler, contained in the Wegeler archives (*Beethoven als Freund der Familie Wegeler-Breuning*) we find the following: " Had it not been for Count Oppersdorf and a few others there would have been a brutal scuffle, for Beethoven had picked up a chair and was about to break it over the head of Prince Lichnowsky, who had had the door forced of the room in which Beethoven had bolted himself. Fortunately Oppersdorf threw himself between them." The cause of the quarrel was Beethoven's refusal to play for the French officers who were Lichnowsky's guests at dinner.

25. Thus Ries. But Czerny tells us that when Anton Halm, showing Beethoven a sonata in 1815, excused certain irregularities with the remark that " Beethoven also has permitted himself many infractions of the rules,"

the composer replied, " I can do so, but not you." He knows exactly what he can do ; he ventures with open eyes. And, after all, we must admit, the " harmonists " of to-day find him very prudent.

26. Ignaz von Seyfried.

27. But observe that it is for his pupil, the Archduke Rudolph, that he accumulates these copies, these *Materialien zum Contrapunkt*. (See Nottebohm, *Beethoveniana*, pp. 154 ff.) And this fact elucidates the tart rejoinder to Halm, quoted on the preceding page. Crutches are good for the weakly !

28. Not only in music but in every department of thought. In the *Bonn-Beethoven Festbuch* for 1927 I have devoted an article to this encyclopædic curiosity, under the title of *Fonti Fortitudinis ac Fidei* ; to this I shall return in a chapter of the second volume of these Essays.
No great creative musician, with the exception of Bach, has had the same passion—and, thanks to the Archduke's library, the same opportunity—for studying the masterpieces of the past, including those of the fifteenth and sixteenth centuries.

29. See the journal of old Gottfried Fischer. The manuscript is part of the Beethoven House collection at Bonn : Thayer gives long extracts from it in his first volume.

30. This fine adagio, before becoming part of the sonata Op. 2, No. 1 (Vienna, 1795), had figured in the quartet in C major, written at Bonn in 1785, when Beethoven was fourteen. He himself regarded it as a lament, and

Wegeler, with his consent, brought it out as a melody with the title *Die Klage*. This is to be found in the appendices to Wegeler and Ries' *Biographische Notizen*.

31. Letter of 15th September, 1787, to von Schaden. It is translated in full in Prod'homme's *La Jeunesse de Beethoven*.

32. In this very Largo e mesto from the sonata Op. 10, No. 3, of which I have just spoken, Beethoven, according to his own avowal, has described " the state of mind of a melancholic." (See the analysis of it in the chapter of this book devoted to the sonatas.) The adagio of the sixth quartet, Op. 18 (published before 1800), bears the title *La Malinconia*.

33. " I have it always," he writes to Wegeler in 1800. " Tell her that I still have a *raptus* sometimes." And again to Bettina, in 1810, " Did I say that? Then I had a *raptus* ! "

34. The painter Kloeber, who made a fine portrait of him in 1818, which he has supplemented in his notes, says : " I often met him on his walks. It was most interesting to see him stop, seem to be listening, look up, then down, and begin writing. I had been warned never to speak to him when he was like this, for if I did he would make himself extremely unpleasant."

35. I would venture to say, *more inhuman*. Let us be careful : here is the key to the Beethoven enigma, to his genius, and perhaps even—yes, so I believe !—to his tragedy. Nature cannot with impunity be violated by

the soul. If the latter tears from it secrets it has withheld from everything else, it will have to pay for them. In Note I of the present volume, on Beethoven's deafness, the reader will see the direct relations I have established, in the light of Dr. Marage's diagnosis, between this perpetual congestion of thought that never ceased its concentration and the catastrophe that overtook the organism.

36. We shall return to this "hunt of the devil" (or rather the "demon") in the great moments of his life.

37. Beethoven, who had heard Mozart, told Czerny that he had "a fine but broken way of playing, no ligato." Czerny adds that Beethoven was especially admirable in legato, and that he treated the piano like an organ.

38. "Whoever has not heard Beethoven improvise," said Baron de Trémont, "has no idea of the depth and the total power of his genius." Someone who heard him about 1790 or 1791 declared that "his playing is different from the ordinary way of treating the piano."

39. Except, perhaps, by means of the Choral Fantasia, Op. 77, if we are to believe Moscheles, who could never listen to it without being reminded of Beethoven's improvisations.

40. *Aus der innersten Tiefe, im den höchsten Hohen und tieffsten Tiefen."* (Reichardt, 1808.)

41. *"Aha! die meisten Menschen sind gerührt über etwas gutes; das sind aber keine Künstlernaturen, Künstler sind feurig,*

sie weinen nicht." Yet immediately after saying this he plays for Bettina his immortal setting of Goethe's immortal lyric, " *Trocknet nicht, Thränen der ewigen Liebe!* " (" Dry not, tears of eternal love.")

42. This man who is so hard with himself, so scornful of the feminine in man and its effusions, in his private life is extremely reserved,—so much so that even his intimate friends knew next to nothing of his love affairs, and chance alone has preserved for us the solitary letter " to the Immortal Beloved." Nor is he any more prodigal of confidences on the subject of his art; and when his art betrays him too openly he feels resentment against it. I will speak later of the hostile silence he preserves with regard to his *Moonlight* sonata.

43. " *Keine Rührung mehr! Fest und mutig soll der Mensch in allen Dingen sein.*"

44. In some recent articles (*Europe*, 15th May and 15th June, 1927), which I shall draw upon later, I have studied the two men together, and shown in what respects they differed from the accepted notion of them.

45. " Often I have cursed the Creator." (To Wegeler, June 1810.)

46. The allegro of the Trio, Op. 9, No. 3 (1796–1798), the superb first movement of the quartet Op. 18, No. 4 (1799–1800) (which foreshadows the *Coriolan* overture), and the *Pathétique* sonata (1798) are striking types of these Beethovenian dialogues, veritable dramas of the passions.

47. A young Courland theologian, one of the two or three friends whom Beethoven, by his own account, loved most. They lived together in 1798/9.

48. Until the epoch at which we have now arrived, Beethoven's hearing had been excellent. He prided himself on the extraordinary fineness and precision of it—" a sense that I had in complete perfection," he writes in the despairing Heiligenstadt Testament of 6th October, 1802; "a perfection possessed by few musicians at any time."

Dr. Aloys Weissenbach confirms this claim : " Until the accident that caused the deafness, his hearing was incomparably fine and delicate " (*unübertrefflich zart und feinhörig*). He adds that even as late as 1814 Beethoven suffered greatly under the least false note (*Auch jetzt noch allen Uebellaut schmerzlich empfindet.*)

On the probable causes and the onset of the deafness see Note I.

49. In the chapter on the sonatas we shall see the ardour with which each new work was welcomed, the young musicians secretly buying and studying the *Pathétique*, which the old professors have laid under a ban.

50. " *Der Tonheros, dessen Genius durch die Entfesselung der inneren Unendlichkeit eine neue Kunstaera geschaffen hat....*"

51. That is to say, the public conquest; for we know now that the youthful Beethoven had been secretly experimenting with all the forms of his art for ten or fifteen years before he gave the public his first symphony.

52. See the Steinhauser portrait of 1801.

53. Count Browne presented him with a horse. Beethoven mounted it a few times and then forgot all about it. A servant stole it, Ries tells us.

54. " At that time he was frank and tolerant in discussions. Whatever did not please him he laughed at with all his heart. . . . Most frequently he laughed at his own thoughts, which he kept a secret from others. Those about him could rarely discover the cause of the explosions in which he so often indulged." (Seyfried.)

55. See Note II, on the Beethoven Sketch-Book of 1800.

56. See, for example, in the recollections of Ries, the story of the comical duel of virtuosity between Beethoven and Steibelt. A quintet by the latter has just been performed. Beethoven, on his way to the piano, takes the 'cello part from one of the desks, turns it upside-down, picks out with one finger a nonsensical theme from the opening bars, and begins improvising on it. Steibelt goes out in a temper and never forgives him.

57. He had always a dislike for teaching.

58. The title of a book by M. André de Hevesy, but an inappropriate term for the two remarkable women who were his faithful and beloved friends, the Countesses Josephine and Therese von Brunsvik. See Note III.

59. His confidant and life-long friend Stephan von Breuning said to his wife, who could not understand how Beethoven could attract, "And yet he has always been successful with women!" (Gerhard von Breuning: *Aus dem Schwarzspanierhause,* 1874.)

60. *Zierlich,* says Müller in 1820. Benedict, in 1823, speaks of his "gentle and nobly shaped mouth." The attractive mouth, set in the tormented face, was also one of the secrets of the charm of Mirabeau, to whom I have already compared Beethoven.

61. *Schneeweissen,* says Schlösser in 1822. It is to be noted that these descriptions date from the later years, after he had turned fifty, when, however, Beethoven's constitution was ruined and his appearance neglected.

62. Thus Müller. The young Charlotte von Brunsvik, Countess Teleki, writing to her sisters in March 1807, tells them of a little Hungarian boy of ten years old whose lovely eyes and precocious intelligence have fascinated her; and she makes the following unexpected comparison, "His physiognomy is just like that of Beethoven; he has the same expressive and lively glance; you can see the genius in his eyes." (La Mara, *Beethoven und die Brunsviks.*)

63. Not, however, the Brunsvik sisters. I cannot find in their letters or intimate journals a single ironic or unkind word about Beethoven; a fact that has struck me forcibly, knowing how easily his appearance lent itself to derision or, more wounding still, to commiseration.

64. *Beethoven, vie intime,* 1926.

65. With the Brunsviks from the spring of 1799, with Giulietta Guicciardi from the summer of 1800. I may refer the reader to the long chapter at the end of this volume (Note III) on *The Sisters Josephine and Therese Brunsvik.*

66. It appears to be proved to-day that these famous letters belong to the year 1812, at which time there was no longer any question, so far as Beethoven was concerned, of Giulietta. (See my article on *La Lettre à l'Immortelle Aimée,* in the *Revue Musicale,* October 1927.) I will return to the matter when we reach the Teplitz period, during which the seventh symphony was written.

67. " *Die mich liebt und die ich liebe.*" (Letter of the 16th November, 1801, to Wegeler.) The idyll seems to have lasted from about June 1801 to the beginning of the following winter. See Note III.

68. " You can hardly believe how sad my life has been, what a desert, for the last two years ; everywhere my wretched hearing appeared to me like a spectre " (*Wie ein Gespenst ist mir mein schwäches Gehör überall erschienen*), he writes to Wegeler on the 16th November, 1801.

69. " For the first time I feel that marriage could make me happy." (To Wegeler, 16th November, 1801.) He had thought of it as early as 1798, in which year he asked the hand of Grétry's " Zémire," the beautiful Bonn singer Magdalene Willmann, who was then engaged at the Vienna Court Opera. But she refused him because

" he was so ugly, and half cracked " (*weil er so hässlich war, und halbverrückt.*) In the following year she married another admirer, who was more satisfactory both to her æsthetic sense and to her common sense.

70. Neither the Brunsviks nor the Guicciardi were free of money cares. Giulietta struggles all her life under a growing load of embarrassments, and has to live by her wits. The Brunsviks have vast domains, the revenues from which, however, are uncertain. And anyhow the girls do not benefit by them. They remain until marriage (Therese never marries) dependent on their mother, who sacrifices them to their brother. Josephine, who was the first to marry, loses her fortune in wretched lawsuits.

71. " Had it not been for my hearing I would by now have gone over half the world. I ought to do so." (Letter to Wegeler, cited above.)

72. " Count Robert sends you his compositions, the fruits of his hours of solitude, which are now frequent ! He is on the point of leaving his country, never to return ; his destiny leads him to Naples, there, remote from men, to seek the happiness that does not bloom for him here. It is sad to think that the zeal he vowed to his country in his youth has to come to flower in a foreign soil ! " (Letter from Giulietta to Therese, 2nd August, 1803, in La Mara, *Beethoven und die Brunsviks.* Hevesy, who quotes from the letter, wrongly assigns it to 1800. See Appendix, Note III.)

Between Beethoven, whom she snubs in the same letter,

and Count Robert Gallenberg, Giulietta does not hesitate for a moment: it is Robert who is the fatal and misunderstood genius.

73. The sonata was published towards the end of the winter of 1801/2 (in February or March 1802). It must therefore have been written shortly after the letter to Wegeler about the *zauberisches Mädchen*.

74. Alexander Wheelock Thayer (continued first by Hermann Deiters, then by Hugo Riemann), *Ludwig van Beethovens Leben*, 5 vols., 1866-1917.

75. He so describes it himself to Bettina, who repeats his remarks in a letter of 28th May, 1810 [to Goethe]. The word "electricity" is frequently used there to explain the sub-conscious of the spirit and the explosions of genius. See my articles on *Goethe and Beethoven* in the review *Europe*, 15th April and 15th May, 1927.

76. The Heiligenstadt agony is in October. In November his letters show him taking up with life once more, almost sprightly, indulging in his usual rough talk, his peasant humour.

77. That of the *Eroica* is in the Berlin State Library. We have at present forty of the Beethoven Sketch-Books, extending from 1798 to 1827, with an interruption of three years, from 1805 to 1808. The complete list, showing the libraries in which they are contained, is given in Josef Braunstein's *Beethovens Leonore-Ouvertüren* (Breitkopf, 1927). Nottebohm was the first to describe them, in four works that are now classics:—(1) *Ein*

Skizzenbuch von Beethoven beschrieben und in Auszügen dargestellt, 1865 (dealing with the sketches from October 1801 to May 1802, comprising those for the sonatas of Op. 31 and the second symphony); (2) *Ein Skizzenbuch von Beethoven aus dem Jahre 1803, in Auszügen dargestellt*, 1880 (from October 1802 to April 1804, including the *Eroica*, the *Waldstein* sonata, the opening scenes of *Fidelio* and the first sketches for the fifth symphony); (3) *Beethoveniana, Aufsätze und Mitteilungen*, 1872; (4) *Zweite Beethoveniana* (a posthumous publication), 1887. Paul Mies, in a remarkable book, *Die Bedeutung der Skizzen Beethovens zur Erkenntnis seines Stiles* (Breitkopf, 1927), has utilised these materials for a study of the laws of Beethoven's creative processes. Braunstein, in the work just mentioned, while paying due homage to Nottebohm, has expressed his doubts as to the latter's sometimes rather arbitrary way of summarising and interpreting the Sketch-Books; Braunstein pleads for a complete edition, if possible in facsimile

78. Not, as Thayer implies in order to support his thesis, during the period of the Testament. Here is the approximate chronology of the chief works that preceded the great crisis of October 1802 : Beethoven finished in 1801 the violin sonatas Op. 23 and Op. 24, the piano sonatas Op. 26 (with the Funeral March), Op. 27, Nos. 1 and 2 (the two sonatas *quasi una fantasia*, the second of which, the *Moonlight*, is published in March 1802), and Op. 28 (the *Pastoral*), and the quintet, Op. 29.

To the winter of 1801/2 belong the three violin sonatas dedicated to the Emperor Alexander, and, in the main,

the three piano sonatas, Op. 31, the six Variations in F major on an original theme, Op. 34, the Rondo in G major, Op. 51, No. 2 (at first intended for Giulietta, and more truly made in her image than the *Moonlight* sonata), the seven *Bagatelles*, Op. 33, and the oratorio *The Mount of Olives*. Finally the second symphony, that demanded a longer concentration, was finished during the summer of 1802.
Miraculous fecundity ! How could such a Spring have been stifled ?

79. The Testament, 10th October, 1802.

80. This famous letter of the 6th and 10th October, 1802, to his two brothers, is too well known for there to be any necessity for me to give it here. The original is in the Hamburg State Library.

81. One of the themes of the *Pastoral* appears in the Sketch-Book between the *Eroica* and the *Waldstein*.

82. " It is so long since true joy echoed in my heart ! O when, O when, Divine One, shall I feel it again in the temple of Nature and of men ? Never ? No ! O, that would be too hard." (The concluding words of the Testament.)

83. All the entries are in ink ; they must therefore have been made in the house in the winter days.

84. The ordinary translation of this term is " development," which seems to me inadequate ; it smacks of the student. We shall see later the true nature of Beethoven's *Durchführung*.

85. With Haydn it is sometimes equal to the first section, and once, even, rather longer.

86. Although in almost all his later symphonies the *Durchführung* is as ample as the first section, in none of them does it attain to such gigantic proportions as in the *Eroica*. Here are the figures, as given by Alfred Lorenz, of the proportions of the first section to the *Durchführung* in the fourth to ninth symphonies: fourth, 154 : 152 ; fifth, 124 : 123 ; sixth, 138 : 140 ; seventh, 114 : 97 ; eighth, 103 : 86 ; ninth, 150 : 141.

87. The design quoted above appears on one of the earliest pages of the Sketch-Book (p. 4). See Nottebohm, p. 28 of the re-issue of 1924.

88. I propose to devote a work to the analysis of the laws that seem to govern the creative subconscious.

89. From about bar 340 to bar 400.

90. In the *Neues Beethoven Jahrbuch*, edited by Adolf Sandberger, 1924.

91. Along with the fifth symphony, which, with even more rigour, realises the same exactitude of proportions: I. 124 × 2 ; II. 123 ; III. 126 + 129.

92. And whose scores he played marvellously on the piano. "His playing of the Handel and Gluck scores and of Sebastian Bach's fugues," says Czerny, "was unique; to the former he gave a fullness of harmony and a spirit that endowed them with a new form." Czerny

also tells us that in 1805, when the French were occupying Vienna, Beethoven was visited by "several officers and generals who were fond of music"; he played them *Iphigénie en Tauride* from the full score, and they sang, "not at all badly" [*gar nicht übel*] the soli and choruses. It is interesting to note that after the meeting Czerny took the full score and made a piano arrangement of it "as I heard him play it." This piano score has therefore an exceptional value for us.

93. *Sinfonia grande, 1804, im August. Geschrieben auf Bonaparte.*

94. A few of them only (I will specify them later) seem to me to have taken the dye of other loved lives, the perfume of which wrought upon him for a moment (the two trios, Op. 70, for instance, dedicated to the Countess Marie von Erdödy). But with a breath he disperses the perfume.

95. i.e., the fifth bar of the theme, the seventh of the movement.

96. I may perhaps be allowed to recall a dream that was once told to me: it was that of a poet absorbed in the creation of an epic. In an Italian square, at the time of the Renaissance, a funeral procession was moving along to the strains of a solemn march. A crowd in mourning was following the hero's catafalque. The dreamer saw the dead man, and, in the same moment, he *was* the dead man: he was at the same time stretched out in the coffin and floating above it, in the hymns of

the crowd and the clear sky.—This complete identification of the visionary with his vision, of the hymned hero and the hymn, is assuredly realised in the adagio of the *Eroica*.

97. Beethoven's way of writing *meilleur* above a sketch he has selected as the best.

98. "*Dann aber beginnt in meinem Kopfe die Verarbeitung in die Breite, in die Enge, Höhe und Tiefe . . . Und da ich mir bewusst bin, was ich will, so verlässt mich die zugrundeliegende Idee niemals . . .*" (1822).

99. In the Sketch-Book of 1800 (*Ein Notierungsbuch von L. van Beethoven*, Breitkopf & Härtel, 1927) we can see how this theme is already occupying Beethoven. It is curious that in the Sketch-Book it should immediately follow the first sketches for the *sonata quasi una fantasia*, Op. 27, No. 1 (the fourth movement, allegro vivace); and the essential similarity between the two, which had been overlooked at first, is now clear, and reveals the primary mood from which they came.

100. The seventh of the *Douze contredanses pour orchestre*, published, without opus number, in 1803 (p. 137 of Nottebohm's Thematic Catalogue, 1868).

101. *Variationen mit einer Fuge* (E flat major), on a theme from the ballet *Die Geschöpfe des Prometheus*, dedicated to Count Moritz Lichnowsky.

102. As regards Handel, see my book on him (Alcan), pp. 144–146, and my article in the *S.I.M.* for May and July 1910 (on the alleged plagiarisms of Handel), in

which I analyse the mechanism of his creative genius. Certain melodies of his slumbered in him all his life, finding the fullness and perfection of their real meaning only twenty or thirty years after their first appearance.

As regards Beethoven we shall have to study the mysterious growth to their final flowering of certain famous themes, such as that of the *Ode to Joy*.

In the Sketch-Book of 1801-1802 the tremendous motive of the first allegro of the sonata Op. 111 appears (twenty years earlier!) as the first sketch for the andante of the violin sonata, Op. 30, No. 1.

103. The Introduction that immediately follows the overture (allegro non troppo).

104. The finale of the ballet (allegretto).

105. Also jottings on the *Murmeln der Bäche* (" the murmur of the brooks "), and the observation (recalling Leonardo's notes in his *Trattato della Pittura*), *je grösser der Bach, je tiefer der Ton* (" the bigger the brook, the deeper the tone ").

All the sketches now mentioned are found in the same Book as those for the *Eroica*.

106. The sketch goes on to indicate the trio in the major.

107. Then comes a sketch of the lay-out of the first movement.

108. In his rapid review of the Sketch-Books Nottebohm has distinguished some thirty vocal and fifty instrumental works (symphonies and sonatas among them) the ideas for which Beethoven has noted down, without ever having completed them.

109. I give this chapter the title of the *Appassionata* because this work forms the peak of the first twenty-three piano sonatas. It is like Mont Blanc towering above the Alpine mass. But before climbing the peak I propose to explore the whole range.

110. According to the accounts (which agree with each other) of Ries and other eye-witnesses, the dedication of the *Eroica* was torn up by Beethoven when the news came of the coronation of Napoleon. The score must therefore have been completed by the beginning of May 1804.

111. Marx and Lenz have difficulty in accepting it as *echt* Beethoven.

112. See Jean Escarra's Introduction to Marliave's book, *Les Quatuors de Beethoven*.

113. See his *Beethoven*, 1927.

114. One of the "glorious moments,"—a humorous allusion to Beethoven's cantata *Der glorreiche Augenblick*, Op. 136, written in 1814 for the Congress of Vienna.

115. "The characteristic features of these compositions, that extend as far as 1817, are : At bottom, the work is essentially exterior and objective. . . . The intimate life of Beethoven, with some rare exceptions, has not yet directly inspired his music ; the artist remains outside." (Escarra, *op. cit.*, p. IX.)

116. "One man, one word !" A favourite motto of Beethoven.

117. *Ich bin nur wenig zufrieden mit meinen bisherigen Arbeiten; von heute an will ich einen neuen Weg einschlagen.*

118. The sonatas were published on the 14th August, 1802. This fact fixes the date of the conversation; Czerny's memory was at fault when he attributed it to 1803.

119. "*Am 2 ten Juni.—Finale immer simpler—alle Klavier Musik ebenfalls.—Gott weiss es—warum auf mich noch meine Klavier-Musik immer den schlechtesten Eindruck [macht], besonders wenn sie schlecht gespielt wird.*" (Cf. Nottebohm: *Zweite Beethoveniana*, p. 446.)

120. Lenz. Vincent d'Indy.

121. Blanche Selva.

122. Escarra, *loc. cit.*

123. It will be found in Thayer, II. 146-147, along with other testimonies. Moscheles' teacher, Dionysus Weber, a man of standing in his day, the founder and director of the Prague Conservatoire, forbade his pupils to go outside the works of Sebastian Bach, Mozart, and Clementi. Moscheles heard his comrades speaking of a new composer who " wrote the oddest stuff possible, such as no one could either play or understand ; crazy music, in opposition to all rule." Little Moscheles [he was then about ten years old] " secretly copied " the *Pathétique*, for, as he says, " my pocket-money would not suffice for the purchase of it. The novelty of its style was so attractive to me, and I became so enthusiastic in my

admiration of it that I forgot myself so far as to mention my new acquisition to my master, who reminded me of his injunction, and warned me not to play or study any eccentric productions until I had based my style upon more solid models. Without, however, minding his injunctions, I seized upon the pianoforte works of Beethoven as they successively appeared, and in them found a solace and a delight such as no other composer afforded me."

124. Article in the *Allgemeine Musikalische Zeitung*, 1797 : " Beethoven's abundance of ideas too often leads him to the wild piling up of ideas one on the other, and the grouping of them in so bizarre a way that the result is frequently only an obscure artificiality or an artificial obscurity." (*Die Fülle von Ideen veranlasst Beethoven noch zu oft Gedanken wild aufeinander zu häufen und sie vermittelst einer etwas bizarren Manier dergestalt zu gruppieren, dass nicht selten eine dunkele Künstlichkeit oder eine künstliche Dunkelheit hervorgebracht wird.*)

125. If it comes to that, it would be more correct to point out the relationship between the opening theme of the *Eroica* and that of the first movement of Stamitz's symphony in E flat.

126. I may refer the reader again to my study of *Israel in Egypt*, where I show what becomes of the insignificant figures of Stradella, Erba and the others when Handel sets to work on them.

127. Twenty similar testimonies relating to the young Beethoven could be quoted.

128. "*Besonnenheit, Selbstdisziplin, Entsagung, Bescheidenheit.*"

129. "*Er hat so präzis geordnet, so energisch geherrscht, wie Mozart kaum jemals, Haydn nur in seinen besten Werken.*"

130. For the benefit of the lay reader, let me say that sonata-form is not the same thing as the sonata. It has a much vaster sense, for it adapts itself to a great number of musical genres,—quartet or symphony, overture or concerto.

131. It is a notable fact that, according to Czerny, Beethoven, when numbering his works, gave Op. 57 (the *Appassionata*) the number 54, for he was reckoning only the works in sonata-form, including among them the *Eroica* symphony.

132. The masterly study of Immanuel Faist—it dates from 1845, and has been re-issued in the new Beethoven collection of Adolf Sandberger (*Neues Beethoven-Jahrbuch, 1924*)—contains a detailed account of the evolution of the piano sonata from Kuhnau and Domenico Scarlatti, the first men of genius to cultivate the form, down to the death of Philipp Emanuel Bach in 1788; it was an epoch of rich flowering, in which all the constitutive elements of the classical sonata were worked out. Faist's list shows fifty-five composers and a total of more than two hundred sonatas in thirty or forty years. (*Beiträge zur Geschichte der Claviersonate, von ihrem ersten Auftreten an bis auf C. F. Emanuel Bach.*)
This essay, that belongs to a now distant past, may be usefully supplemented by Wilhelm Fischer's chapter on

the development of the sonata-form in the monumental *Handbuch der Musikgeschichte* (pp. 717-756) published in 1924 under the editorship of Guido Adler. Fischer's article contains the result of the most recent researches into the subject. He shows how the " return to nature " proclaimed by Rousseau became the watchword of the new style ; the ideal of it was melody, simple and well-defined forms, clear-cut dynamic and rhythmic contrasts, sentiment, and poetry of expression, the conversational manner of good society.

133. I cannot agree with M. Vincent d'Indy when he says of the first movement, in his *Cours de composition musicale,* " Allegro : a word that refers rather to a sentiment expressive of gaiety than to speed of performance." " Gaiety," it is true, was the primary sense of the word. But when it quitted Italy its real meaning was soon forgotten, and it was employed at random. It is for this reason that Beethoven, in a letter to Mosel in 1817 on the subject of Maelzel's metronome, rages against these " indications of the time " (*Bezeichnungen des Zeitmasses*) that come from " the barbarous age of music." " For," he says, " what can be more absurd than the term allegro, that means merry (*lustig*), when the movement often expresses the very opposite to this ? " And again, " As far as I am concerned, I long ago determined to give up these ridiculous terms, allegro, andante, adagio, presto ; Maelzel's metronome makes this possible. I give you my word that I will not employ them in any of my new works." He could not keep his word, however, for other terms were not of general

acceptance. But it is quite clear that " allegro," for him, had no other signification than " fast."

134. We must never forget that this man who, in his art, was so completely master of himself, began publication only when, at the age of twenty-five, he was quite sure of himself and the contour of his personality was already defined.

135. In the Sketch-Book of 1800 the scherzo of the violin sonata Op. 23 occurs to him in the first place in the form of a *Minuetto*, going heavily on its feet, with no elisions, no syncopations.

136. I speak now of the professional musicians, who are rarely, and to-day less than ever, in accord with the larger public.

137. Nagel, in his classic work on Beethoven's sonatas, makes, in this connection, a comparison, that has a touch of regret in it, between the Germans of the past and those of to-day.

138. Beethoven allowed an edition of the adagio of his first sonata, Op. 2, No. 1, to be engraved with words (*Klage : Lament*) by Wegeler. He asked his Bonn friend also to find a suitable text for the theme with variations of Op. 26. Who has not heard other Beethoven adagios adapted for singing ! (Especially that of Op. 2, No. 3, and that of the *Pathétique*.) Disapprove as we may of these sacrilegious arrangements—mostly stupid as they are—they testify to the vocal nature of these instrumental movements. One understands why Beethoven

has written relatively so little music for the voice. His piano and his orchestra *sing* much more than those of his predecessors did : he anthropomorphises them. In process of time they assume more and more the character of direct speech. And this character is particularly noticeable in the sketches. While studying one of those (it is in my own possession) for the famous second movement (the allegretto) of the seventh symphony, I have had the feeling that I was reading an actual monologue in recitative.

139. " The beloved " of that period (1797).

140. The majority of artists of to-day, who, by reaction against the rising democracy out of which they have come, aim at an aristocratic detachment, will not admit the validity of this " public word." I have had occasion to explain what I mean by it when speaking of the *Eroica*. I believe that if the first condition of greatness is to have a great soul, *l'alma sdegnosa* that parsimoniously reserves itself for itself and its imitators—Narcisse and Corydon !—is doomed to sterility. The greatest artists— Handel, Bach, Beethoven—thought for themselves and spoke for all ; their veracious works appeal to large communities.

141. See the celebrated adagio of Op. 106.

142. " Each one," said Beethoven to Schindler in 1823, " perceived in this largo the state of mind of a melancholic, together with all the many degrees of light and shade there are in the picture of Melancholy."

143. In 1823, Beethoven, who was at that time out of humour with the new musical generation, *laudator temporis acti*, recalled the fact that the first hearers of his two sonatas Op. 14 (in E major and G major, 1798-1799) had recognised in them " the conflict of two principles " (*den Streit zweier Principe*) or " a Dialogue between man and woman, or between lover and beloved " (*Dialog zwischen Mann und Frau, oder Liebhaber und Geliebte*)— especially in the second of the sonatas. Writers on Beethoven have wrongly tried to cast doubt on this because they find it inconvenient both to their admiration for the composer and to their own conception of music. We must accept it, however, for what it is—one of those rather trivial plays of fancy, devoid of theoretic importance, in which a great artist likes to indulge himself occasionally. We have only to read the finale of the rondo scherzo of the G major sonata, in which this dualism of motives is most clearly set forth, to recognise the facetious character of it, the deliberate playfulness. *Le Roi s'amuse.*

144. I can indicate here only the more salient types. It will be easy for the reader, however, to detect this alternation in the later Beethoven sonatas—and even, for that matter, among those of this youthful period, in the sequence of the movements of the same sonata. The B flat sonata (Op. 22) is as closed to sentimentality as that in A flat (Op. 26, with the variations) is accessible to it. The sombre and ardent *Moonlight* sonata has on the one side of it the worldly grace of the Op. 27, No. 1 (the first of the sonatas *quasi una fantasia*), and on the

other side the pastoral saunter of the D major (Op. 28), in which there is no trace of passion. Compare with each other, again, the three sonatas of Op. 31, or the *Waldstein* and the *Appassionata*. It seems as if, after each tempest of the soul, the artist, in order to recover his equilibrium, plunges once more into the play of æsthetic or the objective contemplation of Nature.

145. In the finale of this same Op. 10, No. 1, there are foreshadowings of the torments of the finales of the *Moonlight* and the *Appassionata*.

146. Wasielewski suggests the obsequies of Mignon, in *Wilhelm Meister* : " *Kinder, kehret ins Leben zurück . . . Entflieht der Nacht ! Tag und Lust und Dauer ist das Loos der Lebendigen . . .*" (" Children, return to life ! Escape from the night ! Daytime and pleasure and duration are the lot of the living ! "). Nagel, more prosaically, observes that after having conducted the dead man to his last home with a Funeral March, the military musicians return briskly from the cemetery, sounding the double !

147. The Sketch-Book of 1800 gives on pp. 52–56 the theme of the first movement, with this indication : "*Sonate pour M.* —— *váriée tutt a fatto, poi Menuetto, o qualche altro pezzo characteristica come p. E. una Marcia in as moll e poi questo.*" What follows in the Sketch-Book is a different finale from the one we know, and that Beethoven had previously sketched out (so that originally this formed no part of the sonata) ; but the finale indicated was still more superficial. Immediately afterwards we find the trio of the March, and then the

opening of the *Marcia* (but without the designation of " Funeral "). Further on (p. 132-2) the March is found mixed up with the pirouettes of *Prometheus* ; and (p. 137) its rhythm, tapped out on the piano, suddenly eventuates in the first movement of Op. 27, No. 1.

148. I make use of this name, consecrated by custom, without attaching to it any importance beyond that of an association of images, or rather of impressions, happily lighted upon later. It is said to have been invented by Rellstab, the poet of so many of Schubert's Lieder.

149. Of course I do not mean by this that Beethoven improvised out of pure abundance of heart. This great improviser at the piano was never an improviser when he sat down with a pen in his hand. (Moreover, even at the piano he worked out in advance the procedure of his improvisation : the proofs of this are to be found in certain notes from his Sketch-Books that were recently sold in Berlin.)
The sketches for the *Moonlight* sonata, which were discovered a little while ago and published in facsimile by Schenker, show the rigorous way he worked at his ideas. It is clear that a great artist, even when carried away by his heart, knows how to control it, how to hold in the disordered beats of it with a firm discipline. What I wish to bring out is the fact that the laws he thus imposes on himself are not exterior to the emotion : they are the *natural* laws of feeling, released by the mind. And the scientific researches of the most penetrating æstheticians of to-day (cf. Edouard Monod-Herzen's

Principes de morphologie, 1926/7) prove that these *natural* laws are identical at their source with those of the purest art. But in Beethoven's day only a genius could have the instinctive perception of them. Science and the intelligence had not conceived the relationship of them, and refused to admit the legitimate æsthetic of the laws that come from immediate feeling. Beethoven himself, as we shall see, after having hit upon them in a violent access of passion, was infected with doubt, and returned on his steps to the " formal " æsthetic. We shall later meet with a striking example of this in the recoil (glorious however) from the second to the third *Leonora* overture.

150. For the bass also is a melody, the profound sadness of which has nothing of protest about it, as the other has, but accepts sorrow and awaits the end of it : the twelve-bars pedal in the middle of the movement, and the funeral march rhythm on which it concludes, express clearly the deliverance of deep sleep—nothingness.

151. I denounce the treason of almost all the editors, who, shamelessly altering the original accentuation, have substituted the dot (·) for the accent (') in this sharp-cutting accompaniment, in spite of Beethoven's express indication : " *Wo über die Note* (·), *darf kein* (') *statt dessen stehen und so umgekehrt—es ist nicht gleichgültig ♩♩♩ und ♩̇♩̇♩̇ . . .*" (To Carl Holz, 1825). Cf. Nottebohm, *Beethoveniana*, 1872, pp. 107-125.

152. According to a rhythm of thought that is often to be found in Beethoven, the impulse gathers momentum

till the last two leaps (bars 7 and 8) change from a duration of two bars to a single one.

153. Another essential marking that is ignored in modern editions is the *con sordino*, that is expressly indicated and repeated by Beethoven under each of these furious gallopades, as far as the two chords that curb them, the first of which is marked *sforzando*, and both of them *senza sordino* :—

[musical notation: con sordino ... senza sordino]

154. I observe curious resemblances between the allegro of the *Pathétique* and No. 9 of *Prometheus* (the scene of the "Tragic Muse") ; and the composer's markings for the melodrama—*piangendo . . . va in collera*, etc.,—would serve also to explain his intentions in this sonata. It is to be noted that, in the Sketch-Book of 1800, among the sketches for the ballet we find the opening of the *Pathétique* copied textually by Beethoven (p. 49).

155. Insufficient attention has been given to Gluck's influence on the young Beethoven. For myself I have no doubt of it—not as regards symphonic construction, in which the composer of *Orfeo* had not much skill, but as regards dramatic expression, energy of accent, concision of musical speech, breadth and clarity of design, as well as the monumental homophony, the mighty piling up of passion, and a kind of colossal sculpture

that reminds us of the Pergamene school. Gluck had less influence on Beethoven through the other side of his genius—the Elysian perfection of some of his pictures, which are rather affiliated to the eighteenth century ideal, purified by a ray from Pompeii and renascent Greece, than to the monumental and popular ideal of the Revolution and the Empire, of which Gluck was one of the precursors.

Gluck was one of the five musicians whose portraits he had, or wished to have, in his room : in the Fischhoff manuscript we read : " 1815 : *Handels, Bachs, Glucks, Mozarts, Haydns Porträte in meinem Zimmer, sie können mir auf Duldung Anspruch machen helfen.*"

It was not in the theatre, however, that Beethoven obtained his knowledge of Gluck. During his residence in Vienna, as far as about 1807, no Gluck operas were given ; and at Bonn he could have heard, at most, only one of his opéras-comiques. But, as I have already pointed out in the preceding chapter, Beethoven was an admirable interpreter of Gluck's scores on the piano : old melomaniacs preserved the emotional memory of these performances for years after. And what would we not have given to have heard the wild Dance of the Furies (No. 28 of *Orfeo*) let loose under the fingers of the man of the *Appassionata* ! At the mere thought of it I feel a shudder in my marrow.

156. Even in the rondo of the sonata of Op. 28—a pastoral idyll that did not lend itself to oratorical dialectic—Beethoven cannot resist the sonata-form that allows him to work out his impressions musically. And

it is with great art that he accomplishes this *tour de force*.

157. Caution is necessary with this word! It carries no connotation of sentimentality, of which there is no trace in the always virile emotion of Beethoven. I have already drawn attention to his dislike for tearful people. If there were tears in the *Moonlight*, they are tears of rage, tears of fire. And if you listen carefully to the *Marcia funebre sulla morte d'un eroe* in the sonata Op. 26 you will not find the least touch of the Chopin softness and tenderness. Of the two words: *Marcia funebre*, it is the March that dominates the funereal sentiment: Beethoven's heroes die on their feet.

158. Paul Mies, in his excellent study of the sketches (*Die Bedeutung der Skizzen Beethovens zur Erkenntnis seines Stiles*, 1925), ably demonstrates Beethoven's instinctive tendency towards four-square proportions, towards a slightly mechanical regularity of melodic types and the 4, 8, 12, or 16-bar succession of these; as well as the huge effort he made later, in the period of his maturity, to escape from the bondage of cæsuras and strophic divisions and make his melody "infinite." (For example, the Cavatina of the B flat quartet, Op. 130.) This is also the explanation, or one of the explanations, of the fugue-themes to which he had recourse at that time. Yet he never succeeded in more than half disguising the magnetic attraction that square numbers had for him. I shall return to this question in the final volume of these Essays, in which I hope to devote a chapter to "The Mechanism of Interior Creation in Beethoven."

159. I group these two sonatas together because they appeared at the same time, at the commencement of 1803, and because the sketches for them are found in the same book, that of October 1801 to May 1802. Op. 31, No. 3 (in E flat major) did not appear until 1804, and was added to the others in 1805.

160. Czerny, whose indications we do wrong to ignore, for he had studied this sonata with Beethoven, tells us that the first movement should be played with energy, humour and wit (*energisch, launig und geistreich*), and the final rondo very fast, like a whirlwind.

161. The intention of the composer is made more evident by the sketches, in which he notes in the first place the guitar accompaniment, the melody not appearing till later. (Cf. Nottebohm : *Zwei Skizzenbücher von Beethoven aus den Jahren 1801 bis 1803*, new edition, 1924, pp. 36, 37.)

162. August Halm has made an admirable analysis of this in his *Beethoven* (1927). Beethoven has hardly established the tonality before he abandons it, to return to it after a series of modulations that delight in keeping the mind of the listener in a state of uncertainty and suspense. In Halm's opinion the openings of the two sonatas of Op. 31 constitute an historic event in musical evolution ; " they bring with them a complete renewal in music, or, more exactly, in the harmonic tonal essence." And he believes that Beethoven was fully conscious of his discovery.

163. I shall reserve the discussion of his literary readings for a separate chapter. (I have already dealt with them, in part, in the essay entitled *Fonti Fortitudinis ac Fidei* in the *Beethoven Festbuch*, Bonn, 1927.) Beethoven was an ardent reader, all the more so because the loss of his hearing deprived him of the delights of conversation; his misfortune did not prevent him from preserving, to the end of his days, a burning and always alert curiosity that kept him well-informed as to all important European events. We shall have the evidence of this later in his Conversation Books, commencing in 1819. (Cf. my short study of the *Konversationshefte* of 1819-1820, in the Beethoven Numbers of *Vorwärts* and *Le Semeur*, March 1927.) Let us confine ourselves here, however, to his specifically musical readings. He had exceptional opportunities, far beyond what any other great composer has had either the means or the will to utilise: I refer to the magnificent library of the Archduke Rudolf, that now forms an important part of the musical section of the Vienna *Nationalbibliotek*. Insufficient attention has been given to what Beethoven owed to this incessant study of the music of all epochs. He bathed the rock of his own hard genius in it, renewed it, gave it flexibility, especially in the period following his fortieth year, when he retired into himself to practise an inward contemplation like that of the Indian yogi.

164. The firm of Streicher had seceded in 1802 from the great firm of piano-makers Stein-Streicher, that had been established in Vienna since 1794. Beethoven's relations with it were always friendly.

165. "*Streicher hat das Weiche, zu leicht Nachgebende und prallend Rollende der anderen Wiener Instrumente verlassen, und auf Beethovens Rath und Begehren, seinen Instrumenten mehr gegenhaltendes, Elastisches gegeben, damit der Virtuose, der mit Kraft und Bedeutung vorträgt, das Instrument zum Anhalten und Tragen, zu den seinen Druckern und Abzugen mehr in seiner Gewalt hat. Er hat dadurch seinen Instrumenten einen grössern und mannichfachern Charakter verschafft: so dass sie jeden Virtuosen, der nicht bloss das Leichtglänzende in den Spielart sucht, mehr wie jedes andere Instrument befriedigen müssen.*" (Cf. Thayer, II. 556.)

166. In the Sketch-Book of 1803 that Nottebohm has analysed, *Clavier-Uebungen* lie cheek by jowl with the first sketches of the first movement of the *Waldstein*; and the relationship between the two is indisputable. (See pp. 58 and 59 of the new edition by Paul Mies, 1924.)

167. I shall explain what I mean by this when I come to the second and more characteristic of the two sonatas, the *Appassionata*.

168. "... *Ein liebes, zauberisches Mädchen ... die mich liebt und die ich liebe ... Wäre mein Gehör nicht ... O, die Welt wollte ich umspannen ... ohne dieses Uebel! ... Nichts von Ruhe! ... Ich will dem Schicksal in den Rachen greifen ...* etc. *O, es ist so schön, das Leben tausendmal leben!* ... etc."

169. Pp. 27 and 28 of Paul Mies' edition of the *Zwei Skizzenbücher*, 1924.

170. Let me say at once that if this fact is less visible in the majority of the other works of Beethoven, it none the

less exists. Where the microscope of "cellular" analysis sees only the budding of a motive from a few notes, Beethoven already had within him the potential *Idea of the whole work*. The whole oak is in the acorn. But his obscurely gestating consciousness could see the child only after being delivered of it. There is no question here of an after-conceived work of development, at the bidding of the intellect, but of a work of parturition, that is before all things a work of the flesh.

171. It might be a Wagnerian recitative :—

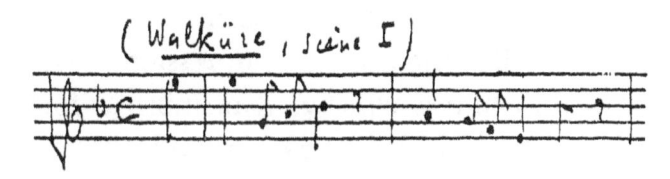

(Walküre, scène I)

Or, further on (cf. the second recitative of the sonata) :—

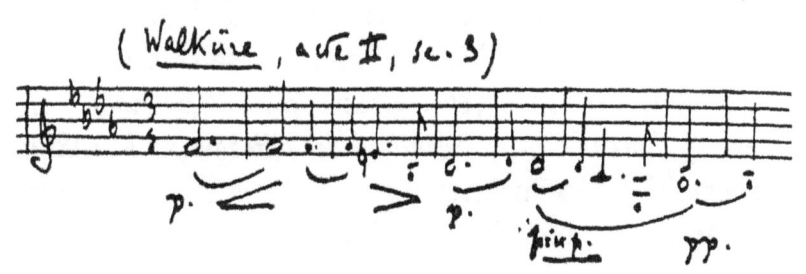

(Walküre, acte II, sc. 3)

Both are motives expressive of prostration. The psychological relationship is beyond question.

172. But the performer must guard against a melodramatic pathos of effect. Beethoven's marking is explicit—"*semplice.*"

173. Cf. my *Empédocle d'Agrigente*, pp. 34, 35.

174. According to Czerny, who is a reliable witness, Beethoven modelled it on the gallop of a horse :—

This, of course, has drawn indignant protests from the critics, those austere guardians of the dignity of art. But we may ask whether these good people have the least conception of the artist and of the creative processus. It goes without saying that a Beethoven would not permit himself the silly amusement of imitating a horse's gallop ! But the acoustic impression of the gallop let loose within him a whirlwind of musical forms. Between the object of the sensation and the perceived impression a whole world lies ; and genius reveals itself in the power with which the external phenomena reverberate in him and become transformed. " In the heart of a musician everything is music," said that son of Beethoven, the little Jean Christophe. " *Bei ihm*," says Czerny, " *wurde jeder Schall, jede Bewegung, Musik und Rhythmus*." ("In him, every sound, every movement, became music and rhythm.") It was the same process by which Leonardo saw smiling or grimacing faces in the crevices of the wall or the flames on the hearth.

Others, such as Nagel, have seen a resemblance between the first phrase of this allegretto and a passage in Mozart's symphony in D major ; but this is to misconceive absolutely the meaning of this music. For if the notes are almost the same, the four-four metre gives those of Mozart a quite different rhythm. Now Beethoven's motive is in the first place rhythm, and melody only in the second place.

175. The progressive calming of the coda of the tumultuous first movement prepares the way for the adagio, which is related to it through the third of the key. And hardly has it exhaled its last sigh of ecstatic lassitude when the flood of the allegretto once more breaks into the tonality of the first movement. But, by Oberon's magic, the sombre D minor, that at first expressed a face in torment, now expresses fantasy and laughter.

176. Remember that the *Pastoral* will not be completed and performed until 1808.

177. Or rather a second or a third, for there is a whole series of them in Beethoven's work. As I have already pointed out, this is one of the main veins of his genius.

178. See Nottebohm, *Neue Beethoveniana*, p. 58.

179. No analogy, of course, with the landscapes of the painter! " *Mehr Ausdruck der Empfindung als Mahlerey.*" "More the expression of feeling than painting.") Notations of the soul, not of the eyes.

180. The lovely *Andante grazioso con moto* in F major, which was published separately, without an opus number, May 1806 :—

It will be found in Breitkopf's collection of *Kleinere Stücke für das Pianoforte*.

This work (the player of which will do well to remember the rôle originally assigned to it at the core of the *Waldstein* sonata) has a delicacy of touch that ought to ensure its being better known. It is an exquisite piece of painting, slightly lost in too large a frame; its dreamy languor shows how young Beethoven's heart was even at that date. But the second motive, repeated three times, has in its outline and the variations of its accompaniment, the values of which vary from the crotchet to the double and triple crotchet, a hint of the heroic fanfare of the andante of the C minor symphony. And in the coda there is an abrupt modulation from F major to G flat minor the lovely melancholy shadow of which evokes the *Wehmut* of one of the songs to *The Distant Beloved*. I have no doubt that Beethoven put into this andante many of his more intimate emotions at this period of his life. Dare I say that this is perhaps why he sacrificed it? Too little notice has been taken of an extraordinary fact—the extended slow movements into which Beethoven poured the deepest depths of his heart, those adagios and largos that were the jewels of his first twenty sonatas and were the special delight of the public of the time, afterwards disappear from his piano sonatas. Either he dispenses with them altogether or he drastically cuts the proportions of them down, reducing them to the rôle of an introductory link to the finale. It is not until we come to the monumental adagio of Op. 106, fourteen years later, that we meet again, in the piano music, with those Soliloquies the gates of which are closed to the external world. It is as if in the maturity of his classical age Beethoven stood on guard against his natural propensity towards sentimental expression. From the *Waldstein* onwards to Op. 106 he reduces the confidences of his adagios to the minimum. The rôle of the two allegros, particularly the last one, is correspondingly enlarged both in extent and in significance.

181. Cf. Nottebohm, pp. 61-63.

182. *Papillons*, Op. 2, *Carnaval*, Op. 9, *Winterzeit*, No. 39 of the *Album für die Jugend*, Op. 68, *Liederkreis*, Op. 39, No. 4, etc. (Cf. Max Friedländer, *Das Grossvaterlied und der Grossvatertanz (Sonderdruck aus der Kretzschmar-Festschrift.*) In this connection it is very curious that this popular melody should have been practically the only one ever used by Beethoven : and it is open to argument whether he did so consciously. Max Friedländer, it is true, mentions a second use of it in his article *Eigenleben von Volksliedmelodien (Sonderdruck aus dem Bericht über Musikwissenschaftlichen Kongress in Basel, 1924)*—the second theme of the rondo of the piano concerto in C major, Op. 15 (1798) :—

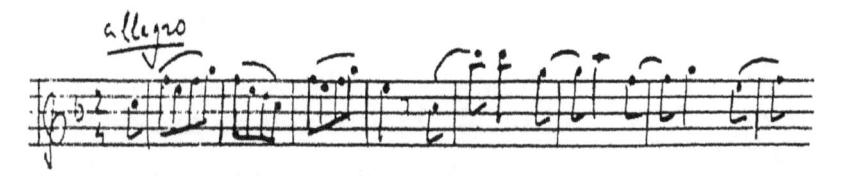

He traces this to " *einer uralten Volksweise.*" But he himself recognises the possibility of such " *Urmelodien,*"

based on the simplest of tonal successions, having been hit upon afresh in all epochs, without any imitation of an anterior model or any knowledge of one. This seems to me a certainty as regards Beethoven, whose constructive mind followed and sought out the simplest paths.

We must accept from Herr Friedländer, then, the surprising fact that Beethoven has not handled a single German *Volkslied*, and that it is very difficult,—almost impossible, indeed—to find in his music any direct influences of the *Volksliedstil*. (All the same, I think we ought to search more carefully not merely his published works but the Sketch-Books. In the *Notierungsbuch* of 1800 I fancy I recognise (pp. 85-86) more than one popular melody flitting across his memory.) It is quite otherwise with the masters who preceded him, including Bach. Now as Beethoven's art, by virtue of its homophonic tendencies, its broad, clear, simple lines, its evident desire to address itself to all, is in essence much more popular than that of any other composer (except Handel), we are driven to believe that this exclusion of the *Volkslied* was æsthetically deliberate on his part. He wanted to make his art a people's art yet all his own. Precisely because he and his art were in essence " popular " in the purest sense, precisely because he spoke naturally a language of the soundest emotions, made to be shared by all, he was able to dispense with the *Volkslied*. His people were within him. These " *uralten Volksweisen* " were indeed the very measure of his thought. When he did not find them at the first attempt he none the less knew that they were germinating at the root of his consciousness; he had only to dig, and he was sure they would leap forth.

183. Cf. Nottebohm, *ibid.*, p. 64.

184. Examples of this are the last movement of the C minor symphony and the splendid second finale of *Fidelio*.

185. At any rate in the maturity of his creative work (1800-1810), which is clearly classic. I will go into this question more thoroughly in connection with the later periods. No doubt his nature and his art became profoundly transformed.

186. The first sketches appear in a Sketch-Book of 1804, in the middle of the work on the second act of *Leonora*; they will be found in Nottebohm's *Zweite Beethoveniana*, pp. 437-442. I have already mentioned how, according to Ries, the theme of the first movement was discovered, hummed, or roared ("*hatte er den ganzen Weg über für sich gebrummt oder teilweise geheult, immer herauf und herunter, ohne bestimmte Noten zu singen*") during a walk in Döbling in the summer of 1804, and how, as soon as Beethoven had returned home, he ran to the piano and, his hat still on his head, ground the notes under an avalanche. But according to Schindler he finished the composition of it in Hungary in the summer of 1806, during a short visit to his friend Count Franz Brunsvik, to whom the work is dedicated. He had the manuscript with him when, in October 1806, he fled in a temper from Prince Lichnowsky's Silesian castle. A torrential rain soaked

it through. When he returned to Vienna he showed Frau Bigot the still damp manuscript, which she dried then and there; and he presented it to her. The manuscript, that still shows traces of the rain, came at a later date into the possession of the Library of the Paris Conservatoire. The work appeared in Vienna in February 1807 as "*LIV Sonate composée pour pianoforte*, Op. 57, with the dedication "*à monsieur le comte François de Brunsvik.*"

187. The essential thing is to define "passion." It is curious to see the amiable disdain with which Czerny, lowering it a few degrees in the scale, transferred the title of *Appassionata* to the youthful sonata in E flat major, Op. 7, "to Babette,"—or at any rate to the first movement of this. The pianists of to-day seem to have no suspicion of the meaning of the work. They make an entertainment, almost a round, of it. Which of them ever dreams of giving it its true character of headlong passion?

188. In this connection perhaps the author of a *Life of Michael Angelo* may be allowed to define the true purpose of a book that many readers have misconceived. I have tried to re-create the Michael Angelo of the *Letters* and the *Rime*, the man in his daily life, the Orestes tormented by the Furies, the Prometheus gnawed by the vulture, the Self-Executioner. I had been penetrated by the cry of his suffering, and I gave it forth again without attenuation, without addition, that the world might know

"*quanto sangue costa*"

the radiant splendour of the work of art. The shadow presupposes the light. The crucified one bore it within him; and I do not forget it. Nor should the public that reads me forget it. The Buonarotti who groans like Job on his dunghill has come down from the scaffolding in the Sixtine, where, his head thrown back, he has just been contemplating Jehovah face to face in the blue gap of the sky. When afterwards he stumbles back to life, he suffers from the vertigo of the whirlwind of God. In my *Life of Michael Angelo* I tried to express this divine vertigo. In my other book on Michael Angelo my first concern was the work and the constructive spirit at the back of it.

189. But before the year is out he reconciles himself with Breuning in a touching letter, in which he reproaches himself and begs for forgiveness; and the excellent Breuning, in the following year, writes an affectionate and enthusiastic poem in honour of his friend, which he has printed and distributed during the first performances of *Fidelio*.

190. The Press gave the composer the paternal advice to " return to his first symphony."

191. " Ill-knit ! " The critics of to-day would say that the seams are of too thick a thread !

192. It is not preserved in its first projected form, though it retains the same movement and the same tonality.

193. Reinhold Zimmermann has recently devoted a fine article of homage to him: *Anton Schindler : ein Leben für*

Beethoven—in the *Beethoven-Almanach der Deutschen Musikbücherei auf das Jahr 1927* (Gustav Bosse Verlag, Regensburg). He shows that Schindler, who has been so often attacked or derided, has in the end been proved right, in the eyes of modern scientific criticism, as against those of his rivals who indulged in Beethoven biography.

194. He did assert it ; as well as he could do in words, which he never handled easily, he defined the frontiers of music and the other arts. Writing to Wilhelm Gerhard of Leipzig on the 15th July, 1817, he excuses himself for not being able to set his Anacreontic *Lieder* to music :

" . . . The description of a picture belongs to painting. The poet can also regard himself as fortunate in this respect [in description] ; he is a master whose domain is not as limited in this respect as mine. But mine extends further in other regions, and the others cannot so easily come to our empire."

" *Die Beschreibung eines Bildes gehört zur Malerei ; auch der Dichter kann sich hierin noch als einen Meister glücklich schätzen, dessen Gebiet hierin nicht so begrenzt ist als das meinige, sowie es sich wieder in andern Regionen weiter erstreckt und man unser Reich nicht so leicht erreichen kann.*"

195. The *Coriolan* overture was written and performed in 1807. In the same year he thinks of writing a *Macbeth* in collaboration with his friend Collin ; and he commences work on the sketches. His admiration for Shakespeare lasted as long as his life ; Schindler says that he was always his favourite poet, and that he knew Shakespeare's works as well as his own scores. He read them in

Eschenburg's translation; and he covered the pages with pencil notes. The third and fourth and ninth and tenth volumes of the set have been preserved; and the underlined passages have been shown in Albert Leitzmann's *Ludwig van Beethoven, Briefe und persönliche Aufzeichnungen*, 1921, Vol. II, p. 273 ff. They throw a light on Beethoven's thoughts as he read *Othello, Romeo and Juliet, Much Ado About Nothing, All's Well that Ends Well, The Merchant of Venice*, and *A Winter's Tale*. Schindler also rescued from the dispersion of Beethoven's library after his death a copy of *The Tempest* in Schlegel's translation, but in an edition of 1825; we can therefore learn nothing from it with regard to the epoch when he was writing the *Appassionata*.

196. But wrongly so! I have already reminded the reader that Beethoven protested against the leading place among his symphonies being assigned to the C minor. He himself gave it to the *Eroica*.

197. I can understand, though I cannot share it, the curious antipathy towards this sonata of some thoughtful and sensitive but rather cold connoisseurs, such as August Halm. If these heavy, emphatic, somewhat banal outlines were not vivified by the most intense passion, they would be nothing more than phrases of debate, gestures of the forum. By a sort of bravado that is only the characteristic of his style carried to its extreme, Beethoven has deprived his picture of everything in the way of a circumambient atmosphere, of landscape, and, —like Michael Angelo in his heroic nudes,—gives us only

the huge bodies naked and red, bulging with muscle. So much the better! The bodies are merely the tense network of the swelling muscles.... But how formidable is the voltage with which the apparatus is charged! If Herr Halm has not felt an electric shock from it he must be well " insulated "! Whoever has tried to bring out the meaning of the first allegro of the C minor symphony on the piano knows that no other work of Beethoven is so difficult to seize upon, for it demands an uninterrupted expenditure of energy; the line of passion is bare and unbroken, without a detail, a shadow, an ornament to afford a moment's distraction.[1] In this respect the first allegro of the *Appassionata* occupies an equivalent place among the sonatas. But here the line is much finer, broader, and more varied; it is filled with a richer blood.

198. "... *welche Beethoven selbst für seine grösste hielt,*..." says Czerny.

199. Between the *Appassionata* (Op. 57) and the two sonatas of Op. 78 (dedicated to the Brunsvik brother and sister) there came, besides the three Rasoumovsky

---

[1] I am reminded of Gluck's letter to the Bailli du Roullet after the completion of *Alceste* (1st July, 1775):—
"I go almost crazy when I run through it. The nerves are on the stretch too long, and from the first word to the last there is no relaxation of the emotion.... I have not been able to sleep for it for a month: I seem to have a hive of bees buzzing perpetually in my head.... I am now beginning to understand the skill of Quinault and Calzabigi, who have stocked their work with minor characters to give the spectator relief and afford him a little tranquillity. An opera like this is not an entertainment but a very serious occupation...."
There are no "minor characters" in the *Appassionata* and the first allegro of the C minor symphony. No, "this is not an entertainment"! And I can understand a Europe that has lost its bearings since the war not being able to find its way about in it. Beethoven's music is "a very serious occupation."

quartets, the fourth, fifth and sixth symphonies, the violin concerto, the fourth piano concerto, the Erdödy trios (Op. 70), and the *Coriolan* overture. I mention only the masterpieces.

200. Note this remarkable preoccupation, the expression of which corresponds to the latest researches of present-day æsthetic : " *die Wissenschaft der Kunst* " ! Here are Beethoven's own words :—

" . . . *dieses sein geistiges Kind ihm vor allen anderen die grössten Geburtsschmerzen, aber auch den grössten Aerger gemacht habe, es ihm daher auch am liebsten sei, und dass er der Aufbewahrung und Benutzung für die Wissenschaft der Kunst vorzugsweise werth halte . . .* "

201. *Ein Skizzenbuch von Beethoven, aus dem Jahre 1803.*

202. Treitschke and the biographers who have followed him are in error when they say that Beethoven received the libretto of *Leonora* in the winter of 1804/5. He had already written part of the work before the first performance of Paër's *Leonora* (24th October, 1804). The first date we can be sure of is that of a letter from Charlotte to Therese von Brunsvik, 20th November, 1804, in which she says that Beethoven has played to Josephine von Brunsvik " several magnificent pieces from the opera he is writing." And on the 24th November Beethoven's brother Karl writes to Breitkopf : " My brother is at present greatly (*so sehr*) occupied with his opera."

203. Nottebohm, *Zweite Beethoveniana*, 1887, pp. 409–460.

AAb

204. At any rate in the form in which it has come down to us ; for it appears that Beethoven had already composed it to another text.

We lack the sketches for Nos. 6-11 of the score, which must have been made in another Sketch-Book.

205. As late as 1823, when he is ill in a watering-place, he writes to his nephew that he would very much like to enjoy " lovely nature " ; " but we are too poor, and one must write or have nothing to live on." (" *Mais nous sommes trop pauvres et il faut écrire ou de n'avoir pas de quoi* " [in French in the letter ; 16th August, 1823].)

206. Scene No. 7. Arrival of Pizarro. Scene between Marcellina, Leonora, and Rocco.

207. Cf. Thayer, II. 466-474.

208. *Allgemeine Musik-Zeitung*, Leipzig, 8th January, 1806.

209. For Beethoven never succeeded in having his title *Leonora* retained, because of the possible confusion with Paër's *Leonora* : he had to agree to the title of *Fidelio*, that never pleased him.

210. The performances were deplorable. The exasperated composer refused to conduct the second performance ; he did not want to hear his music massacred again. " I say nothing about the wind instruments. But to have all the pianissimos, crescendos, decrescendos, fortes, and fortissimos erased from my opera is

enough to make a man give up writing." (Letter of 10th April, 1806, to Meyer, who sang Pizarro.)

211. *Zeitung für die elegante Welt*, 10th May, 1806.

212. *Der Freimüthige* (Kotzebue's paper), 11th September, 1806.

213. The pontiff whom I have just cited,—the critic of the *Freimüthige*—speaks with animosity of those friends of Beethoven " who, lauding works of this kind to the sky, force their opinion noisily on others, pursue every other talent with envious hatred, and would like to erect for Beethoven an altar on the ruins of all the other composers."

214. Thayer, whose curious *parti-pris* makes him constantly try to rehabilitate the Viennese and German public and critics at the expense of Beethoven, tries to dispute Breuning's testimony (in his letter to Wegeler of 2nd June, 1806). He goes as far as the ridiculous argument that Breuning could not have been present at the performances, for he was *Hofkriegssekretär*, and had too many other occupations as well. He cannot even understand how Breuning could have found time to re-cast the libretto of *Fidelio*. But " *qui veut trop prouver . . .* " He confutes himself, since Breuning *did* re-cast the libretto. Moreover, he found time to help in the long and painful revision of *Fidelio* in the Lichnowsky palace, as well as to write an enthusiastic poem for distribution at the performances of March/April 1806. His friendship for Beethoven recognised no obstacles:

could he have been elsewhere than by his side at a time so serious as this, in a cause he had at heart? For the rest, the *Zeitung für die elegante Welt*—that does not come under suspicion, for it treats Beethoven's work harshly —is obliged to mention " *die niedrigen Kabalen.*"

215. Bettina speaks indignantly of it in 1810.

216. The terzetto and the quartet in canon in the first act, and the duet of Marcellina and Leonora, that was later omitted from *Fidelio*.

217. It was not ready for the first performance (23rd May, 1814), and the *Ruins of Athens* overture had to be played in its stead! But it was ready for the second performance on the 26th.

218. He recalls it in one of the finest studies of his *A travers Chants*.

219. He confesses this with a moan to Treitschke in April 1814.

220. It should therefore have a more solemn movement than is usually given it to-day.

221. The flighty Giulietta: the criminal affairs of Countess Erdödy—to mention only the two women whose love and friendship kept the first place in his heart.

222. Diary of Fanny Giannatasio del Rio, 15th June, 1817.

223. In spite of a few great interpreters of the chief part. But *Leonora* is not merely a rôle : it is a musical drama, a tragedy with chorus ; and neither the directors nor the producers seem to have suspected this.

224. A recent study by Hermann W. von Waltershausen, *Zur Dramaturgie des Fidelio* (in the *Neues Beethoven Jahrbuch*, 1924), points out clearly the ordinary errors in the interpretation and the staging of the opera. It may not be superfluous to indicate here a few of those that concern the age and physical appearance of the hero.

Florestan is not a *jeune premier*, an amorous tenor ; he is a man of forty, matured in politics and already aged by experience. The player should bring out the virile, resolute, stoically resigned character of the man, which is clearly painted in the music, especially in the original version. Leonora, on the other hand, is a rather frail young woman, with nothing about her of the vociferous, full-breasted heroism of the massive Wagnerian Brynhildes. The nineteenth century grand opera and the Bayreuth stage have deformed the optic and acoustic of the theatre. Waltershausen rightly reminds us of the incongruity between this enormity of figure and of lung-power and the type of dramatic singer of Mozart's time, who was formed in the Italian art of *bel canto*. The *mezzo* register was then necessary not only for the tragic soprano but for the *buffonista* and *vocalisante* (the Queen of Night, for instance). The singers of that day were not specialists, as ours are, in a restricted register in which they are " forced " to the point of monstrosity, like a melon under glass. Suppleness and delicacy were demanded of the singers, as of the orchestra. And the delicate portrait of the young Wilhelmina Schroeder-Devrient (see the *Beethoven-Almanach der Deutschen Musikbüchereri*, 1927) shows us the ideal type of a Leonora of Beethoven's time. In the first act the music clearly indicates her fragility, her weariness, her excessive nervous excitement. Leonora is a heroine only through love, and could not maintain herself at this tension for long : she is broken, she faints.[1] This slenderness of figure alone justifies the costume she wears, that becomes grotesque upon the visceral amplitude of our Valhalla Gargamelles.

Professor Josef Turnau, the Intendant General of the Breslau theatres, also gives some interesting advice in his study *Die Inszenierung des Fidelio* (in the same publication). He shows that everything in the setting should be subordinated to the central idea : there should be a contrast and progression between the two poles of light and shade. His suggestions for modulating the light in accordance with the music are not to be despised, on condition that researches of this kind are not allowed to degenerate into a decadent puerility. In the Vienna performances we saw how, when the curtain rose on the final scene, after the release of the prisoners, the vibrations of the daylight were in harmony with the brilliant whiteness of the orchestral and choral symphony in C major. But the essential thing is to give

---

[1] Berlioz describes one bit of Schroeder-Devrient's acting in the middle of the violent prison-quartet, when the trumpets sound the deliverance: "I still see her, with her trembling hands stretched towards Pizarro, laughing convulsively."

the whole performance a character of monumental unity.

225. He gives the palm to the libretti of *Fidelio*, *La Vestale*, and *Le Porteur d'eau*. Of these three subjects, two were directly inspired by events of the French Revolution.

226. Beethoven became conscious of it himself only in the middle of the first act ; when he began the work he saw as yet only the admirable action. And not the least striking of his discoveries was the one he suddenly made of the epic grandeur of the subject, when, after having drawn the character of Pizarro, he identified himself with the anguish and the heroism of Leonora.

227. *Mes Récapitulations*, 3 vols., Paris, Louis Janet, 1836/7 : " *Un trait sublime d'héroïsme et de dévouement d'une des dames de la Touraine, dont j'ai eu le bonheur de seconder les généreux efforts.*" Bouilly administered the department, at Tours, during the Terror.

It is a remarkable fact that the other opera libretto that Beethoven admired, *Les Deux Journées, ou le Porteur d'eau*, had been suggested to Bouilly by another event of the time,—" by the act of devotion of a water-carrier towards a magistrate related to him "—[i.e., Bouilly].

228. *Léonore ou l'Amour conjugal, fait historique espagnol en deux actes*, music by Gaveaux, performed for the first time at the Théâtre Feydeau, the 1er *ventôse an VI* (19th February, 1798).

" The action takes place in Spain, in a State prison a few leagues from Seville."

This disguise, that was at least justified at that time by considerations concerning living people, proved insufficient. When Carvalho revived *Fidelio* at the Théâtre Lyrique, in the days of Berlioz, in order to make it more picturesque he transported the action to Milan in 1495; Leonora became Isabella of Aragon; Florestan, Jean Galeas; Pizarro, Ludovic Sforza; and Fernando, Charles VIII! How sadly this romantic tinsel weakens the rough reality of the original subject!

229. *Zur Dramaturgie des Fidelio*, 1924. (See above.)

230. I am not referring to the French *Léonore* of Gaveaux, which Beethoven knew. Hermann Abert has noted some superficial reminiscences, notably in the vocal canon quartet. In Berlioz's opinion Rocco's song about gold was the only one in which Gaveaux could stand the comparison.

231. Thayer (Vol. II, Appendix I.) gives a list of the Cherubini operas that Beethoven may have heard in Vienna: 1802, *Les Deux Journées, ou le Porteur d'eau*; *Médée*; *Lodoïska*; *Der Bernardsberg*; 1803, *L'Hôtellerie portugaise*; *La Prisonnière*; 1806, *Faniska*.
(Cf. R. Hohenemser, *L. Cherubini*, 1913; Kretzschmar, *Ueber die Bedeutung von Cherubinis Ouvertüren und Hauptopern für die Gegenwart;* and especially Arnold Schmitz: *Cherubinis Einfluss auf Beethovens Ouvertüren* (in the *Neues Beethoven-Jahrbuch*, 1925).

232. Arnold Schmitz points out also the resemblance between the opening of the overture to *Le Porteur d'eau* and the unison introduction to the *Leonora No. 3*.

233.

[musical notation: Cherubini: Ouverture d'Elisa / Léonore, ouverture n° 2.]

The influence of Cherubini on the forms of the coda in Beethoven's overtures has been particularly brought out by Schmitz.

234. Cf. Schmitz.

[musical notation: Cherubini. Ouverture d'Elisa / Léonore: Ouverture n° 1.]

235. "Ah! break not yet, exhausted heart!"

236. Cf. Nottebohm, the Sketch-Book of 1803. Marcellina's aria necessitated four long sketches and many smaller ones. The duet between Marcellina and Jaquino, over which lies the shadow of Mozart, costs Beethoven, bar by bar, terrific trouble before he finds the suitable accent and melody; so also with the three numbers that follow. Nor did even this first disproportionate labour suffice; Beethoven preserved nothing of all this but Marcellina's aria.

237. 'Cello, oboe, and bassoon, *soli*. This duet (No. 10), that is quite out of place in the drama, is suppressed in

performance. But it deserves to be known; it might enter into the concert repertory.

238. So again with the trio (Marcellina, Leonora, Rocco, No. 6).

239. In the mournful year 1817, when the song *Resignation*, Op. 137, is his *sole* original work. I will return to this in due course.

240. *An die Hoffnung*, Op. 32; words by Tiedge.
When I wrote these lines of the text, I did not know how the facts justified me. This song *To Hope* was written by Beethoven for Josephine von Brunsvik (Countess Deym), whom he loved and by whom he believed himself to be loved, as perhaps he was. In those days Josephine was the sole confidante of his musical creation. He had just played to her the opening scenes of *Leonora*. (See, at the end of this volume, Note III on the Brunsvik sisters.)

241. *Leonore, Oper in drei Akten*, Klavierauszug. Breitkopf, 1905. This edition, with a preface by Erich Prieger (Bonn, November 1905), was published on the occasion of the centenary of the first *Leonora* (20th November, 1805).

242. "*Sprechend oder singend*" has been written in the score.

243. Berlioz is the only one to have felt deeply the significance of them.

244. A page of sketches shows us that once again this instrumental motive arose in the subconscious before

the composer's intellect had recognised the significance of it. Beethoven intended it at first for the finale of the G major concerto. (Cf. *Beethoveniana*, pp. 13, 14.)

245. *Zweite Beethoveniana*, p. 415.

246. Josef Braunstein has shown that Beethoven was indebted, for the opening of this instrumental introduction, to the opening of his *Trauerkantate* for the death of Joseph II.

247. " *Dieses Stück wird durchaus sehr leise gespielt und die sf. und f. müssen nicht zu stark ausgedrückt werden.*"

248. Leonora : " *O mehr als ich ertragen kann!* "

249. Of the quartet in the first act.

250. " He first shall know who it is that rends his proud heart ! "

251. " *Als Rächer, als Rächer, Pizarro!* "

252. Florestan's reply is accompanied by wood-wind and horn.

253. Berlioz has described " the voices that answer each other, in burning apostrophes, in the midst of the orchestral tumult and of this passage for strings—as it were the cries of an excited crowd." He sees in this scene " a miracle of dramatic music " to which he " knows no pendant in any master, ancient or modern."

254 *Allgemeine Musikzeitung*, 8th January, 1806.

255. I find less felicitous the transfer to Florestan, who is embarrassed by his fetters, of the stumbling orchestral motive, *meno allegro*, in F major, that first of all depicted the heroic Leonora relapsing into feminine weakness the moment she knows her husband is saved.

256. In the second version Beethoven makes Leonora first of all sing alone, then the other voices *soli* ; and he tightens up the chorus.

257. Let us first of all settle the chronology of the four overtures : Josef Braunstein's excellent work, *Beethovens Leonore-Ouvertüren, eine historisch-stilkritische Untersuchung* (Breitkopf, 1927), enables us at last to correct the errors in which, following Seyfried and Nottebohm, criticism had become entangled.

The No. 1 was written in 1805, for the first *Leonora* (in three acts), but was not performed with it ; for after being heard in private at Prince Lichnowsky's house it was by common consent put aside (see Schindler). It was not published during Beethoven's lifetime : it was first issued by Haslinger, in 1832, as Op. 138.

The No. 2 was substituted for it by Beethoven at the performances (in three acts) of 1805. For reasons I shall give later, its tremendous originality made it incomprehensible to the public.

For the revival in 1806 (in two acts) Beethoven wrote the No. 3, that is now known everywhere. The No. 2 was published for the first time (after his death) in 1843, in an abridged form ; then in 1853 and 1905, edited by Jahn and by Erich Prieger. Recently a new manuscript version of it has been discovered.

The No. 4,—the *Fidelio* overture—was written for the revival of the work in its final form, in 1814. Although the least important of the four—perhaps for this very reason, indeed—it has always been used since that date to introduce the opera.

258. The contemporary overture, as practised by Mozart and after him by Beethoven in his first overture, the *Prometheus*, is in essence a slow Introduction followed by an allegro " first movement " in sonata form, with reprise, but without *Durchführung*.

259. Braunstein has pointed out that Wagner, who discussed the *Leonora No. 3* at divers times and in very diverse ways, seems to have been strangely ignorant of the No. 2, for in his essay *Ueber die Anwendung der Musik auf das Drama* (1879) and in the article *Ueber Franz Liszts symphonische Dichtungen* (1857) he reproaches Beethoven for having stopped suddenly half-way, and for not having rejected the *reprise*, that checks the course of the musical drama. Now this is precisely what Beethoven had had the audacious genius to do in the No. 2, which is the true precursor of the symphonic poem of Liszt and of the whole nineteenth century.

260. *Zur Dramaturgie des Fidelio*, 1924.

261. In the same year he writes the G major piano concerto, the violin concerto (Op. 61), the fourth symphony, and the *32 Variations on a theme in C minor* : a whole world of beauty, a new world conquered. We shall return to it.

262. It must be understood that I speak here only of the first chain of these Alps : at the back of that there rises another chain.

263. I pay my tribute to the admirable labours of M. G. de Saint-Foix, who has been a pioneer in this case, as, with the assistance of T. de Wyzewa, he was in the case of the youth of Mozart.

264. " *Ihr meine Brüder . . . sobald ich tot bin, und Professor Schmidt lebt noch, so bittet ihn in meinem Namen, dass er meine Krankheit beschreibe, und dieses hier geschriebene Blatt füget Ihr dieser meiner Krankengeschichte bei, damit wenigstens so viel als möglich die Welt nach meinem Tode mit mir versöhnt werde.*"

265. The original has disappeared ; a copy of it was preserved by Seyfried, who published it in the appendix to his *Studien* (1832). Theodor Frimmel was the first to remind us of it ; he published the complete text in his *Beethoven Handbuch* (2 vols., Breitkopf, 1928). At the end of this chapter I reproduce the whole of the section that concerns the auditory apparatus.

266. Letters to Amenda (June 1801) and Wegeler (29th June and 16th November, 1801) ; Heiligenstadt Testament (6th October, 1802) ; conversations with Dr. Aloys Weissenbach (1814) and Charles Neate (1815) ; also a few testimonies given by his friends—Ries, Czerny, the Giannatasio del Rio family, Schindler, Seyfried, etc.

267. A summary of it will be found in the excellent *Beethoven Handbuch* of Theodor Frimmel (1928) : articles

Taubheit, Krankheiten, Leichenöffnung. A whole volume has been devoted by Dr. Waldemar Schweisheimer to the influence of the malady on Beethoven's life and work (*Beethovens Leiden, ihr Einfluss auf sein Leben und Schaffen*, 1922). See also a short bibliography of the subject in my *Vie de Beethoven* of 1903 (1927 edition, p. 13, Note 1).

268. It is said that Schuppanzigh once surprised Beethoven, in the last period of his life, striking a bootjack violently against some hard object to see if he could hear anything—and failing.

269. *Comptes rendus des séances de l'Académie des Sciences*, Vol. 186, pp. 110 and 266 : séances of 9th and 23rd January, 1928.

270. " *Wisse, dass mir der edelste Theil, mein Gehör, sehr abgenommen hat, schon damals als Du noch bei mir warst, fühlte ich davon Spuren und ich verschwieg's, nun ist es immer ärger geworden* . . . " Beethoven begs Amenda to " keep this matter of my hearing a great secret, and not to confide it to anyone whatever." Consequently he still thought in 1801 that no one else had remarked it.

271. " . . . *Nämlich mein Gehör ist seit drei Jahren immer schwächer geworden, und das soll sich durch meinen Unterleib, der schon damals, wie Du weisst, elend war, hier aber sich verschlimmert hat, indem ich ständig mit einem Durchfall behaftet war und mit einer dadurch ausserordentlichen Schwäche, ereignet haben* . . . "

272. " . . . *wo ich manchmal in Verzweiflung war* . . . "

273. "... wirklich elend. Wirkliche schreckliche Koliken..."

274. "... ein Tee fürs Ohr..."

275. "... nur meine Ohren, die sausen und brausen Tag und Nacht fort."

276. "... Die hohen Töne von Instrumenten, Singstimmen, wenn ich etwas weit weg bin, höre ich nicht... Manchmal auch hör ich den Redenden, der leise spricht, kaum, ja, die Töne wohl, aber die Worte nicht; und doch, sobald jemand schreit, ist es mir unausstehlich.."

277. It is a curious fact that, according to Schindler, the left ear seems afterwards to have withstood total deafness longer than the other.

278. *Es ist nun wahr, ich kann es nicht leugnen, das Sausen und Brausen ist ewas schwächer als sonst, besonders am linken Ohre, mit welchem eigentlich meine Gehörkrankheit angefangen hat, aber mein Gehör ist gewiss um nichts noch gebessert; ich wage es nicht zu bestimmen, ob es nicht eher schwächer geworden. Mit meinem Unterleib gehts besser..."*

279. In the interval he confided to Wegeler the moral resurrection that had been wrought in him by the love of "*ein liebes zauberisches Mädchen*" (Giulietta). To her he owed his first happy moments since he had fled from the company of men two years before.

280. "*Meine Jugend—ja, ich fühle es, sie fängt erst jetzt an. Meine körperliche Kraft, sie nimmt seit einiger Zeit mehr als jemals zu und so meine Geisteskräfte. Jeden Tag gelange ich*

mehr zu dem Ziel, was ich fühle, aber nicht beschreiben kann ... O, es ist so schön, das Leben tausendmal leben!"

281. "*... Aber bedenket nur, dass seit sechs Jahren ein heilloser Zustand mich befallen, durch unvernünftige Aerzte verschlimmert ...*"

282. "*... Aber welche Demütigung, wenn jemand neben mir stund und von weitem eine Flöte hörte, und ich nichts hörte, oder jemand den Hirten singen hörte und ich auch nichts hörte. Solche Ereignisse brachten mich nahe an Verzweiflung; es fehlte wenig und ich endigte selbst mein Leben.*"

283. "*Nur sie, die Kunst, sie hielt mich zurück. Ach, es dünkte mir unmöglich, die Welt eher zu verlassen, bis ich das alles hervorgebracht, wozu ich mich aufgelegt fühlte, und so fristete ich dieses elende Leben, wahrhaft elend ...*"

284. "*Kein Geheimnis sei dein Nichthören mehr, auch bei der Kunst!*"

285. "*Er hat einmal einen furchtbaren Typhus bestanden; von dieser Zeit datirt sich der Verfall seines Nervensystems und wahrscheinlich auch der ihm so peinliche Verfall des Gehörs.*" Observe that this indication might agree with that of the Fischhoff manuscript : we might diagnose an infectious influenza that took an intestinal form. The experiences of the last few years have shown us a number of cases of otitis as a result of such infections.

286. Dr. Marage : *L'Audition et ses Variations*, 2nd edition, 1924 ; *Physiologie de la Voix*, 1925 ; *Education et rééducation des centres auditifs*, 1913.—Also a number of articles bearing on the same questions.

287. Especially these—Beethoven's deafness first of all affects the higher tones; it is accompanied or preceded by whistling and buzzing; he *hears* a low voice but does not *understand* it; he cannot endure shrill speech.

288. I ought to mention that on this point Dr. Marage disagrees with the German diagnoses summarised by Frimmel (*Beethoven-Handbuch*; article *Taubheit*), who comes to the conclusion that there was an otosclerosis, and says that recent studies of this malady show that the higher tones are the first to disappear. Dr. Georges Canuyt, director of the Ear Clinic at the Strassburg *Faculté de Médicine*, also decides, in his study *La Surdité de Beethoven*, on " a bilateral otosclerosis of trophic and hyperæmic form, juvenile type." I lack the qualifications to take sides in the debate.

289. On this point, however, it has to be observed that as the fall only happened in 1802, its effects have nothing to do with the buzzings, which preceded it; though it may have violently accelerated the development of the deafness.

290. Beethoven knew it well: he calls it his " usual malady." See the letter of 1805 to Seb. Mayer : " Since yesterday I have had colic pains " ("*Kolikschmerzen, meine gewöhnliche Krankheit*").

291. Dr. Marage has told me of a curious case that is analogous: the auditory troubles of a tenor at the Opera, that were caused by an intestinal intoxication, and were cured by appropriate treatment.

292. For the Beethoven centenary, 28th March, 1927 (published in the *Festbericht* of the *Beethoven-Zentenarfeier*, Vienna, 1927, and in the *Revue Musicale* for April 1927). Cf. Chapter I of the present volume.

293. I cited several testimonies from his earlier works, anterior to his departure from Bonn.

294. I am engaged on a book on these two personalities.

295. He adds in another letter : " I have known several cases of complete deafness as regards all sounds, but without hummings ; the subjects were a prey to profound melancholy and wanted to live alone, remote from everyone. There were no congestive formations and no periods of excitation. If Beethoven's deafness had been of this order I doubt whether he would have ever been the great musician he was. . . ."

296. This is the aspect that Beethoven presents to those who observe him in the act of composition. The extent to which his very pains could be accompanied by creative euphoria is shown by an occurrence vouched for by Wegeler, who was an eye-witness of it : two days before the first performance of his first piano concerto, in C major (probably the spring of 1800), Beethoven, while suffering terribly from intestinal pains, wrote the joyous rondo of the concerto. (Cf. *Beethoven als Freund der Familie Wegeler*, p. 44.)

297. Dr. Marage : *Fonctionnement de l'oreille à l'état pathologique*, 1910.

298. " For," he says, " supposing the labyrinthine origin to be established, this species of malady always begins with hummings. Now the letter of 1801 to Amenda seems to indicate a 60 per cent. loss of hearing. To arrive at that stage would take at least three years, during which there has been a gradual diminishing of the capacity to hear high notes. Add two years of hummings without deafness, and we arrive at 1796."

299. Cf. p. 144.

300. Dr. Marage: *Fonctionnement de l'oreille à l'état pathologique.*

301. This would seem to lend some probability to the story told by the singer Lablache, who pretended that Beethoven, when dying, had made this extraordinary remark to him : " Do you hear the bell ? They are changing the scene ! " (" *Hört Ihr die Glocke ? Die Dekoration wechselt* " : the allusion being to the Vienna theatres, in which the signal for a change of scene was given by a bell). See Lenz : *Beethoven, eine Kunststudie,* I. 78 (1885). It has been denied hitherto that Beethoven's deafness permitted him to hear bells. But the bells sounded within him !

302. *Obductionsbericht über den Leichnam des P. T. Herrn Ludwig van Beethoven welcher in Gegenwart des Herrn med. Doctors und Professors Wawruch in seiner Wohnung pathologisch untersucht und hierüber nachstehender Befund erhoben wurde.*

303. " The translation is literal, so far as this is at all possible in French, and tries to depart as little as possible

from the original elsewhere; but this is not always possible, it being necessary to be more precise in French." (Dr. Wennagel's note.)

304. "We may translate as either 'their' or 'its' zone of origin; the German wording lacks precision. It seems probable, however, in the light of what has gone before, that the remark that follows applies to both sides of the fourth ventricle and not to the right side alone." (Dr. Wennagel's note.)

305. "The sense of this might also be: 'The convolutions of the brain appeared to be of double depth and more numerous than ordinarily. The remainder of the cerebral substance was much softer and contained a larger proportion of water.' The uncertainty is the result of the word *sonst*, that is so lavishly used in German, where it is of great service to the writer who is not bent on giving his thought precise expression; but it is very embarrassing for a translator who wants to convey the logical sense of the text. In the same paragraph the word in parentheses, *geräumiger*, has not been translated. Its meaning is so vague that the author of the German text seems to have desired to indicate his own lack of comprehension. Or has there been an incorrect interpolation later?" (Dr. Wennagel's note.)

306. Inadequate as a post-mortem report as vague as this may be for the medical science of to-day, the description has still a certain interest for us, for it is the only one that tells us what appearance Beethoven's ear presented. (R. R.)

307. Gustav Nottebohm : *Zweite Beethoveniana*, Leipzig, 1887 (pp. 230 ff. : *Ein Skizzenbuch aus dem Jahre 1800*).

308. *Ein Notierungsbuch von Beethoven*, vollständig herausgegeben von Karl Lothar Mikulicz,—Breitkopf, Leipzig, 1927.

309. There is also a facsimile reproduction of a notebook of twenty pages, of the period of the Ninth Symphony and the Diabelli Variations (W. Engelmann, Berlin, 1913). See also the recent publications of the *Beethovenhaus* at Bonn : *Beethovens Unbekannte Skizzen und Entwürfe* (three Parts, 1924).

310. Of the works sketched out in this book, *Prometheus* was first performed on 28th March, 1801 ; the sonatas Op. 23 and Op. 24 appeared in October 1801. Nottebohm conjectures that Op. 26 was intended for the marriage of Count Moritz von Fries, that took place on 15th October, 1800.

311. But the word " Funeral " never appears ; and the naïve carelessness with which the young composer associates the most diverse, not to say the most antithetical, emotions is shown not only in his note preliminary to the composition of the sonata and in the airy conjunction (p. 57) of the March with the smile of the *Spring* (the motive of the first movement of the violin sonata, Op. 24), but in the astounding turn of chance that makes him suddenly fall from the rhythm of the Funeral March, that he has been repeating indefinitely, plump into the first bars of the sonata *quasi*

una fantasia, Op. 27, No. 1 (p. 137). It is clear that no painful thoughts possessed him; he is the free artist playing with his emotions.

312. Cf. Beethoven's letter to Matthisson, 4th-August, 1800: "You know yourself what changes a few years make in an artist who is always going further [*der immer weiter geht*]: the greater the progress one makes in art, the less one is satisfied with one's earlier works."

313. Almost all his female friends,—from the good Princess Lichnowsky, Therese and Josephine Brunsvik, Giulietta Guicciardi and the Countess Erdödy, down to the "Dorothea Cecilia" of Op. 101 (the Baroness Ertmann).

314. With very few exceptions, writers upon Therese von Brunsvik have hitherto drawn upon their fancy with a regrettable levity. Very few have gone direct to the sources; and these sources, until to-day, were extremely incomplete. The best and most exact books on the Brunsviks are those of La Mara: *Beethovens Unsterbliche Geliebte, Das Geheimniss der Gräfin Brunsvik und ihre Memoiren* (Breitkopf, Leipzig, 1909), which is completed and corrected by *Beethoven und die Brunsviks*, Leipzig, 1920. M. André de Hevesy's books: *Petites amies de Beethoven*, Paris, 1910, and *Beethoven, vie intime*, Paris, 1927, make use of some interesting documents and are well written, but they lack historical solidity; their main thesis will not stand, for it rests on presumptions without proofs. Let me add that the hasty perusal of some letters and fragments from Therese's *Journal* has not allowed M. de Hevesy to recognise the exceptional

grandeur of the character, the intelligence and the life of Therese von Brunsvik. Irony has an easy task of it with saints and with the heroes of the spirit; but irony is inadmissible here.

Anyone who desires to know Therese thoroughly must go direct to the vital documents—her own writings. These are of two orders:

1. Her *Memoirs*, begun in 1846, continued in 1852, and interrupted in 1855 (that is to say, written when she was between seventy and eighty). The liveliness of the memory is astonishing for so great an age; and certain pages are delightful in the charm of the impressions they communicate. But it goes without saying that we must not rely implicitly on the correctness of every date; her memory may have stumbled; and the story is told with a certain irregularity of sequence that is explained by the incredible activity of Therese and the many tasks she undertook to the end without bending under them. These *Memoirs* were published integrally by La Mara—this, indeed, is her chief merit—in her first book (1909). Unfortunately when she published in 1920 her second book, in which she abandons her former thesis, she did not reproduce the *Memoirs*. Now the second book has so thoroughly put the first in the wrong that the latter is not likely to be reprinted, and has become unprocurable. An independent publication of the *Memoirs* is very desirable to-day, in France no less than in Germany.

2. Much more important, but still more inaccessible, is Therese's *Journal intime*, that is still unpublished. It

belongs to the Baroness Irène de Gerando, *née* Countess Teleki, the last inheritor of the blood and the memories of the Brunsvik family. Therese kept up her *Journal* regularly from 1809/10 to about 1853. It does not record the whole inwardness of her life or even all the events of it; but it enables us to penetrate to the depths of that religious soul, to the sanctuary of her faith, her doubts, her sorrows, her struggles. It is a magnificent confession, the riches of which cannot be set forth in a short study. I am indebted to the friendship of Mlle. Dr. Marianne de Czeke for the opportunity to read the entries for the whole of the first six years (1809-1814), that cover the main epoch of the Beethoven problem. And if these pages have not brought me the hoped-for key to the enigma, I have found in them a treasure I was not searching for—a great soul of the type of Beethoven's own.

315. The year 1928 was to see one erected to her in Hungary; the hundredth anniversary was celebrated of the first crèche opened by her in Central Europe, under the name of "*Kinderbewahranstalt*," "*Engelgarten*" (1st June, 1828). At her death there were in Hungary 88 Children's Homes, without counting the other educational and benevolent establishments to which Therese had left all her property. On this occasion the Hungarian Government had the noble idea of issuing a selection from her writings, chosen by the pious and learned zeal of Mlle. Dr. Marianne de Czeke. The volume is to appear in the series *Fontes Historiæ Hungaricæ Ævi Recentioris*, founded by the

Society for Hungarian History, under the title of: *Korompai Gróf Brunsvik Teréz Naplói és Iratai. Szerken tetle, bevezeléssel es magyàrázó jegjretekkel ellátta Dr. Czeke Marianne.* (*The Journals and Writings of Countess Therese Brunsvik de Korompa, selected, annotated, and prefaced by Marianne de Czeke, Dr.Ph.*). Two volumes of extracts are planned. The publication of the *Journal* in its entirety would mean at least four large octavo volumes of 600 pages each.

316. The eldest of the four young girls, Therese, was twenty-five in 1800; the youngest, Giulietta, was sixteen.

317. *Charakterbild der Gräfin Therese Brunsvik, vom Standpunkt der Psychologie und der Vererbungstheorie.*

318. The dates of birth and death of the four Brunsvik children are as follows :—
   Maria Theresia (our Therese) 1775-1861.
   Franz de Paula (the friend of Beethoven) 1777-1849.
   Josephine (who first became Countess Deym, then Baroness Stackelberg) 1779-1821.
   Karoline (Charlotte, Countess Teleki) 1782-1840.
   Giulietta Guicciardi (1784-1856) was their first cousin ; her mother,
   Susanna Brunsvik, was the sister of the Brunsvik girls' father, Anton II.
I shall not have to speak of the youngest of the three Brunsvik sisters, Charlotte, who was neither the least amiable nor the least sacrificed of them all. But her

character was better balanced, more resigned, than that of the others; and her life flowed along quietly in the remote Wallachian castle in which she had been shut up by a misanthropic husband, a man of great parts, but bizarre and savage, with a jealous love for her. It is from her that the last surviving representatives of the Brunsvik family proceed. Franz, Count von Brunsvik, Beethoven's close friend, we shall meet with again in the chapters that follow.

319. "All of us had chronic fevers. My mother had a quartan fever four years in succession; she did nothing for it, and made no change in her way of living." This carelessness was dearly paid for later: the Brunsvik race was decimated by " nervous fever " (as it was called in those days); and Josephine, Therese's favourite sister, suffered from it till her death.

320. " Our good mother was a sceptic on the subject of education. She denied that education and instruction had any influence on the character or the intelligence: what a man is to be, he becomes; it is written. Anything that men may do to change him is either futile or harmful."

321. " A young gentleman gave me Klopstock's Odes: these were my Bible. Another gave me the poems of Matthisson and of Salis: I was intoxicated by them all. I wrote prose and verse; I learned by heart; I could remember a piece after having read it once or twice. . . . We were left to ourselves, and we poetised to our heart's content."

322. They were no longer infants in point of age, but their life in the country had kept them younger than their twenty years; and Therese never lost her youthfulness of heart.

323. i.e., one of the trios, Op. 1. One would like to think that the poetic largo in E flat major of Op. 1, No. 2, was the first communing between Therese and Beethoven.

324. In French in the text; Therese, especially in her *Journal*, constantly mingles French and German; whole pages are in French, which was the *langue favorite* of her mother. "She could not understand," Therese adds in her *Memoirs*, "how I could find any pleasure in the prolixity of German."

325. Therese had had piano lessons from an organist and choirmaster of St. Peter's Cathedral, Vienna.

326. To Therese and Josephine.

327. Count Joseph Deym, the director and proprietor (under the name of Müller) of a celebrated Art Gallery. Therese's account of the meeting with Deym, how he was overwhelmed at the first sight of Josephine, his dexterity in getting into the good graces of the mother, the scene of the compulsory betrothal, the despair of the weeping Josephine, who, after having uttered the fatal "Yes," throws herself on her sister's neck, imploring her to marry Deym in her place—all this forms

one of the best pages, ironic and at the same time moving, of the *Memoirs*. It should be better known.

Deym was not lacking in worth or undeserving of esteem. Josephine did not refuse him hers, nor even, generously enough, her affection when Deym, in the following year, was partly ruined, and then repulsed by the mother who had insisted on this imprudent marriage. But Josephine's tender letters to her sisters reveal her melancholy and her hope that her loved ones shall be happier and freer in their choice. (See La Mara : *Beethoven und die Brunsviks.*)

328. Josephine's letter of 28th October, 1800. This, however, was the period in which Beethoven's sufferings were at their height.

329. Her father, Count Guicciardi, had just been appointed Hofrat of the Bohemian Chancery at Vienna.

330. This miniature, that was part of the Beethoven inheritance, now belongs to Dr. Breuning, of Vienna.

331. Correspondence of the three sisters : " You know that she understands how to show herself off " (" *dass sie sich geltend zu machen versteht* ") (January 1801). Elsewhere they make merry over Giulietta's choice, in the tableaux vivants, of the rôle of Niobe, " to make herself interesting " (" *um sich interessant zu machen* ").

332. Beethoven's letter to Wegeler, 16th November, 1801.

333. The tradition of the neighbourhood is that Beethoven wrote the *Moonlight* sonata in the park at Korompa.

334. The later attitude of the family was to keep away from the embarrassing subject. Giulietta's granddaughter, Baroness Gisela Hess-Diller Gallenberg, who has been good enough to give me some valuable details, writes thus: "Any allusion to the friendship of Giulietta and Beethoven—who was treated simply as a music-teacher—was absolutely forbidden among us. My sister and I were in despair at this, and always suffered under it."

335. Reproduced in La Mara's *Beethovens unsterbliche Geliebte*.

336. It is the same spruce Beethoven, a romantic gentleman *à la* Chateaubriand, that Isidor Neugass painted at his own request: the picture, which he himself sent to the Brunsviks, is now in the possession of Mme. Hugo Finaly, in Florence. (The widow of the last Brunsvik, who died in 1899, became, by her second marriage, the Marchesa Capponi; and the Beethoven relics have gone to Italy.)

337. "... *die mich liebt und die ich liebe.*"

338. In French in the text. But Beethoven adds: "*Il* [Gallenberg] *était pourtant plutôt son amant que moi.*"

339. "I heard through her of his [Gallenberg's] distress, and I found a man of means who gave me 500

florins to help him. He was always my enemy, and that was just why I did all I could. . . . When she came to Vienna [in 1822] she sought me out in tears, but I scorned her." (Remainder of the conversation with Schindler, 1823, written in French.)

340. "Julie played *sehr hübsch* Beethoven's clarinet trio." (Letter of Josephine.)

341. Letter of Josephine, January 1801.

342. "For the first time I believe that marriage might bring happiness. Unfortunately she is not of my class; and in any case I could not marry; so I must extricate myself gallantly" ("*ich muss mich nun noch wacker herum tummeln*"). (Letter to Wegeler, 16th November, 1801.)

343. M. A. de Hevesy has inadvertently dated it 1800. There can be no doubt whatever that the correct date is 1803, for the letter refers to (1) Beethoven's oratorio *The Mount of Olives*, that is to be given at the Augarten (the first performance was on the 5th April, 1803, and the Augarten concert on 4th August) : (2) some "new works" by Beethoven,—*Bagatelles*, Op. 33, and the Variations dedicated to the Odescalchi, Op. 34 : the former appeared in May 1803, the latter in the course of the same year.

344. "I have spoken to Beethoven. . . . I have scolded him about it ["*ich zankte ihn darüber aus*"], and he promised me everything."

It is in this same letter that she speaks of her "Count Robert" as a romantic hero whom his destiny compels to leave an ungrateful country, "to seek in Naples the happiness that does not bloom for him here." The fatal young man, however, did not forget to take away with him the finest flower in Vienna. But the rose has its thorns. . . . The marriage soon turned out unhappily, and the infatuated pair were very unfortunate in material affairs.

345. Pepi's letter to Therese, 6th April, 1802, in which they discuss the *con sordino* of the sonata.

346. "*Welche alle vorhergehenden vernichten.*"

347. Count Wolkenstein's letter to Therese, 18th June, 1806. He confides to her his love for Josephine and the overwhelming effect on him, at their first meeting, of "her magic force" ("*ihre Zauberkraft.... Ihrer unbewusst, entzücket sie um so mehr.*" (La Mara.)

Therese draws a ravishing portrait of her in 1809, in which she humbly depreciates herself in comparison with her, and says: "There are certain persons who, by means of a strong will, have succeeded in attaining to a height on which they can afterwards let themselves go without risk; they stay there without ever being in danger of becoming common or mean; in characters of this kind everything, even indifference, is ennobled. I have an example under my own eyes: never will Josephine be common, however freely and unconcernedly she may give herself. She is always gracious and distinguished; she has acquired a perfect tact, perfect fineness of taste; and everything that lacks this is repugnant to her.... And the purity of her taste for what is and what is not beautiful!" (Her unpublished *Journal*: in French in the original.)

348. Josephine's letter of October 1803: "Beethoven is so eager [*eifrig*] in his task and he insists [*verlangt*] that I shall be equally so; you can imagine what that means!"

349. There is no need for me to go into details regarding the material situation of the Deyms at this period, or to speak of the Art Gallery that Deym owned and administered, an immense building with eighty furnished rooms to let. The details will be found in La Mara's two books and in Therese's *Memoirs*.

350. The whole Brunsvik stock, so refined in mind and heart, had fragile nerves. Josephine died of a nervous consumption (*Nervenschwindsucht*). Of her six children, five died young. Her mother suffered from nervous fevers. Her brother Franz was ailing until maturity, and mentally not quite normal. Therese, the weakest in her youth, had most resisting power, and survived them all. But she was in constant warfare with her own nature.

351. Josephine, who was ill, had had to rent a country house at Hietzing; and Therese, who was with her, writes in June 1804: "We have visited Beethoven, who looks very well [*sehr gut aussieht*]; he has promised

to come to see us. He does not mean to travel this summer; and perhaps he will stay at Hütteldorf, so that we shall be near each other."

It is noticeable that the account given by Therese, Charlotte and Pepi of Beethoven's moral and physical condition that year (the summer of the *Appassionata*) does not agree with that of his faithful companion Breuning. While the latter is disturbed about Beethoven's nervous fever and his gloomy mood, Beethoven is always laughing and radiant when he is with the three sisters. But perhaps it was they who brought the sun to him.

352. Cf. La Mara.

353. " Beethoven comes very often. . . . It is a little dangerous, I confess. (" *Das ist etwas gefährlich, gestehe ich dir.* . . . ") (19th December.) Already at the end of the preceding month we find Therese, who is away from Vienna but has been kept informed by Charlotte, writing cautiously to Pepi not to make so much music, out of regard for her health; and the passage I have cited from one of Charlotte's letters shows that Therese had expressed her apprehensions to her.

354. In French in the original.

355. She adds that it is " a great misfortune." (29th May, 1810: Therese's unpublished *Journal*.)
But even the word " rarely " does not exclude all possibility; and the three Brunsvik sisters were capable

of considering Beethoven as not only their equal but their superior. For the rest, their brother Franz was later to make a bourgeois marriage with a musician.

But I ought to add that Josephine in the later days expresses a very lively sense of aristocratic pride, that is often recorded in Therese's *Journal*. This characteristic seems to have become more pronounced and obstinate in her after her second marriage, to Baron Stackelberg. Perhaps the remembrance of certain humiliations in Viennese society in the earlier days of her union with Deym still rankled in her.

356. "*Beethoven . . . dem innig Geistesverwandten . . . Josephinens Haus und Herzensfreund! Sie waren für einander geboren und lebten beide noch, hätten sie. sich vereint.*"

357. *An die Hoffnung* (*To Hope*); the words are taken from Tiedge's *Urania*.

358. "*Der gute Beethoven . . .*" (24th March). It was a few days before the first public performance of the *Eroica* (7th April, 1805), to which Josephine refers in her letter.

359. Beethoven was then at work on *Fidelio*.

360. In the chapters that follow I shall return to the later life of the Brunsviks. Here I remain within the limits of the dates assigned; these limits contain the whole story of the love of Beethoven and Josephine.

361. She was isolated in spirit, certainly, but not detached from the world, in which she had some

brilliant triumphs. It may be useful to recall these, for there has arisen a legend of a Therese deformed and ill-favoured, and the "well-informed" will tell you that it was her "ugliness" that barred her from being loved by Beethoven. I must admit that, unlike them, I have not received the confidences of Beethoven, who, if I may believe a famous letter of his to Franz von Brunsvik, was always glad to embrace her. But it seems to me that she did not lack admirers in aristocratic circles. Not to speak of her "Toni," who loved her and was loved in return, we shall see, later on, *blasé* great gentlemen like the Grand Duke of Tuscany in her court; and even after she is forty Baron Podmaniczky will weary her with his pursuits and his proposals of marriage, which she will refuse for four years. We know her features only from a solitary portrait of her in her youth,[1] a bad copy of which, probably by her own hand, is in the Beethoven House at Bonn. The original, by Kallhofer, is in the castle of Korompa. Thanks to the courtesy of the Countesses Chotek I am able to give an excellent reproduction of it—for the first time— in the present volume: it is of quite another character —fine, intelligent, energetic features, a pure and ardent expression, an intense look, an attractive mouth, a vigorous sap. A description of a bust of her, in a letter of 1808, speaks of "her ardent and yet veiled glance,

---

[1] By mistake the amusing picture of the two sisters that is reproduced in M. A. de Hevesy's *Beethoven, vie intime* (p. 32) is inscribed "portrait of Therese and Josephine." In reality, the family assures me, it represents Josephine and Charlotte. Here we have an example of the power of imagination; for M. de Hevesy, taking the pretty Josephine to be Therese, fancies he recognises, under "the cunningly-folded veil" that "conceals the shoulders," the supposed deformity of Therese.

and the charming smile that never leaves her" ("*Ihr lebendiger und doch umschleierter Blick, das liebenswürdige Lächeln, das Sie nie verlässt . . .*"). Do we not seem to recognise these characteristics in the intimate sonata, Op. 78, that Beethoven dedicated to her?

She had a fault of figure of which we should never have known had not she, and she alone, referred to it in her *Memoirs* and in her *Journal*—a proof that it was not very noticeable and that she succeeded in disguising it. What precisely was it? In a poem inserted in the *Journal* (*Des Mägdleins Rosen*), in which she reviews her past in a spirit of melancholy, she appears to hint at an accident and a broken rib:—

> "*Der schöne schlanke Gliederbau
> Des muntern Kindchens ward
> Zertrümmert und eine Rippe brach* . . ."

("The lovely slender frame of the merry child was shattered, and a rib broken.")

But perhaps this is only a poetic licence, for it hardly seems likely that the child with the broken rib should become the keen dancer (admired and sought after by Archdukes) that Therese was at that time.

Elsewhere she speaks of "*einem gekrümmten Rückgrat*" ("a curved spine"), and of the "bandage for the shoulders," that she put on only in the mornings. Perhaps her sedentary life at one period in her youth, when she read and dreamed too much, may have given her a tendency to a slight curvature of the spine. In a note of 1809 she prescribes for herself: "I must straighten my figure by extreme vigilance, and, if possible, appear quite erect." (29th March.)

Two seasons at Karlsbad (1807–1808) and the simple and healthy open-air life she led after 1809 seem to have entirely restored and strengthened her. In the half-century that remained to her she showed extraordinary powers of resistance, for she never took care of herself. Nor was she spared crushing fatigues and trials of all sorts, ruin, mourning. "My whole life," she writes at a later date, "is like a battlefield" ("*Einem Schlachtgemezl gleicht Dein ganzes Leben*"). She preserved an invincible energy to the end.

362. The reader must not take this to mean that I believe Therese to be the "Immortal Beloved" of 1812. That is quite another question, which I shall consider at the proper time. Here I will only say that after having scrupulously studied all the intimate documents that are accessible as yet (for the family letters are still withheld from us), and after having for a long time discussed them in a friendly way with Mlle. Dr. de Czeke, who was good enough to let me see them, I have arrived at a different conclusion from hers. The hypothesis of the "Immortal Beloved" does not seem to me incompatible with what I know of the true character of Therese and of the circumstances of her life at the date indicated. As for the documents themselves, they present a sufficient number of odd coincidences with the accepted story for a historian who is more imaginative than scrupulous to find in these data just what he is looking for. I will not allow myself to be "drawn." I reserve the mystery,

meanwhile waiting for more definite facts to be brought to light.

In any case, putting aside entirely the problem of the "Immortal Beloved," it is certain that Therese and Beethoven were very close friends in the years between 1806 or 1807 and 1812.

363. "*Ergebenheit, innigste Ergebenheit in dein Schicksal!* ... *O harter Kampf!*" ... (Beethoven's *Journal*, 1812.)

364. "*Dulde und entbehre!*" (Therese's *Journal*, about the same period.)

365. I must add that the dates of the *Journal* take it out of the time-limits of the present volume. With the exception of a few detached leaves, it is kept up regularly only from the spring of 1809 onwards—the epoch when, under the influence of certain profound moral impressions, (it was six months before she went to Pestalozzi) and painful inward crises, Therese had a veritable "illumination." I shall return to this subject shortly.

366. Some of the most moving "Reflections on myself" (with which her *Journal* opens) were written at Pisa, during a sad journey in which she was quite alone, abandoned by those she loved : in her hotel room she had no other company than the tic-tac of her little watch. ... "*Ich erinnere mich noch in Pisa, dass ich so allein gelassen wurde, dass mich der Gang meiner kleinen Uhr als das einzige Mobile erquickte, das mich umgab.*" It was the 12th April, 1809, the Wednesday of the week after Easter. A fortnight earlier, in Florence, on Wednesday in Holy Week, she had had that celestial illumination the

whole secret of which she does not communicate to us,[1] but the profound vibrations of which endured throughout her life, so that Wednesday was always a holy day, to be consecrated to absorption in God. (Some of the pages of her *Journal* are reserved exclusively for her " Holy Wednesday.") We breathe again with her the atmosphere of those days,—the bells of Florence, the mourning in the churches, the contagion of regrets, nostalgic memories and self-collection. . . . Holy Wednesday. . . . From the bottom of these Christian hearts there rises, with the tears evoked by the Passion, all the melancholy of their sins committed, of the bruises inflicted by life. The hearts that are truly Christian do not dream of attenuating them, much less of turning them into self-adornment. They say their *mea culpa*. Therese does not fail in this duty of loyal and lucid humility. And when, after the unrolling of the veils of Holy Week, after the sunlit sleep of Easter Week, the monotony of ordinary days returns, increased, for Therese, by the solitude of Pisa, that august field of death, and by the abandonment of her by her family, she takes up her pen (12th April, Anniversary Wednesday) and opens the door to a Confession that will continue for half a century.

367. It is impossible to be crueller to a woman than Therese often is to herself; she castigates herself with insulting judgments.

---

[1] A year after, on 28/29th March, 1810, she writes: " A year has gone by since the day when the grace of the Eternal placed me in a situation in which I was granted a deep glance into my inward self and into the inwardness of the moral life. From that time dates a complete reform of my way of thinking and of my very being. I began to penetrate into what I am and what I should be; and I commenced the great reform."

368. "*Dieser ungezügelten Phantasie*" ("this unbridled fancy"), she writes of herself. "*So bin ich ein Imaginationsmensch—dieser müssten Schranken gesetzt werden*" ("I am a creature of imagination: I must set bounds to this"). (1809.)

369. The soul outruns the expression: she was too ardent, too complex, too unsettled. To train her in style there would have been needed genius not only of the heart but of the profession, the discipline for which could not be learned by anyone of her class, her world, and a life as agitated as hers. Therese, who speaks or reads a number of languages, ancient and modern, writes equally ill in German and in French; the two jostle each other in her *Journal*. But from the confusion of this incorrect style there flash out occasionally lightnings of passion, of grief, of heroism, and striking intuitions. The truly noble, truly veracious soul struggles under the envelope into which it is exiled. And she knows herself to be an exile, betrayed by herself; at times she gives magnificent expression to this.

370. Published in part in La Mara: *Beethoven und die Brunsviks*, pp. 57, 65.

371. "This feeling that governs the weakest of my actions, this inner contentment (*Befriedigung*) that makes me indifferent to everything else, this profound disquietude, this anxiety (*Bangigkeit*), this ravishment (*Wonnerauch*), this inexpressible stirring of the soul, this complete transformation (*Umwandlung*) of all my moral

being. . . . I comprehend otherwise, I see otherwise, everything appears to me in a higher, clearer light, as if a veil had been torn from my eyes. . . . I live a new life. . . . And I weep with the happiness that fills me." (February 1805.)

372. Charlotte's letter to Therese, 18th February, 1805 : " Oh ! do not surrender yourself to any illusion about love ; try to rouse yourself from this lethargy before it is too late ! " Charlotte knows well that her " Tesi is often subject to illusion " ; she knows her " excessively excited imagination."

373. Elsewhere : " Often I feel within me a violent shock ; I find myself in an abyss, without knowing how I came there."

" It seems that everything is over for me, everything is in ruins. O God, save me ! " Very often in the *Journal* it is a question of combat against her " *Sinnlichkeit* " : " *Mein Kampf soll gegen meine Sinnlichkeit sein* " (" My fight must be against my sensuality " : 1809). " *Ich bin der Sinnlichkeit gefangen gegeben. Sie ist es, die mich beherrscht* " (" I am a captive to my sensuality. It is this that rules me " : 1810).

And however we may try at times to limit the bearing of this confession, it remains true that we constantly feel she is on the verge of being carried away, in spite of her energy and her lofty reason, by the first surprise of the senses and the imagination :—

" *Der Augenblick beherrscht mein besseres Wollen, auch das augenblickliche Gefühl herrscht* . . . (" My better will is the slave of the moment. The feeling of the moment governs me!" May 1810).

For so proud a woman, what an impulse of revolt, and what humiliation!

"That I should give myself up without resistance to the first temptation! When shall I be strong and sure of myself? What anguish! . . . Have I really knowledge of the passions that are involved?"

374. "*Hat Beethoven seine oder unsere Zeit erquickt? Seine Zeit hat ihn nicht verstanden. Christus, sans comparaison*" ("Has Beethoven quickened his time or ours? His own time did not understand him. Christ, *sans comparaison*": i.e., "without comparison being intended"). (Therese's *Journal* in the last years: cf. La Mara: *Beethoven und die Brunsviks*, p. 93.)

375. "*Nach den Genies kommen zunächst diejenigen, die sie zu schätzen verstehen.*" (2nd February, 1805.)

376. ". . . *diese hübsche Finger spielen die Sonaten Beethovens in einer Weise, die dem Meister und seinen Jüngern den Kopf verdreht.*" (27th August, 1808.)

377. According to Therese's *Memoirs*, they performed oratorios.

378. "Astronomy, physics, chemistry . . . are quite within the scope of a child, and certainly of a girl of genius. These things are made for women, and it is only absurd prejudice that has deprived us of them." (*Journal.* 1810.)

379. Brusque manners, a rough tone... "*meinen rauhen Ton,*" as she accuses herself later. The early days spent in the wild Puszta had given her some cavalier ways and impetuosity of speech and a violence in discussion of which it was difficult to cure her, and that often drew on her the disdainful reproof of the aristocratic Josephine. In her *Journal* we see her as prompt to throw herself on people's necks as to get in a passion with them, and, in the one case as in the other, to surrender herself absolutely, reveal her closest secrets, to regret it the moment after,—and then begin again!

380. "I disdained to be the Egeria of the Florentine Numa," she writes later (1818). Cf. La Mara.

381. 10th November, 1804 :—"He always asks after you." (Charlotte to Therese, 20th November, 1804.)

382. "*Küsse deine Schwester Therese, sage ihr, ich fürchte, ich werde gross, ohne dass ein Denkmal von ihr dazu beiträgt, werden müssen.*" (11th May, 1807. Cf. Thayer, III. 30.)

383. "Everyone is getting married; only you and I won't think of it." (Therese to Franz, 14th October, 1804.)

384. Notably the Rasoumovsky quartets, which Franz was in no hurry to return to him. (16th November, 1807.)

385. "*Leb wohl, theurer Bruder, sey es mir, ich habe keinen, den ich so nennen könnte....*" (Summer of 1812. Cf. Thayer.)

386. Beethoven's letter to Therese, a copy of which the happy and flattered young woman sends to Josephine. (2nd February, 1811.)

387. So, at least, we are assured in Therese's *Memoirs*. Recent researches, however, reveal no trace of the execution of this project; and at a later date Therese mournfully expresses her regret at not having a house of her own and being always compelled to live with others.

388. In a letter that figured in a sale in Berlin in December 1921 (cf. Leo Liepmannssohn's catalogue No. 47 of autographs), and that belongs to the summer of 1808 (not 1807, as the catalogue erroneously says), Therese writes: "*Beethoven sah ich die letzten Tage sehr viel* . . ." ("I have seen Beethoven very often these last days"). And she asks that a portrait of him just painted by a certain Neigart shall be sent to Pepi. In March 1807 again, when the younger sister Charlotte sees a child whose glance and expression remind her of Beethoven, the first thought that occurs to her is, "How I wish Pepi could have seen him!"

389. "*Da übertrug er sein Feuer der Liebe in meinen Geist! . .*" ("It was there [at Yverdon] that he transplanted his fire of love into my bosom"). "*Dort lernte ich kennen, was mein Geist bedurfte: Wirkung auf das Volk. Das Wort war gefunden. Von da an hörte alle egoistische Selbstbildung auf; dem Vaterland weihten wir aus als Erzieherinnen seiner Massen. Ihnen Kräfte, Zeit, dem künftigen Geschlechte Liebe!*" ("There I learned what it was my spirit needed—

action on the people. The word was found. From that time there was an end of my egoistic self-culture; we dedicated ourselves to the Fatherland, as educators of the masses. To them our strength, our time! To the future generations our love!") (The *Memoirs*.)

390. My opinion at present—so far as I have been able to study the documents that have been communicated to me—is that, if it be not at all impossible that Therese may have met Beethoven at the indicated place and time, and that she may have provoked in him, in one of her moments of exaltation and passionate weakness, the crisis testified to in the famous letter to " The Immortal Beloved," it is practically certain that in that case Therese would afterwards master herself and return the letter to him. For she no longer belonged to herself, she could no longer dispose of herself for a life of matrimony: she was now caught up in a whirlwind of duties, the most pressing of which was not her religious and social mission (that still needed some years to develop in her) but the ruin of her sister Josephine, the domestic catastrophe that had befallen her family, in these very months that exacted of her a complete devotion to them and their salvation—an absolute sacrifice. I hope to deal with all these events, for which this is not the place, in a special study of Therese von Brunsvik.

391. Their characters are singularly alike: we are surprised to find Therese expressing thoughts that have the ring of certain famous words of Beethoven: " I no longer wish to confuse goodness with weakness. I was

never good, though I thought I was : *true goodness is allied to strength.*" And again : " Sterile goodness is a veritable feebleness of mind and character. . . . A man who is satisfied with it is a good animal; but if he adds pretensions to it he is the unhappiest and most contemptible of beings." (*Journal*, 1809.)

Elsewhere Therese expresses in the same terms as Beethoven her detestation of "*Kleinlichkeitsgeist*" (" smallmindedness "). "*Er ist mir verhasst*" (" I hate it "). (*Journal*, 1816. Cf. La Mara, p. 86.)

And how heroic a spirit ! Are these words Therese's or Beethoven's :—" *Ohne Gefahr und Kampf ist kein Sieg* " (" Without danger and battle there is no victory ") ?

Elsewhere she underlines again and again a favourite thought of Beethoven's, that he has set to music : " *Edel sei der Mensch, hülfreich und gut!* " (" Let man be noble, helpful and good ! ").

Yet why be astonished at such similarities of thought when we see, from the *Journal* of 1811 (16th April), the place Beethoven held among the directors of her mind :—

" *Welch himmlisches Vergnügen, in schönen Seelen und ihren Schriften, das Erhabene, das Göttliche im Menschen zu finden : Goethe . . . Herder vor Allen, und van Beethoven . . . etc.*" (" What heavenly pleasure to find, in beautiful souls and their writings, the sublime, the divine in man : Goethe . . . Herder before all, and van Beethoven ! ").